Analyzing Public Discourse

Martha Cooper

Northern Illinois University

WAVELAND PRESS, INC.

Prospect Heights, Illinois

Consulting Editors

Joseph A. DeVito
Robert E. Denton, Jr.

For information about this book, write or call:

Waveland Press, Inc.
P.O. Box 400
Prospect Heights, Illinois 60070
(312) 634-0081

Copyright © 1989 by Waveland Press, Inc.

ISBN 0-88133-407-3

Printed in the United States of America

7 6 5 4 3 2 1

Table of Contents

3 The Anatomy of Controversy 39

4 Good Reasons Fit the Audience 63

5 Good Reasons Structure the Audience's Response 95

6 Good Reasons Withstand Objection 117

7 Good Reasons are Ethical 135

8 Ideology, Propaganda and Implicit Discussion of Public Issues 153

Acknowledgements

Like most books, this text has benefited from the supportive assistance of many people other than the author. I have benefited from the knowledge and wisdom of many excellent teachers from high school through graduate school. Their influence has left imprints on this text that are not easily specified but are worthy of acknowledgement. In addition, several people deserve special thanks. My colleague, Richard Johannesen, offered advice concerning several chapters and was especially helpful regarding Chapter 7. Ann Chaney, a graduate student, checked sources of data for several chapters. A number of undergraduate students read early drafts of Chapters 1, 2, 8, and 9; thanks go to Jim Doherty, Ron Bell, Andrea DeLeon, and Sally Mordini. In addition, my entire Rhetoric of Controversial Issues class at NIU used the manuscript in draft form as a text and, in that process, provided helpful feedback. Carol Rowe, Editor, and Robert Denton, Consulting Editor, at Waveland Press were especially helpful in providing suggestions for Chapter 10. Neil Rowe, Publisher at Waveland, and Bonnie Highsmith, Production Manager, were both enthusiastic and patient during my preparation of the manuscript. Finally, my colleague and husband, Charles Tucker, read and commented on the entire manuscript and provided a consistently supportive atmosphere for my work.

Preface

Numerous social commentators, such as Richard Sennett and Robert Bellah, have suggested that the public sphere has changed considerably during the last few decades. Yet, John Dewey's observation that community, or the public sphere, exists only by virtue of communication persists as a fundamental principle of public life in our society. It is the workings of that connection between community and communication that this text intends to explore. More specifically, the text is designed to meet the following four objectives: (1) to assist students in understanding the nature and function of communication in public controversies, (2) to assist students in developing skills for evaluating argumentative messages about public issues, (3) to help students understand the ways in which communication structures our perceptions of reality and informs our opinions on controversial matters, and (4) to encourage students to participate in the exercise of free speech in our society.

My intention in this text is to provide a mature treatment of public argument that will encourage the student to evaluate public discourse critically rather than reducing public discourse to a set of formulaic rules that may either confuse the student or lead to an increased alienation from and hostility toward the public sphere. Within this context, four features of the text deserve mention.

First, the text integrates related material that has frequently been compartmentalized. For example, argumentation texts have traditionally provided some excellent tools for analyzing arguments but have typically presented these tools in the context of preparing students to become academic debaters rather than more critical consumers of public argument. Similarly, texts in rhetorical criticism, typically designed for upper-level speech communication majors, have often presented their methods of analysis in the context of public address rather than public discussion that may take other, nonoratorical forms. Texts on public opinion in the field of political science have included chapters on communication but have rarely availed themselves of the critical tools provided by the field of communication. By assuming a rhetorical perspective toward public discourse, this text attempts to integrate the critical tools common to the study of argument and rhetorical criticism with the political perspective common in the study of public opinion and free speech.

Second, this text provides critical tools for analyzing messages rather than providing messages for analysis. The few books available for students enrolled in introductory courses in rhetorical criticism or message analysis characteristically have devoted little space to critical methods and much space to collections of speeches. Consequently, the student's attention is directed more toward the product of rhetorical activity and less toward the analysis and evaluation of public discourse. Although public address is still important, contemporary public discussion is just as likely to take the form of a news interview, an editorial, or a documentary film. Therefore, this text emphasizes critical methods that are applicable across forums and forms.

Thirdly, this text explores public discourse from the audience's point of view. Typically, introductory texts are oriented toward the source, speaker, or advocate's point of view. However, research is consistent in showing that listening, or playing the role of the audience, is a far more typical role for most people. Given the increased emphasis on the receiver of communication, both in scholarly work and in legislative documents concerning education, an orientation designed to assist people in becoming better audiences seems appropriate.

Finally, this text attempts to blend contemporary theories with fundamental principles from the rhetorical tradition. Traditional tools for microscopic rhetorical analysis, such as distinguishing among ethos, logos, and pathos, identifying fallacies, and so forth, are treated in the context of more contemporary macroscopic theories, such as Perelman's idea of the universal audience, Habermas' construct of the ideal speech situation, Noelle-Neumann's theory of the spiral of silence, and so on.

The ideas, theoretical principles, critical tools, and examples in this text are the product of my own experience teaching undergraduate students about public discourse. The text will find its primary use in introductory courses in message analysis characteristic of many courses that fulfill a requirement for general education in the humanities. In my own experience with such courses, the material contained in this text is best supplemented with a multiplicity of actual messages of different types which students may analyze according to the principles and suggestions contained within the text. In addition, the text may be used as a supplement in either traditional public speaking courses or political communication courses. However the text is used, I trust and hope that the result will be students who both appreciate a society that relies on communication as its preferred method for resolving disputes and who are better equipped to participate in the marketplace of ideas.

Martha Cooper
Northern Illinois University

Chapter 1

Communication and Public Issues

A fundamental paradox for most of us is our sense that we are unique, autonomous individuals at the same time that we are members of a community. Many of us find great joy in our connections with others and experience loneliness and anguish when we feel isolated or estranged from others. Yet, the normal traumas of life—death, divorce, a simple move to a new geographic location— underscore the sensation that regardless of our social connections, our close relationships, our membership in identifiable groups, and so forth, we are individuals who are born and die as individuals, simply making connections of a variety of types with others along the course of life.

Social critics have made a point of recognizing that individuals in contemporary society frequently have been preoccupied with their private interests (the problems associated with their own autonomous lives) rather than with public interests (the problems associated with the life of the community). Richard Sennett, in *The Fall of Public Man,* argues that we spend increasing amounts of our time and energy focusing on our individual needs and wants rather than community interests.[1] Christopher Lasch, in *The Cult of Narcissism*, has also noted our preoccupation with ourselves as opposed to others.[2] And a recent study of our moral life as Americans has concluded that for most of us "the touchstones of truth and goodness lie in individual experience and intimate relationships," rather than public life.[3] These same commentators suggest that just as any of us can reflect on our own loneliness, and sometimes even despair when we find ourselves apart from others, our preoccupation with our own private lives often spawns a longing for a greater sense of community and public life. Surveys indicate that many Americans yearn for the idealized "small town," in which people operate cooperatively and act like friendly neighbors instead of like nameless, faceless bureaucrats.

Our relative inexperience with public life suggests the need for considering just what constitutes a *public* perspective, for examining the nature of the *public sphere.*

Public Sphere

When we think about what is involved in public life, it is helpful to conceptualize our life as an existence within various spheres of influence. In a very concrete sense, we can think of that part of our life that goes on at home, at work, at school, at the club, and so forth. Frequently, we describe ourselves in categories that refer to the various spheres of influence in which we live. "I'm in college." "I belong to the Catholic church." "I'm a Democrat." "I work out at the Rec Center." "I like football." These types of self ascriptions explain to ourselves and others who we are in terms of the groups we belong to, how we spend our time in those groups, in short, how we spend our lives. Some of who we are depends on our private life, for example, "I'm married." Some of who we are depends on our public life, for example, "I'm for equal rights." Knowing which part is which depends on our understanding of the public sphere.

Most scholars define "public" by contrasting it with "private." For our purposes, we can begin the same way. A neat and concrete way of contrasting the two comes from the distinction made by economists between private goods and public goods. The economist, when considering types of goods, focuses on who obtains the benefit from consuming a particular good. If an identifiable, distinct individual obtains the benefit, the good is classified as private. If a number of people share in the benefit, making distinctions difficult as to who exactly benefits how much, then the good is classified as public. For example, a soft drink typically is consumed by a single person who derives most, if not all the benefit of the refreshing thirst quencher and so is a private good. But a highway benefits everyone who uses it, many people at the same time, and is a public good. Televisions are usually bought individually, by particular people, and provide an entertainment benefit to the buyers and are, therefore, private goods. Public education is bought, or paid for, by many people simultaneously and dispensed to, and benefited by, many other people simultaneously, and is therefore a public good. Private education, on the other hand, may be paid for only by the benefactor in which case it is a private good, or may be contributed to by a number of people simultaneously, in which case it may be a public good. The distinction made by economists suggests an essential component of the public sphere: *it affects groups of people, rather than single individuals, at any given time.*

The idea of a group of people who are affected by something simultaneously was discussed at some length by John Dewey in the book, *The Public and Its Problems.*[4] He argued that a public was any group of individuals who are together affected by a particular action or idea. Dewey noted that the public sphere is defined by the effect of an action or idea, rather than by who takes the action or offers the idea. Just because a "public" official takes a particular action, the action is not necessarily one that belongs to the public sphere. If the action, for example taking a vacation at Camp David, does not affect a community of people, then it belongs to the private sphere rather than the public sphere. However, if a public official offers a proposal to cut aid to higher education while he is on vacation at Camp David, then his action belongs to the public sphere because his proposal will affect a community of people—students, their parents, academic administrators, the taxpayers, and so forth. Conversely, if a private individual takes an action that affects a community of people, then the action exists in the public sphere despite the fact that it was exercised by a private individual. For example, if a movie star renounces the use of drugs it is not necessarily a public act. But if, by renouncing the use of drugs, the same movie star makes a number of people aware of the problems associated with drugs and by example encourages others to do likewise, then the act is a public one.

Dewey's perspective holds two important implications. First, his explanation suggests that no single public exists. In other words, any particular action or idea might affect a group of individuals, but another action or idea might affect another group of individuals. For example, if an administrator at a university in Chicago suggested erecting a statue to honor Martin Luther King in the campus plaza, that suggestion would probably affect all the members of that university community. However, a student at a small college in South Dakota would probably not be affected by the suggestion. Moreover, citizens of Chicago who lived several miles away and rarely, if ever, visited the campus would be unlikely to be affected by the question of the statue. However, those citizens might also constitute a public if the issue changed from one of constructing a statue to one of whether or not bars and taverns in their neighborhood should be allowed to do business after midnight. In short, Dewey's definition suggests the possibility of many different publics, corresponding to many different actions and ideas, all existing simultaneously.

The second implication of Dewey's explanation is that a public exists as the result of an action or idea, rather than as the context for the action or idea. Ordinarily we use the term "public" as if it existed continuously, throughout time. When we hear about "public opinion," "the public good," "the public interest," and so forth, our tendency is to think that the "public" exists, sort of in the same way that the NFL, the Republican Party, or the local Kiwanis Club exists. In other words, our talk about "the public" suggests that it exists in some organized, readily identifiable way; although particular individuals may come and go, "the public" is some enduring organization with a defined structure that began long, long ago and will exist forever. Conceived in this way, we can begin to believe that our actions and ideas could be presented to this stable, highly defined "public." Contrary to this view, Dewey's suggestion is that only those people who are together affected by an action or idea constitute "the public." Consequently, "the public" is a constantly changing entity, depending on the particular action or idea in focus.

Based on Dewey's idea, then, we can add to our earlier generalization about the nature of the public sphere. In addition to the concern for groups of people, rather than individuals, *the public sphere is constantly in flux as actions and ideas change.* Which group belongs to the public sphere depends on which action takes place and which idea is offered at any given time. Because many actions and ideas can exist at any given time, many publics may exist at the same time.

Given the two characteristics of the public sphere just discussed, you may be wondering how any aspect of our existence can belong to the private sphere. In other words, it seems as though anything we do might have influence on someone else and anything we think, assuming that we let someone else know we thought it, could possibly affect someone else, in which case we would be operating in the public sphere. Hence, it is helpful to continue with a third defining characteristic of the public sphere.

Most of us, by means of our own self-reflexiveness, can reflect on our own thoughts or behaviors and intuitively sense whether or not we are acting or thinking in our private world or our public world. We may have a sense of our private image and our public image, our private personae and our public personae. We have developed a repertoire of ways that we present ourselves in public and a similar repertoire of ways for our private presentation. Think of the clothes you choose to wear in public versus those that you choose to wear at home. Or consider the details about your life that you commonly discuss with people who are just acquaintances versus the aspects of your life that you reveal only to your intimate friends and relatives. You may present the image of a confident, independent woman who is not particularly interested in marriage when you chat with some classmates at the Union, but you may present an image of someone who is worried about whether she'll find the perfect job and who would like to have the marriage question settled by making it official with her boyfriend when you talk with your best friend late at night. These differing images provide a basis for thinking about the persona common to the public sphere as opposed to the private sphere.

One way to explore the persona common to the public sphere is to return to the concerns and methods of life common in the Classical world of Ancient Greece and Rome. In the Classical world, particularly during the height of civilization in the Greek city-states, the welfare of the community was often given much greater importance than the welfare of individuals who lived within that community. Frequently, people made decisions about their own individual behavior not because of the importance of that behavior for them individually, but because of the implications of that behavior for the larger community. For example, a young man might be educated to practice moderation regarding food, drink and sex — not because such moderation would enhance his own life-style (e.g., avoid a heart attack, AIDS, and so forth) — but because, as a future leader in Greek society, he could set a better example for others by practicing moderation. Similarly, the ancient Greek citizen would choose his friends not just because he enjoyed their company and found the relationship satisfying, but also because he and they shared an image of what constituted the common good. Thus, in the ancient world, people found it natural to think of themselves first as members of a community, and second as autonomous individuals, separate from the community.

In contemporary society, our private, individual lives are very real to us. In contrast, we often must struggle to think of ourselves as a member of a public. In other words, it is easier for us to think of ourselves in terms of our individual career goals, our preferred romantic partners, and our most appealing pastimes, than to think of where we fit and what our preferences are concerning community affairs.

Several factors probably reinforce our sense of individualism and inhibit our sense of publicness. The *mobility* of contemporary society, wherein most of us have moved to different locations several times before we reach adulthood and expect to move several more times during the course of our lives, makes a geographic sense of community difficult. The *managerial* nature of our governments, by which being a public official is a full-time job and the specialization and interdependence of labor divides our professional lives from our civic lives, encourages us to feel somewhat alienated from the political system. We may wonder what difference our opinions really make since there are so many full-time, professional managers of public affairs whom we don't see as particularly accountable to those of us not involved in government. The *diversity* of the other people we interact with on a daily basis—as people from a variety of cultural backgrounds and traditions find themselves working, playing, and doing business together—inclines us to question whether or not we really belong to the same community and encourages some of us to seek more comfortable surroundings where our neighbors and business partners share our cultural background. Finally, the *psychology of our own culture* emphasizes the importance of being independent and self-sufficient, encourages us to "make it on our own," "be our own person," and "march to the beat of our own drummer," and discourages us from finding fulfillment in the community and expanding our public selves.

Still, the paradox of self and community exists, and we find ourselves drawn to others and their concerns from time to time. When we watch a movie about the brutality in Central America and wonder how "we" (the United States) can help to solve the problems there, when we listen to rock stars sing "We Are the World" and consider what "we" (probably through some organization) can do to help stop world hunger, when we hear about motorists on the Los Angeles freeways taking shots at one another and wonder how "we" (the government, the transportation industry, or someone) can deal with this problem, when we find out that a local school board has just added several books to the "restricted list" in the local school library and "we" (just us) immediately have an opinion one way or the other on the matter, our public personae are emerging. Thus, we have discovered a third characteristic of the public sphere: *within the public sphere, people exhibit a concern for the common good, the good of the community.*

The public sphere, then, is not a real place to which you could walk or in which you could sit down and have a conversation. Instead, it is an orientation that people take to parts of their lives. When something happens that seems to affect groups of people rather than single individuals, the public sphere is emerging. The public sphere is constantly in flux as actions and ideas change. The groups, or other people, that we find with us in the public sphere may change as the actions and ideas change from time to time and place to place. Finally, we can recognize that we have entered the public sphere when we find ourselves motivated by the needs of others as well as ourselves, by the needs of the community, rather than our own personal needs.

Public Issues

Now that we've explored the nature of the public sphere, we are ready to investigate the nature of *public issues*. Generally, an *issue* is defined as a contemporary situation with a likelihood of disagreement. More specifically, a public issue is a situation with a likelihood of controversy that arises from our sense of ourselves as members of a community, that affects the community's interests, or requires community involvement. Some examples will help to clarify just what a public issue is.

The question of what to do about terrorism is a good example of a public issue. Already there is disagreement as to whether "we," the nation, should negotiate with terrorists who take our citizens hostage or refuse to negotiate and instead retaliate against the terrorists. In the case of terrorism, the "we" that is affected is potentially anyone and certainly the large community of Americans, who seem to be prime targets. Similarly, the response to terrorism seems to require community action—diplomatic negotiation by representatives of government or military action by the armed services. In addition, even the individual who expects never to travel abroad, and thereby never to become an object of terrorist attack, may be interested and concerned about this issue because it seems to affect the larger community. For example, several wealthy benefactors have contributed financial assistance to both governmental and private efforts to free American hostages in the Middle East. In these cases, the benefactors probably did not expect to gain personally, but offered assistance out of a sense of community spirit.

Sometimes public issues grow out of private concerns. For example, in the summer of 1980, Candy Lightner's 13-year-old daughter was killed by a hit-and-run drunk driver. Ms. Lightner's grief and anguish was the driving force in establishing an organization called MADD (Mothers Against Drunk Driving), an organization that has consistently worked to solve the problem of drunk driving and console the victims of this social ill. Although individuals who belong to MADD may find personal comfort and satisfaction in their involvement, they deal primarily with the community's interest in maintaining a safe transportation environment and conduct their work through community action. Drunk driving, at the initiative of groups like MADD, became a public issue because the effects of the private act of driving drunk were felt by all members of the community who tried to avoid the drunk driver and, when unsuccessful, became victims of the drunk driver. At present, there is fairly little disagreement about whether or not driving drunk is good or bad; however, there still exist some people who consider driving drunk to be their choice. There is considerable controversy about the appropriate actions for preventing drunk driving as advocates disagree about whether or not to raise the drinking age, mandate severe penalties for driving drunk, or severely restrict the availability of alcohol. Thus, like terrorism, drunk driving is a situation with a likelihood of considerable disagreement that affects community interests.

Typically, we understand the nature of public issues more clearly as they exist in our present-day realities than when we consider them in the abstract. Public issues exist at a given point in time within a given context. There is a historical reality to public issues in which the time and place of the public issue help to specify the community whose interests are at stake in the controversy. Similarly, the historical reality of a public issue helps to specify the opinions, thoughts, and actions people will likely have about a public issue. The key to catching a glimpse of both the historical reality of a public issue and the issue itself is the ability to recognize communication about a public issue. Hence, a discussion of the relationship between communication and public issues is in order.

Communication as an Expression of Public Opinion

There are many technical definitions of communication offered by scholars for various purposes. However, for our purposes at present, you may think of communication as simply *the expression of ideas or thoughts by one person to another*. It is just such expression that allows an observer to recognize the existence of a public issue. For example, we only recognize unemployment as an issue if it is talked about; unemployment may lay dormant as a latent issue for months or even years until public discussion begins. For example, public opinion polls show that the last time Americans thought that unemployment was a serious public issue the unemployment rate was between 6 and 7%. Several years later, the unemployment rate was 9%, but not many people were talking about it, and public opinion polls showed that unemployment was not considered to be among the most important public issues at that time. Similarly, the advertising of tobacco products only became a public issue when representatives of the American Medical Association began to advertise it through interviews on television and lobbying efforts in Congress. And, of course, if terrorist attacks were not publicized and talked about, it is unlikely that terrorism would be perceived as a public issue. The explanation for why this happens will be discussed later in this book, but for now it is helpful just to remember that communication about a public issue is necessary for us to recognize the existence of the public issue.

Not only does communication alert us to the existence of a public issue, but communication also alerts us to the areas of disagreement about a public issue and contributes to the eventual resolution of disagreement about a public issue. To explain this process, it is helpful to explore the meaning of another concept, *public opinion*. Public opinion is *the shared judgment of a group of people about public issues*.

Important Public Issues **as reflected by Public Discussion and Public Opinion Polls**		
1947	**1967**	**1987**
Soviet/U.S. Relations	Racial Violence	AIDS
Atomic Energy	Vietnam War	Nuclear War
Communism	Morality and Sex	Iran/Contra Scandal
Marshall Plan	Rock Music	Pornography
Labor Problems	Birth Control	Televangelism

How do the public issues from the three time periods differ?
How many of these public issues do you have an opinion about?
What public issues would you list for the present year?
Why do some public issues seem to fade away?

Political philosophers and the officials of governments, especially democratic governments, have been concerned with public opinion for centuries. The traditional wisdom has been that government officials need to conform to the shared judgment of their citizens or those government officials may lose their offices. In other words, if governments do not stay within the bounds of public opinion, the officials responsible for deviating may at best lose the next election and at worst lose their lives. At the same time that philosophers and politicians alike have recognized the power of public opinion, they have also worried about the wisdom of public opinion. Frequently, politicians and others have questioned whether or not the public is informed enough, intelligent enough, public spirited enough, and wise enough to decide how to deal with public issues. A brief and selected review of the ways in which public opinion has been considered by various political philosophers highlights the importance given and caution with which public opinion has been treated.

In the Classical world of the Athenian democracy, public opinion played a vital role. The public persona common to Athenian citizens allowed the community to take for granted a concern for and ability to decide about public issues. Consequently, government officials were chosen by lot on the assumption that any Athenian citizen was able and willing to perform the duties of public service. In their writings on political philosophy, Plato and his student Aristotle, observed that the highest form of government gave the most credence to public opinion. They named and explained the three types of government accordingly. In a monarchy, one person ruled. In an aristocracy, a few people ruled. But in a democracy, many people ruled. When many people ruled, public opinion had its largest impact. Of course, many types of people (e.g., women, slaves) were excluded from the ranks of "citizenship" and consequently their opinions did not contribute to the public opinion, but still the Greek ideal of participative democracy was a model of public opinion influencing government policy.

Centuries later, during the Age of Enlightenment in France, political philosopher Jean Jacques Rousseau issued three generalizations about the nature of public opinion.[5] He argued first that opinions originate in social relationships, not supernaturally or because of man's nature. In other words, Rousseau believed that public opinion was the product of interaction and communication between people and that at different times people would reach different agreements, making public opinion always dependent on the particular circumstances rather than dependent on some innate characteristic of human nature. Thus, warfare might be acceptable to the public in some circumstances at some times but not in other circumstances at other times.

Secondly, Rousseau argued that governments rest on opinion, rather than on laws or coercion. Put simply, if government actions violated public opinion frequently and importantly enough then revolution was likely. The contemporary circumstances of Poland provide some evidence for Rousseau's argument. Laws and government coercion were unsuccessful in stemming the foundation and initial rise to power of the Solidarity movement. Even after heavy oppression of the Solidarity Union by government officials, there still exists a literal "underground" community in Poland in which educational, cultural, and political events are conducted in chambers underground many of the churches there. The ultimate results of the struggle between Solidarity and the official Polish government is still in question, but if Rousseau is to be believed, it is only a matter of time until public opinion will conquer the official Polish regime. The transfer of power in the Philippines from Marcos to Aquino serves as another example of this characteristic of public opinion as described by Rousseau.

Finally, Rousseau argued that social change cannot be too far ahead of public opinion. In other words, even if government officials are enlightened and exert strong leadership to implement new policies, if public opinion is not also on the side of new policies, those policies will fail. A chapter from American history verifies Rousseau's observation. Prior to the great agricultural disaster in which land that had been productive turned into a Dust Bowl, government officials had tried for some time to get farmers to alter their planting practices in order to slow down the opportunities for soil erosion. However, public opinion was not in line with either the perception of disastrous erosion or the need for new agricultural techniques. The government's efforts failed, and millions of acres of farmland became unproductive for a time. It is easy to imagine other cases, from discontinuing the practice of littering to racially integrating communities and schools, in which social changes were forced to wait on the requisite public opinion changes.

Close to the time of Rousseau's reflections, the founding fathers of the United States were also considering the role and importance of public opinion. During the debates about the Constitution, three distinct positions regarding the role of public opinion were voiced by three of the most famous early Americans.[6] Alexander Hamilton did not trust the public because he believed many were ignorant about the complex matters of government and given to emotional responses that would be unstable as a basis for making policy. Therefore he favored a representative system of government in which the wealthy class, less affected by their own petty self interest, would carry on the work of government. Madison shared Hamilton's concerns that ordinary citizens would be uninformed and likely to act only on their narrow self interests, but was most concerned that the new government be able to promote cooperation. He argued that the representative form of government could best take into account competing private interests and uphold the public interest. Thomas Jefferson disagreed with both Hamilton and Madison. Jefferson argued that the public was able to make informed, stable, and consistent judgments because of two factors. The citizenry was of equal status and shared a common history. However, Jefferson too favored a representative system because he believed that the new country was too large and the population too dispersed to successfully use a system of participative democracy.

The arguments presented by Hamilton, Madison, and Jefferson point to three ideas about public opinion and its role in a democracy that have become traditional. First, public opinion must be well informed to warrant attention. In other words, officials are much more likely to ignore uninformed opinion than informed opinion. Second, public opinion must remain fairly stable over time to be taken into account. If opinion was constantly shifting back and forth, for and against, chaos would result in the realm of policy making. Third, strong and constant principle must underlie public thinking about different issues for public opinion to have impact. In other words, shared values that imply the existence of some consensus about the goals of a society need to undergird the various public opinions about particular decisions.

In order for public opinion to be taken into account, it must be expressed in some way. In a participative democracy, such expression can occur straightforwardly as the citizenry debates and discusses issues of public importance. However, because of the decisions of those like Hamilton, Madison, and Jefferson, the United States operates in the realm of a representative democracy rather than a participative democracy. Moreover, the large populations, diversities of individual and cultural perspectives, and geographic mobility of most citizenries, makes direct expression of opinion in a defined forum unlikely in most communities. The lack of a forum for direct expression of public opinion has made study of that opinion somewhat problematic. In recent decades, within democratic societies, political scientists have studied public opinion primarily in two ways. They have examined voting behavior as a way to investigate the expression of public opinion, and they have studied public opinion polls. The polls certainly provide a direct expression of opinions; however, they do not provide much elaboration of those opinions because polls tend not to provide open-ended questions. An alternative to using either voting behavior or public opinion polls as the method by which to study public opinion formation is to focus on the public discussion of public issues.

The importance of public discussion of a public issue is apparent if we examine the life cycle of a public issue. In a review of the study of public opinion, Katz described four stages of public opinion formation:

1. salience of some problem (issue) for a number of people, even a small minority
2. the discussion of the problem, resulting in increased salience
3. the formation of alternative solutions and the narrowing of alternatives
4. the final mobilization of opinion to affect the collective decision, either through a majority vote (as in an election or referendum) or through the assessment by leaders of the strength of mobilized opinion.[7]

Public discussion is important to each of the last three stages Katz described. It is during the second stage that public discussion of the issue converts the issue from a latent and potentially private one to a public one. As more and more people talk about the problem, the problem is perceived as a public issue. During the third stage, public discussion centers on alternatives and focuses attention toward particular solutions. In the final stage, public discussion about the solution that has been reached is likely to occur. For example, a government official may announce and explain a plan of action or the news media may report and analyze the results of an election.

Given the importance of public discussion to public opinion formation, it is not surprising that many political philosophers have noted the centrality of communication to the formation of communities. John Dewey, for example, wrote: "Men live in a community in virtue of the things which they have in common; and communication is the way in which they come to possess things in common. . . . What they must have in common in order to form a community, or society are aims, beliefs, aspirations, knowledge — a common understanding — like-mindedness as the sociologists say."[8] Similarly, Richard McKeon stated: "The primary function of communication is to establish relations between men. It provides a bond of association and community."[9] Drawing on the work of McKeon, Hauser, a professor of Communications, wrote: [Communication's] end not its beginning, is community — community in action, in common resolution to a common problem. On this interpretation a productive rhetoric *establishes* our bonds of communal sharing, *makes* us a community, and *leads* us to discover what in our experience there is to know. . . ."[10]

In review, then, it is through communication that public issues become noticed, that public opinion begins to be formed, that communities begin to recognize themselves as sharing a common problem and aspiring to a common solution, and that public issues are finally resolved.

The Nature of a Rhetorical
Perspective Toward Communication

Because of the centrality of communication to public issues and public opinion formation, the study of public discussion is important. The study of public discussion is a study of the verbal and nonverbal expressions of people as they talk about public issues in diverse forums with diverse forms. In other words, one may examine the expression of public opinion as it appears in speeches, movies, advertisements, slogans, buttons, newsletters, and all the other forms of communication, wherever the messages present themselves.

Some guidelines regarding what we are looking for as we examine a multiplicity of messages in a variety of forums and forms are necessary to define our inquiry. Because our interest is in determining the nature of public opinions about public issues, we are interested in investigating the public discussions that express a point of view about a public issue. As we investigate that public discussion, we are interested in looking at: (1) how the opinion was formed, (2) how the opinion was expressed, and (3) how the opinion is likely to influence other opinions.

In addition to these guidelines, it is helpful to refine the definition of communication that we have been using thus far in order to further specify just what type of communication we are investigating. Traditionally, communication scholars have described their studies of public discussion of public issues as the study of *rhetoric*. The term, "rhetoric," originated with the ancient Greeks and was used to refer to the practice of public persuasion. For our purposes, a definition of rhetoric provided by Gerard Hauser is particularly helpful. Hauser argues that *rhetoric is the management of symbols in order to coordinate social action*.[11] If we examine his definition in detail, we can see how the definition fits an investigation of the expression of public opinion about public issues.

Three ideas about the nature of rhetoric comprise Hauser's definition. First, is the idea that rhetoric uses symbols. Symbols may be verbal, consisting of language, or nonverbal, including the use of pictures, physical actions, nonlinguistic sounds, spatial arrangements, and so forth. A primary feature of symbols is that they present a meaningful idea, thought, opinion, or belief. In other words, when a person uses symbols, he or she is making a message. Therefore, a rhetorical perspective involves examining a set of symbols in order to uncover the message.

Because examining symbols is so important to a rhetorical perspective, it is helpful to review the various types of symbols. Most messages are comprised of both verbal and nonverbal symbols. As we examine verbal symbols, or language, we are interested in individual words, phrasing, the arrangement of sentences, and the claims that are made. The use of space, motion, objects (physical appearance, color, shape), and paralanguage (tone in spoken discourse and punctuation in written discourse) comprise the nonverbal symbols of a message. Depending on the particular message, some types of symbols may be more prominent than others. A couple of examples may illustrate the diversity of symbol-use.

Many advertisements combine the use of verbal and nonverbal symbols. Verbally, certain words — usually those that are crucial to the thesis of the message — may be repeated and may serve as the subjects for the sentences. The copy may be organized into paragraphs or phrases that highlight the particular advantages or features of the concept, product, or policy that is advocated. The particular words used may connote action, passivity, strength, weakness, or a variety of other meanings.

Nonverbally, every printed advertisement consists of a layout, or spatial arrangement that directs the reader's eye from one part of the message to another. Ideas in the advertisement may be highlighted by the placement of a picture or "headline" at the top or bottom. White space may be used to block off parts of the message, creating a sense of division or association among the ideas. The actual print may be slanted or a picture may portray action that induces the reader to engage in the motion of the message. Objects featured in a picture or a logo or appearing alone in part of the advertisement may suggest additional meanings within the advertisement. Similarly, style of type (e.g., block, script), punctuation, and the use of features such as boldface or italics may underscore certain ideas and downplay others.

A familiar advertisement from the U.S. Army illustrates the type of symbol-use just described. The advertisement features a picture of college students in a collegiate scene dominated by fall colors at the top of the page. Two-thirds of the way down is a "headline" in block-type capital letters, "JOINING THE ARMY MAY BE THE SMARTEST THING YOU CAN DO FOR YOUR COLLEGE EDUCATION." Below the headline are five paragraphs of copy and a chart that describe the benefits of the G.I. Bill and the Army College Fund as well as the more general benefits of joining the Army. At the bottom right is the familiar slogan of the Army's recruiting campaign, "ARMY. BE ALL YOU CAN BE," in smaller, blocked capital letters. This particular advertisement is rich with symbols. The words emphasize being smart, financial success, college education, and being the best that you can be. The idea of college life (and being "smart") is highlighted with the picture. The use of objects, such as the books that the young, attractive people are carrying, the clothes they are wearing, the architecture of the buildings in the background, induces the reader to believe they are viewing a collegiate scene. Within the picture, the students are shown at the top of a stairway, suggesting a feeling of success that comes with being "on top." The fall colors of the mature trees in the background of the picture suggest the beginning of a new academic year, a time when most of us feel optimistic and energetic. The chart, which depicts the monetary contributions of the G.I. Bill and Army College Fund during years two to four of college, features a "bottom line" notion as it relates to individual finances. The clean, block-style of print looks "smart," reinforcing the bold-faced headline. Meanwhile, the accompanying information regarding contributions that the student is required to make are placed in the smaller print.

Non-print messages include the same types of symbols, but sometimes in different ways. Advocates in face-to-face situations also rely on words and phrases arranged into discrete units. However, these direct advocates tend to rely on paralanguage (pauses, changes in rate, volume, and pitch) to punctuate their ideas and to signal discrete ideas. In addition, they may use bodily movement (gestures, facial expressions, eye contact, and so forth) to add to the meaning conveyed through their words. Similarly, their physical appearance and the objects they display may carry additional meaning. And, as they present their messages, the physical layout (the spatial arrangement) of the place may influence the meaning or may even be altered by the advocates themselves as they move about a committee room or lecture hall.

Mediated messages add other nonverbal cues to the spoken or printed verbal symbols. Within a media presentation, for example, background music or sound effects may be used as paralanguage to punctuate the message. Motion may take the form of alternative forms of video editing such as quick-cuts that seem to speed up the action or freeze-frames that slow it down. Spatial arrangement may be determined in part by camera shots and angles that sometimes present the viewer with long shots, other times provide a panoramic view, and other times zoom in for a close-up. The viewer may find herself looking down on the action at one point and up toward the focus of attention at another. Regardless of the form of the message, however, both verbal and nonverbal symbols of the type listed will carry the meaning of a given message.

The second idea imbedded in Hauser's definition is that rhetoric is concerned with the "management" of symbols. When people "manage" something they act with a purpose in mind. Hence, a rhetorical perspective assumes that the people using the symbols are acting purposefully, or intentionally. Because we are concerned with the "management" of symbols, we are concerned with how the symbols are put together to do something, to achieve a purpose. Of course, human intentions do not always work perfectly. Sometimes the best of intentions go awry. Consequently, we are just as interested in the likely result of a message as the original intent of the message-maker.

Again an example can clarify the importance of taking into account the purposiveness of a message. During the 1986 Superbowl, the sportscasters were surprised during the first defensive series by the Chicago Bears. For the first several plays, Gary Fencik, playing safety, dropped back rather than closing a gap on the line. The sportscasters commented that this action would probably encourage the

New England offense to run toward the gap in the line. Then on the third play, when Fencik made the same move, Dave Duerson rushed the gap from his position in the defensive backfield, thereby plugging the hole. With a stroke of insight the sportscasters commented that it looked like Chicago had been trying to trick the New England Patriots into running a play to the left that would not result in any gain. From a rhetorical perspective, what had happened is that Chicago had presented the Patriots with some nonverbal symbols in the form of Fencik's movement in order to lure New England into a trap. In other words, Chicago had "managed" symbols in order to evoke a response by their opponents that would give Chicago the advantage.

The third component of Hauser's definition specifies that the symbols are managed "in order to coordinate social action." In other words, regardless of the particular intention of a particular message-maker, or source, the general purpose of rhetorical communication is to coordinate community action. The emphasis Hauser gives to community action makes his definition particularly appropriate for the study of "public" discussion in which community interests and actions are the focal point. When we assume a rhetorical perspective, we are looking for how the management of symbols results in establishing social relationships among people such that a community is formed and subsequently community opinions are expressed and solutions are reached.

Implicit in the idea that rhetoric coordinates social action is the idea that rhetorical communication involves a transaction between people when a message is sent and received. The communication creates a community by constructing a relationship among people. Most usually in public discussions, at least one party to the transaction constructs the message and assumes the role of source, or advocate. At least one other person receives and interprets the message, thereby assuming the role of receiver, or audience. Frequently, there are several people involved who alternately assume the roles of advocates and audiences. The advocates try to construct their messages strategically, and the audiences try equally to diligently interpret the messages they receive. When we assume a rhetorical perspective we are interested in who is involved in the transaction and what roles they are assuming — are they advocates or audiences or both? As we examine the roles that the participants assume, we are interested in how they use their roles strategically to respond to symbolic messages.

To summarize, it is possible to examine the public discussion of public issues by assuming a rhetorical perspective toward communication. When we do so, we are interested in analyzing messages about public issues. Our examination includes an examination of the symbols used, an investigation of how those symbols are used purposively, and an exploration of how the symbol use establishes social relationships in which people assume different roles and establish themselves as a community. Such investigation describes how opinions are expressed and helps us to speculate about how opinions were formed and what influence those opinions are likely to have on others.

The Influence of Rhetoric on Public Life

Thus far we have taken the existence of public issues and public opinion and public discussion as given and discussed the general nature of each of these concepts. Earlier in this chapter, we observed that in contemporary society many people feel alienated and somewhat cynical about whether or not their opinions make a difference. Yet political philosophers like Aristotle, Rousseau, and others have contended that public opinion does make a difference in the way governments and societies operate. Hence it is helpful to review how public discussion, as a driving force in the formation of public opinion, affects our lives.

Two types of social change emanate from the power of public opinion. Informal social change occurs when informal customs or traditions are altered. Formal social change occurs when laws or their interpretations are changed to prohibit or allow particular actions by the government or its citizenry. There are numerous examples of both types of changes occurring as the discussion of public issues encourages shifts in public opinion.

Informal changes are some of the most interesting. For example, in the 1950s and early '60s, litter was quite common along our highways. It was difficult to drive anywhere on vacation without confronting glass bottles, tin cans, and paper strewn along the highway. In West Virginia, where the fog was often heavy and the sideline of the highway was rarely painted, people used to joke that it was still easy to stay on the road because you could tell where you were by watching your headlights reflect off of the beer cans on the side of the road. Today, you see litter along the roads very rarely; it is simply unacceptable anymore to throw whatever garbage you have outside the window of a car. This informal change occurred over a period of several years during which there was much talk about litter. Government officials and private citizens alike mounted anti-littering campaigns. People talked, joked, and seriously lamented the littered environment until public opinion, or community interest, was mobilized to change the informal custom.

Littering may seem like a trivial example, but a more recent example can hardly be dismissed in the same way. Consider drunk driving. A generation ago, drunk driving was acceptable. People used to brag about how well they could handle an automobile while they were under the influence. Judges rarely gave DUI offenders harsh sentences. Many states did not even have open container laws. Yet within only about six years, primarily as a result of public discussion of drunk driving as initiated by MADD and other similar groups, public opinion has shifted. Not only have many laws been changed, but social customs have changed as well. "Designated drivers," bars that offer taxi services, restricted hours for the sale of beer at sports stadiums, and a general attitude of concern for "friends who drive drunk" are all informal changes that have resulted from the public outcry against drunk driving.

Another example of informal social change has occurred in the area of male-female relations. Twenty years ago, all formal language used masculine pronouns and male-oriented terms. Women were often explicitly discouraged from entering certain career fields or professions, and the idea of women competing in interscholastic sports was limited at best and nonexistent at worst. Although conditions of perfect equality do not yet exist, change has occurred. Public discussion of equal rights and equal opportunity and subsequent shifts in public opinion are in large part responsible for these types of social changes.

Formal social change also results from public opinion as mobilized by public discussion. For example, both the Constitutional Amendment that prohibited the sale of alcohol and the subsequent Amendment that repealed that action resulted from mobilized public opinion. Similarly, the Civil Rights Act was in large part the result of a decade of public discussion about the issue of racial segregation and integration. The eventual withdrawal of United States troops from Vietnam likewise reflected the growing public opinion of the time that our involvement in Southeast Asia was at least unproductive and at worst immoral.

Sometimes formal changes take the form of judicial rulings or administrative policies rather than actual statutory changes. In 1973, the Supreme Court offered the prevailing opinion of the times as one of their reasons in the *Roe v. Wade* decision for ruling that states could not make abortion illegal. Similarly, in the late 1970s, then President Jimmy Carter attempted to solve the energy crisis with measures that focused on conservation because of his allegiance to public opinion polls that indicated Americans believed the availability of energy was a problem at the same time that they deplored wasteful practices.

Because public discussion is central to the formation of public opinion, which in turn influences both formal and informal change, the study of public discussion offers a valuable opportunity for both understanding and participating in social change. This book is intended to offer a communication perspective for understanding and evaluating public discussion. The chapters that follow elaborate the rhetorical perspective outlined in this chapter. We will be exploring a variety of ways to analyze messages and their effects on public affairs.

Summary

The public sphere is concerned with matters that affect groups of people rather than single individuals. The public sphere is constantly in flux as ideas and actions change. For any particular issue or problem, the "public" may consist of a different group of people. When people engage in public discussion, or operate in the public sphere, they generally exhibit a concern for the common good. Public issues are those matters within the public sphere about which there is a likelihood of disagreement. Public opinion is the shared judgment of a group of people about a public issue. Public opinion is most often expressed through communication. Public discussion of public issues not only assists in making those issues salient, but also helps to focus attention on particular alternatives and to reach resolution of the controversy.

A useful perspective for analyzing public discussion is the rhetorical perspective that understands public discussion as the management of symbols in order to coordinate social action. By analyzing symbolic messages about public issues, we can better understand both the formation of public opinion and the influence of public opinion on social change, both formal and informal social change.

Notes

[1]Richard Sennett, *The Fall of Public Man* (New York: Knopf, 1977).

[2]Christopher Lasch, *The Cult of Narcissism: American Life in an Age of Diminishing Expectations* (New York: W.W. Norton, 1979).

[3]Robert N. Bellah, Richard Madsen, William M. Sullivan, Ann Swidler, and Steven M. Tipton, *Habits of the Heart* (Berkeley: University of California Press, 1985), p. 250.

[4]John Dewey, *The Public and Its Problems* (Chicago: Swallow, 1954).

[5]Jean Jacques Rousseau, "The Social Contract," in *The Social Contract and the Discourses,* trans. G.D.H. Cole (New York: Dutton, 1913).

[6]See, W. Lance Bennett, *Public Opinion in American Politics* (New York: Harcourt Brace Jovanovich, 1980), pp. 30-39.

[7]D. Katz, "Attitude Formation and Public Opinion," *Annals of the American Academy of Political anad Social Sciences* 367(1966):150-62.

[8]John Dewey, *Democracy and Education* (New York: Free Press, 1916), p. 4.

[9]Richard McKeon, "Communication, Truth, and Society," *Ethics* 67(1957):93.

[10]Gerard Hauser, "Searching for a Bright Tomorrow: Graduate Education in Rhetoric During the 1980s," *Communication Education* 28(1979):264.

[11]Gerard Hauser, *Introduction to Rhetoric* (New York: Harper and Row, 1985), p. 3.

Suggested Readings

Bellah, Robert N., Richard Madsen, William M. Sullivan, Ann Swidler, and Steven M. Tipton, 1985. *Habits of the Heart.* Berkeley: University of California Press.

Bennett, W. Lance, 1980. *Public Opinion in American Politics.* New York: Harcourt Brace Jovanovich.

Dewey, John, 1954. *The Public and its Problems.* Chicago: Swallow.

Hauser, Garard A., 1985. *Introduction to Rhetoric.* New York: Harper and Row.

Hennessy, Bernard C., 1975. *Public Opinion, 3rd Ed.* Belmont, California: Wadsworth.

Lippman, Walter, 1965. *Public Opinion.* New York: Macmillan.

Sennett, Richard, 1977. *The Fall of Public Man.* New York: Knopf.

Chapter 2

Contemporary Public Discussion and the Rhetorical Situation

In the previous chapter, we described three characteristics of rhetorical communication that were implied by the definition of rhetoric as the management of symbols in order to coordinate social action. In this chapter, we will add a fourth characteristic of rhetoric, or public discussion, which stems from the nature of publics as reactions to actions or ideas: *rhetoric is situated*. In other words, messages constructed during public discussions of public issues are responses to particular situations, to the particular controversies sparked by the public issue in question. Because, as we discussed in the last chapter, the public sphere comes into being when a group of people perceive that they will be affected by a particular idea or action, what is said is influenced by the nature of the situation and subsequently may alter the situation. When people make messages that do not take the situation into account, their messages are usually deemed irrelevant by others. Conversely, as indicated by the discussion of the influence of public discussion on formal and informal social change in the previous chapter, when messages are attended to and perceived as relevant the situation may be altered in terms of social changes. In this chapter, we will explore both the general nature of the rhetorical situation and investigate ways for analyzing the rhetorical situation unique to any particular discussion of a public issue.

The Rhetorical Situation

Professor Lloyd Bitzer explained the general nature of the rhetorical situation in a landmark essay by the same name.[1] His central thesis was that certain complexes of persons, events, objects, and relations invite public discussion which, if it is fitting to the situation, alters the situation. His suggestion rests on the belief that rhetoric is powerful enough to alter some situations, and recognizes that the situation which provokes a rhetorical response exists for a limited period of time in a particular place. A clear implication of Bitzer's idea of the rhetorical situation is that analysis of rhetoric, particularly public discussion, requires analysis of the rhetorical situation that invited a rhetorical response.

In his explanation of the rhetorical situation, Bitzer lists three components of any particular rhetorical situation that can provide three areas for analysis by anyone interested in investigating a rhetorical situation: (1) *exigence*, (2) *audience*, and (3) *constraints*.

The *exigence* is defined as *an imperfection marked by urgency.* In other words, the exigence is the reason why someone is motivated to make a message, or to engage in public discussion. For example, in the case of MADD, a single mother whose daughter had been killed by a drunk driver was motivated to speak out against drunk driving. The existence of drunk drivers who threatened the safety of the highways constituted the imperfection, and the recent death of a daughter and the accompanying grief gave this imperfection an urgency that Ms. Lightner could not ignore. Similarly, when officials of the Soviet Union recently proposed elimination of all medium range nuclear missiles in Europe, officials of the United States felt a need to respond. The global threat of holocaust attendant to the existence of massive numbers of nuclear weapons is a continuing imperfection, and the new proposal offered by the Soviets combined with a perceived need by many Reagan Administration officials for some type of arms control agreement before Reagan's term ended gave an urgency to the imperfection.

The exigence to which an advocate, or public discussant, responds may be either historically real or merely perceived by the source of the message. For example, in the case of arms control, the threat of nuclear war and the existence of thousands of missiles is real. We could look at, feel, and even count the missiles, and we could find plenty of experts willing to assess the degree of risk regarding nuclear war. However, the desire to reach an arms control agreement before the end of Reagan's term in office is an exigence that arises in the perceptual frames of his staff and, perhaps, Reagan himself. People's sense of history and desire for a President to "go down in history" encourages them to be aware of the fact that up to 1987 Reagan was the only President since the dawn of the nuclear age *not* to reach an arms control agreement with the Soviets. The urgency of the imperfection felt by members of the administration was the result of inner realities — beliefs, values, motives — rather than external realities. Both types of exigencies are equally legitimate; either is sufficient cause for a rhetorical response, that is for the management of symbols in order to coordinate social action.

In the case of arms control, we have at least two exigencies operating simultaneously. Both the need to reduce the threat of nuclear war and the need to solidify Reagan's place in history work together as dual exigencies for discussion of the issue. Further analysis of this situation might reveal other exigencies as well. For example, the recent public appearances of Gorbacev, the Soviet leader, have resulted in a new, more appealing image of Soviet leadership in the international community. Anxiety about the Soviets assuming the role of "the good guys" internationally could provide a third exigency for a response by the United States. In any case, this example points to another characteristic of the exigency in a rhetorical situation. There may be more than one. The reasons people engage in public discussion may be many and varied even for a particular episode of public discussion.

The second element of the rhetorical situation is the *audience*. Bitzer defined the audience as *those people with both an interest and an ability to deal with the exigence*. This definition suggests that the audience is not just anyone who hears or reads or sees a public message but is that group of people who are interested and are able to do something about the imperfection marked by urgency.

If we return to the example of arms control, we can see how the various exigencies point to different audiences. In the case of the exigence of reducing the threat of nuclear war, it is likely that all the world's people who are informed enough to know about the possibility of nuclear holocaust are interested in the exigence; however, a much smaller group of people are in a position to do something about reducing the threat. Officials of government, who have the power to make the policy decisions that could either launch or prevent a war, are the most obvious audience. Members of the military, who would carry out the orders, and peace activists, who make efforts to reduce the threat, are also audiences who have some ability to deal with the exigence as well as an interest in it.

In contrast to the exigence of reducing the threat of nuclear war, the exigence of elevating the historical importance of Reagan's presidency suggests a different audience. Scholars of history, political commentators, and journalists all have an interest in the enduring values of a President's term of office. These same people, by virtue of their power to record and disseminate their judgments to the larger population, have the ability to slant the historical record either in favor of, or against, the Reagan Administration. Thus they are a primary audience given the exigence. Future generations of ordinary people, however, will make judgments regarding the worth of the President's actions. Hence, ordinary people of future generations constitute another potential audience for this exigency. And, of course, with widespread public opinion polling that periodically questions ordinary citizens about their perceptions regarding how well the President is doing his job, ordinary citizens both in the United States and abroad constitute another audience for this exigency.

If the third exigency, the need to reestablish the United States as "the good guy" internationally, is considered then other potential audiences emerge as important. World leaders have an interest in, and ability to, assess the relative value of aligning themselves with East or West and establishing international relations accordingly. These leaders are also subject to public opinion in their respective nations, and because public opinion emerges from the general populace, citizens throughout the world may constitute an audience.

Just as there may be more than one exigence, there may be more than one audience for any particular rhetorical act. However, we may determine the audience only after investigating the exigence because the audience is composed of only those people with both an interest in, and ability to deal with, the exigence.

The third component of the rhetorical situation is the collection of *constraints* that exist for the rhetorical response. Constraints are *both limitations and opportunities for what can be said in what ways*. Constraints arise from the nature of the exigence, the nature of the source, the nature of the audience, and the general time, place, and conditions of the rhetorical act. Again some examples will help to clarify the nature of constraints.

If we consider the example of a representative from MADD speaking to a community organization about drunk driving, we can explore both the limitations and opportunities for what may be said in what ways. One set of limitations on what can be said arises from the exigence, the problem of too many drunk drivers on the local highways and streets. Both the discussion of the problem and the solutions offered are limited by those factors relevant to the problem of drunk driving. If other topics, such as the need for funds by MADD or the upcoming summer picnic for interested members of the organization or the quality of instruction at the local high school, are to be discussed they must somehow be discussed as relevant to the exigence or the nature of the rhetorical situation will change with the introduction of new and different exigencies. Similarly, both opportunities and limitations arise from the nature of the speaker. If the speaker has experienced the anguish of losing a loved one to an accident precipitated by alcohol abuse, then the opportunity for personal anecdotes presented sincerely with the added credibility of personal experience suggests itself. Conversely, if talking about an episode that the speaker has experienced evokes the experience of severe grief and anguish, the negative and emotional feelings of the speaker may serve as limitations for what he or she chooses to discuss. The audience furnishes limitations and opportunities as well. The discussion of the problem as well as the solution needs to conform to the audience's understanding of the facts and inclinations toward viable solutions. If the prevailing attitude toward alcohol in the community is liberal and includes a sense that drinking to excess is socially acceptable and a way of life, limits on what can be said may exist. If the audience is composed of people who rarely drink at all, there may be opportunities for offering more far-reaching solutions than otherwise. Recent events and places well known to members of the audience may furnish opportunities for ways to elaborate on the message. For example, a recent automobile accident or wild party may serve as an example from which the speaker can work his or her message. Suggestions might be made for local events at which designated drivers (people who agree not to drink so they may chauffeur friends home) would be present. The particular time and place of the discussion may also offer limitations and opportunities, ranging from what audio-visual materials can be used to enrich the discussion to how long the message can be to maintain the interest of the audience.

We will conduct a fuller discussion of constraints in the context of another example letter, but for now it is enough to remember that constraints can arise from any aspect of the situation and furnish both limitations and opportunities for what can be said in what ways. To review, when people engage in public discussion they generate messages in response to rhetorical situations. If their messages fit the situation, their messages have taken into account the exigence, the audience, and the constraints.

Dynamics of the Rhetorical Situation

If we combine our knowledge about the rhetorical situation with the characteristics of rhetorical communication discussion in Chapter 1, we can gain a clearer picture of how public discussion operates. In general, public discussion is a dynamic activity in which the people involved often switch roles and the situation may be constantly changing. As suggested by the diagram below, a source, or advocate, constructs a message that is composed of symbols that are then received and interpreted by an audience. All of this happens within the context of a particular situation.

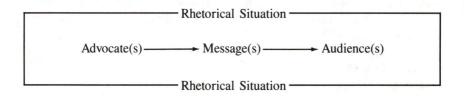

When public discussion occurs, the roles of advocate and audience do not necessarily remain stable. Frequently, whoever receives the message about a public issue may have a response to the message, and therefore become an advocate. Thus, it is helpful to think of audiences as potential advocates, who may respond to an advocate's message with their own messages. When that happens, the original advocate becomes an audience. Therefore, it is equally helpful to think of the advocate as a potential audience. For example, when a news commentator interviews a political candidate concerning her views of the state of AIDS research and treatment, a public discussion is transpiring. Initially, the political candidate may play the role of advocate, explaining and defending her perspective toward the appropriate public actions regarding AIDS. However, if the news commentator follows the candidate's statement with additional questions that suggest there may be problems with the candidate's perspective, then the commentator has begun to act as an advocate for an opposing point of view, for which the candidate has become an audience. Moreover, if the interview is televised, a second audience of television viewers also exists. If, on the other hand, the interview is conducted in a forum where viewers may call in to make statements or ask questions, for example the "Phil Donahue Show," then the viewing audience is also a group of potential advocates, who may construct their own messages on the subject. The diagram below more accurately describes public discussion, given the flexibility of roles assumed by the advocates and audiences during public discussion.

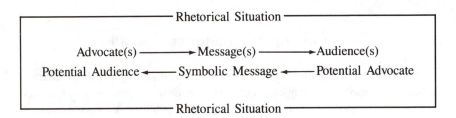

Notice that the rhetorical situation surrounds the action of the advocates and audiences. In other words, public discussion both occurs within the context of the rhetorical situation and influences the rhetorical situation. In addition, characteristics of the advocate(s), message, and audience(s) influence both the context for the public discussion by furnishing constraints and helping to shape the exigence and influence the outcome of the public discussion by eventually altering the situation.

We have already discussed how characteristics of the advocate, the audience, and the context can provide constraints on the message. However, a few words about how a message can influence the situation are in order. Traditionally, as we observed earlier in this chapter, advocates are presumed to construct messages that conform to the rhetorical situation. In other words, the message is assumed to fit the rhetorical situation. When a message fits the situation, the result of the public discussion is likely to be a movement toward a solution to the exigence that provoked the discourse to begin with. For example, if an exigence, the need to slow the spread of AIDS, provokes the Surgeon General to make a public statement in which he advocates safer sex through the use of condoms, then his message will likely reduce the incidence of AIDS if his audience is of a mind to accept the use of condoms as a viable way to deal with AIDS. If, however, the audience is opposed to the use of condoms or even opposed to the activity of sex under most circumstances, then the Surgeon General's message would not fit the constraints of the audience and the exigence would not be solved.

Sometimes, however, advocates can construct messages that do not fit the rhetorical situation and still experience a measure of success from their public discourse. This is because advocates are sometimes able to redefine the nature of the rhetorical situation through their discourse. Two contemporary scholars of communication, Robert Branham and Barnett Pearce, have described four principle means by which communicators may respond to the situation in which they speak through their discourse: conformity, nonparticipation, desecration, and contextual reconstruction.[2]

Conformity involves adapting the message to the situation at hand. By adapting the message to the constraints of the situation, an advocate furnishes the audience a way to deal with the exigence that conforms to their needs, abilities, and expectations. The examples discussed so far are all examples of conformity. *Nonparticipation* occurs when an advocate refuses to participate in a rhetorical situation. For example, in 1969 a group of antiwar advocates were on trial in Chicago for conspiring to provoke riots and other disturbances during the National Democratic Convention in 1968. Ordinarily, defendants in a criminal proceeding, especially one with the heavy political overtones of the "Chicago Seven" trial, are expected to speak out in their own defense, to take the stand and tell their story. However,the seven defendants followed an initial display of "outrageous" behavior with silence, thereby refusing to participate in the rhetorical situation by any conventional standard of what constituted participation. Their silence made a statement about their view of the legitimacy of the trial. In other words, their nonparticipation actually sent a message about their opinion regarding the rhetorical situation. Their supporters were delighted. Their opponents were disgusted. Through their nonparticipation, they created a new rhetorical situation in which the issue no longer was whether or not the group was criminally responsible but whether or not the political-judicial system was legitimate.

A third means of response, according to Branham and Pearce, is *desecration*. When an advocate desecrates a rhetorical situation, he or she responds to the situation with a message that so violates the standards of appropriateness in that situation that the effect is to question the legitimacy of the situation. Hence, the effect of desecration is similar to that of nonparticipation, to question the legitimacy of the situation. The means for achieving that effect, however, responding with an inappropriate message, is different from offering no message. The antics of the anti-war protestors before their silence provide an example of desecration. By coming into court dressed in judicial robes, bringing in birthday cakes, and so forth, the defendants violated the decorum of a judicial procedure. Their messages, more common to a party than a trial, resulted in reflection by many as to what exactly the rhetorical situation was.

A final means by which to respond to a rhetorical situation is *contextual reconstruction*. An advocate reconstructs the context by presenting a message that recognizes the situation at hand but alters the exigence as perceived by the audience. Branham and Pearce provide a classic example of contextual reconstruction with their analysis of the "Gettysburg Address." Abraham Lincoln acknowledged the situation for his speech when he commented that "it was altogether fitting and proper . . . to dedicate a portion of that field as a final resting place for those who here gave their lives that that nation might live." However, he also noted that such an exigence was impossible to meet: ". . . we cannot dedicate — we cannot consecrate — we cannot hallow this ground." Instead, Lincoln reconstructed the situation with a new exigence: ". . . it is for us, the living, rather, to be dedicated here to the unfinished work which they who fought here have thus far so nobly advanced." Thus, Lincoln used his address as a means by which to transform the event from one of burial to one of rebirth. A more contemporary example of an advocate reconstructing the situation occurred during the Iran/Contra Hearings. Some, if not all, of Oliver North's popularity when he testified before Congress stemmed from his ability to shift attention away from his participation in activities of questionable legality and toward the desperate needs of the "Freedom Fighters" of Nicaragua. Following a suggestion that North be allowed to present his slide show on the need for military assistance for the "Contras," Senators and Congressmen engaged in lengthy debate about whether or not he should be allowed to make his pitch. They appeared to recognize that if he was allowed to shift the topic of discussion accordingly he might redefine the context.

In review then, public discussion arises in situations that seem to require a communicative response. Those situations can be defined by describing the exigence, the audience, and the constraints. As discussion proceeds, the original advocate may play the role of audience and the original audience may play the role of advocate. Similarly, the result of an advocate's message may be a revision of the audience's expectations, and thus the constraints and even the exigence may shift. As public discussion occurs, that discussion may alter the situation that initially encouraged the discussion. The message, whether it fits the constraints or reconstructs the exigence, will likely alter the situation.

Advocates, Audiences and Issues in Contemporary Society

As the preceding discussion suggests, any particular situation will have particular advocates, audiences, exigencies and constraints. However, it is possible to observe the prototypical rhetorical situations for a given society at a given time. In other words, we can explore who is likely to engage in public discussion under what circumstances. Aristotle did precisely that during the fourth century B.C. in Ancient Greece.

In the *Rhetoric*, Aristotle classified three types of oratory common to public life in Greece according to three types of judgments likely to be made on the basis of what was said. We can think of those three types of judgments as resulting from three different types of exigencies. In other words, Aristotle observed three different reasons for public discussion, each of which had its own unique constraints.

The three types of oratory Aristotle catalogued were: *deliberative, forensic,* and *epideictic.*[3] Deliberative oratory consisted of public discussion that was designed to reach agreement about public policies, the future courses of action that should be followed by the polity, or self-governing citizenry. Forensic oratory was concerned with past actions by individuals and whether or not those actions implied guilt or innocence regarding the individual's relationship to the larger community. Epideictic oratory consisted of public discussions that would result in praise or blame of individual actions by the polity as a whole based on present-day standards. If we look for the exigencies that provoked these three types of public address, we find that the need to decide which policy would be best required deliberative oratory, the need to determine legal guilt or innocence required forensic oratory, and the need to agree about what was praiseworthy and what was not required epideictic oratory.

Aristotle's three divisions arose in a society in which every person was his own advocate. Although an individual might seek help in writing his address, he himself was an active advocate on public matters. Moreover, the audience to which the advocate in Ancient Greece spoke was fairly stable. In Book I of the *Rhetoric*, Aristotle devoted considerable time to description of the nature of the Greek audience at that time. Contemporary society is, of course, quite different from that of Ancient Greece as we saw in Chapter 1. However, we can explore the basic types of situations in contemporary American society in much the same way as Aristotle described the rhetorical situations of his day.

Let us begin by considering the prototypical exigencies that provoke public discussion in contemporary American society. W. Lance Bennett, a political scientist, has identified three origins for public issues.[4] He suggests that some issues are structural, some are agenda, and some are crisis issues. His classification of the origin of issues is an attempt to explain what accounts for something becoming an issue that is subsequently discussed and about which opinions are formed that urge a resolution of the issue. We can explore each type of issue as a type of exigence that is likely to provoke public discussion.

Structural issues arise because of the structure of society. In other words, some points of controversy are embedded in the prevailing political, economic, or social structure. For example, given the nature of the United States economy as a mixture of private and public interests, cycles of employment and unemployment and inflation and price stability will probably always exist. Consequently, many economic issues are likely to surface, be resolved, and resurface. The exigencies are built into the system. Similarly, the current geo-political reality of the world is such that we are divided into autonomous nation-states, or sovereign states. So long as world government remains the dream of only a few rather than a reality, sovereignty is likely to result in some international conflicts of interest. Consequently, issues of war and peace will emerge and reemerge as structural issues.

Agenda issues, on the other hand, become issues because some elite group of people place them on the public agenda through a persuasive campaign. By "elite" group, I mean a group of people who organize themselves so that they may function as opinion leaders. In other words, either because of their special status as members of a particular profession or holders of a particular office or because of some special expertise and knowledge that they possess, they assume a position of "expert" that may influence other people who do not consider themselves expert on the matter at hand. By pointing out a problem, social ill, or other situation, these elites may construct an agenda issue. Consider for example, the issue of drug abuse during 1986. Nancy Reagan, from her position as First Lady, began a campaign against drugs that has since become identified as a campaign to "Just Say NO." If we examine the statistics from that time period we find that the number of people using and abusing drugs in 1986 was not very different from the number using and abusing in 1980. However, Mrs. Reagan and her followers helped make drug abuse an issue by making it part of their public speaking agenda. The agenda-makers need not be public figures or celebrities, although that does help them secure the media attention they need in order to influence the public agenda. Consider, for example, the plethora of environmental issues raised during the late 1970s and early 1980s. In these cases, the elites were groups like the Sierra Club and Greenpeace. By organizing fairly ordinary citizens into a cohesive group that studied, became informed about, and kept watch on various erosions of environmental quality, these people constructed agenda issues ranging from the need to protect baby seals to the need to save redwood forests from industrial development. The anti-drunk driving campaign we examined earlier in this text also provides an example of an agenda issue.

Sometimes we find ourselves confronted by some natural or manmade disaster. When this happens, we are confronted with *crisis issues*. For example, in 1976 some ordinary families near Niagara Falls, New York, noticed slimy substances oozing up through the ground in their backyards. Simultaneously, they worried about the large number of miscarriages experienced by the young mothers in the neighborhood and the strange illnesses that many people living there were suffering. This crisis of the leaking of hazardous wastes at Love Canal spawned an issue concerning hazardous waste. In 1987, Continental Airlines was plagued by a number of crisis situations. Their airplanes were involved in several "near misses" in the course of a couple weeks; their pilots landed at the wrong airports or took the wrong flight paths at about the same time. During the same period a Northwest Airlines jet crashed shortly after taking off at Detroit. All but one aboard died. For a good month afterward, there was much public discussion of airline safety, a crisis issue at that time.

Usually an issue is provoked primarily by one of the three origins that Bennett identified. However, it is not unusual for the exigence to be somewhat complex and the origin of the issue to be a complex of factors. For example, a crisis may be used by an elite group to promote an issue on the public agenda. Or a particular elite group may be concerned with a particular aspect of the structure of society such that their discussion originates because of a structural feature but through their expertise the issue reaches the public agenda. Thus issues may sometimes find their origins in more than one of the places identified by Bennett.

Just as we examined the typical exigencies in our society, we can investigate the typical advocates and audiences. In contemporary society individual roles are highly defined, and specialization and division of labor in our complex society has resulted in the growth of special institutions in which public discussion occurs and particular professional careers in which advocacy is the primary function. Even so, discussion of public issues may occur almost anywhere, from Congressional chambers to household living rooms. Hence, it is helpful to think about the difference between formal advocacy, where the forum is an established institution and the advocates are professionals, and informal advocacy, where the forum is anywhere and the advocates are amateurs.

We can begin by considering *public institutions and formal advocacy.* From the local to the national level, our system of government has created a variety of institutional forums for formal advocacy. Discussions of public policy occur in city councils, state legislatures,and the U.S. Congress and Senate. In these settings, discussion and debate is frequently carried on exclusively by elected representatives. However, almost as often, the public hearing is used as a means for advocacy in which any citizen and some noncitizens may participate. Despite their alleged "fact-finding" goal, hearings frequently offer the opportunity for interested individuals who are not professional advocates to voice their opinion. Whether it is a question of creating a new transit system for the city or a question of what happened when the U.S. sold weapons to Iran and used some of the funds to resupply the Contras, ordinary people may be solicited to speak about their opinions, interests, and involvements.

Public issues arise in other formal institutions as well. The judicial system offers an array of forums for advocacy. Although some are designed primarily to deal with private disputes in civil proceedings, many, particularly at the appellate level, provide the apparatus for formal advocacy about public issues in which professional attorneys engage the issues. Similarly, many administrative agencies, such as the Environmental Protection Agency (EPA), the Federal Communications Commission (FCC), the Occupational Health and Safety Agency (OSHA), and others, hold public hearings in which any interested party may present their views and conduct deliberations in which only their appointed members engage the issues.

Common to all public institutions in which formal advocacy occurs is a highly defined situation for public discussion, in which some formal procedure for discussion has been established and some people have been designated as advocates. The rules, roles, and norms within these situations furnish some of the constraints for message-making in these situations and therefore must be taken into account if we are analyzing public discussion in these forums.

In addition to formal advocacy that occurs in highly defined formal institutions, much discussion about public issues occurs informally in a variety of places. Informal advocacy comes in many forms. For example, friends may discuss the threat of nuclear war in an informal conversation. Or millions of television viewers may watch a docu-drama about incest in America. Or college students may reflect on posters that appear on their campus regarding race relations. *Informal advocacy is characterized by the lack of formal rules for discussion and diversity of advocates and audiences.*

The lack of formal rules for discussion in the case of informal advocacy implies that anyone may take the role of advocate. However, when anyone decides to make a message abut a public issue, the elements of the rhetorical situation still exist. For example, if two friends engage in a conversation about the status of women's rights, chances are they are responding to an exigence for which each feels the need to clarify personally where they stand on this issue. Are women really equal to men? Does contemporary society make equal opportunity relatively easy or relatively difficult? Should they support new legislative actions to promote women's rights? Because their discussion transpires outside the purview of a formal institution that could formally change the legal status of women in our society, they as audience have no ability to make formal changes. However, they do have the ability to form their own opinions on the matter, opinions that may at some point be taken into account by the policy makers. In this situation, each friend may play both the roles of advocate and audience as each responds to shared or different exigencies. Constraints arise not only from the particular place and time in which they converse but from their relationship as well. If they are long-time friends, they may be aware of particular beliefs, biases, moods, and expectations that will limit or open the terms of discussion. Because they are engaged in a friendly conversation, their procedure for discussion will not be as formally defined as a court of law, but they will likely follow the patterns of turntaking common to ordinary conversation.

Other examples of informal advocacy illustrate the range of options open to those who engage in such discussion. Let's return to our two friends who are interested in women's rights. If, as a result of their discussion, they decide to become actively involved in a local chapter of a women's rights group, they may engage in another type of informal discussion of public issues. The group they join may hold a workshop or sponsor a lecture on the subject in which members of the community are invited to attend. In this case, the exigence may simply be the need to raise community awareness on the issue. As the event is organized, the situation will be more formally defined than the prior conversation. If the group decides to broaden their efforts by circulating posters, buttons, and pins that promote women's rights (e.g., a button that reads, "59 Cents," the average amount a woman earns as compared to a dollar by a man), then the situation may become even less formally defined than the prior conversation. In both cases, the audience becomes larger and at the same time less involved with the advocate. The constraints furnished by the friendship relationship fall away. Meanwhile, constraints resulting from the lecture format and the expectations of the audience for the public lecture come into play in the first case, and constraints unique to the type of social interaction that results in people wearing and noticing buttons, posters, or pins comes into play in the second case. In the lecture the role of advocate will be fairly stable, while with the use of posters and buttons the advocate may be played by a number of people or none at all.

Given the description of formal and informal advocacy thus far, you may be thinking that perhaps another characteristic that distinguishes the two is the type of social change that each precipitates. It would be easy, but misleading, to suggest that formal advocacy results in formal social change while informal advocacy results in informal social change. In fact, both result in both types of change. For example, just the existence of a formal public hearing regarding flood control may result in raising homeowners' awareness of the dangers of building or living on a flood-plain such that planned development in such areas is halted without any formal legislation prohibiting it. Similarly, enough informal discussion about the dangers of improperly discarded toxic waste may cause lawmakers to take notice and pass legislation that regulates such disposal. Hence, both formal and informal advocacy can manifest public opinion in ways that lead to social change. The difference between the two exists in the rigor and codification of the nature of the rhetorical situations in which the two types of discussion arise.

Media and the Multiplicity of Messages about Public Issues

In contemporary society, we frequently receive our information about public issues secondhand. In other words, we rarely actually attend and witness a debate between public officials regarding public issues; we rarely visit Congressional chambers to observe discussion by public officials. Instead, more often we rely on the mass media to select and transmit the important arguments of the day to us through articles in newspapers or magazines or programs on television. Therefore, the role of the media in public discussion requires investigation.

If we conceptualize public discussion as occurring as an event in which people play roles as advocates and audiences in response to an exigence, we may conceptualize the *media as choreographers of public discussion*. In other words, the media may orient us toward recognizing some exigencies and ignoring others at the same time that the media suggests who is the advocate and who is the audience. Scholars of communication and political science have conducted extensive research on the role of the mass media in the formation of public opinion in order to elaborate how the media influence our understandings of the various elements in the rhetorical situation. Those studies have resulted in two theoretical concepts that are important to the student of public controversy.

The first theoretical concept that requires exploration is the characterization of the function of the mass media in public discussion: the *agenda setting function*. From at least the early 1920s, the idea that the mass media could play a powerful role in shaping people's opinions was voiced by numerous intellectuals. The effects of newspapers and other print materials for years had suggested that a carefully crafted article could persuade the citizenry to support particular policies in addition to merely informing readers about those policies. "Yellow journalism," the persistent sensationalist discussions of the need to go to war in Cuba by writers like William Randolph Hearst of the *New York Examiner* and Pulitzer of the New York *Sunday World* that resulted in public support for Teddy Roosevelt and the "Rough Riders," was one of the more notable examples of the influence of the mass media. Similarly, during World War II, there was great concern for how officials in Nazi Germany were using the mass media for purposes of propaganda, to manipulate the opinions of the masses in Europe. Even so, there persisted the idea that if media were used in a nonmanipulative way the primary function of the media would be to present an objective account of the facts.

In 1972 however, two scholars, McCombs and Shaw, put into writing what others had surmised for some time, that even "objective" type news reporting played an influential role in the forming of public opinion. The reason, they asserted, was because the media played an agenda setting function.[5] In other words, if an event, controversy, or position on a public issue received media coverage it was more likely to be considered an important event, controversy or position by the reading, listening, or viewing public. If the media talked about something, other people in other contexts were also likely to talk about the same thing. The point that McCombs and Shaw made was different from the observation of the manipulation common to propaganda that had been observed by others. They were not suggesting that the media told us what to think, but merely that the media told us what to think about. In other words, those issues that receive media coverage are more likely to attract public concern, and thereby to provide focal points for controversy.

A variety of studies have provided some support for the idea that the media sets the public agenda. For example, one study of magazine coverage of fluoridation of water and nuclear power from 1950 to 1975 found a correlation between the amount of media coverage and the public reaction against those issues.[6] Similarly, a year-long study of the 1976 presidential campaign showed that Jimmy Carter's movement to the front of the Democratic pack of contenders that year correlated with extensive media coverage of his campaign.[7]

Although the agenda setting function of the media has been documented, reviews of the body of research in this area suggest that the media's function is not a simplistic one. In general, massive and intensive coverage of an issue makes that issue more salient, or more important, than other issues. However, there are exceptions. A study of the Watergate scandal that resulted in Nixon's resignation from the Presidency, for example, concluded that discussions by the Supreme Court, the Congress, and other influential citizens were contributing causes of public concern along with media coverage.[8] Other scholars have demonstrated that sometimes media coverage makes the advocates more important than the issues.[9] In other words, extensive coverage can elevate the importance of public institutions and the particular public officials in those institutions without really influencing the perceived importance of the issues discussed by those officials in those institutions. Thus, the agenda setting function of the media influences not only the exigencies to which the tuned-in citizenry is likely to grant importance, but also helps determine which advocates will be given a greater hearing.

The ability of the media to set the public agenda is explained in part by a second theoretical concept emerging from media studies: *the gatekeeper theory*. The notion that the media act as gatekeepers means that the media have the power to choose what will and will not be covered, which news they will let in through the gate and which they will shut out. Obviously, the events, issues, arguments, and so forth that take place any particular day far exceed the capabilities of the news profession to cover all of them. News broadcasts typically last only a half an hour and magazines and newspapers have limited amounts of space. Moreover, readers, viewers, and listeners have only so much time to spend checking out the news. Consequently, decisions about what will be covered and to what extent influence what arrives on the public agenda.

Because decisions about coverage have enormous impact as to what issues are perceived as important and which advocates are perceived as credible, it is crucial to explore the variety of decisions made by the media. First, the media must decide whether or not to cover an event or issue, whether or not to put someone on the story. Assuming that is done, then they must choose how much coverage to give the story — how much time to give it on the evening news, how much space to give it in the paper or magazine. Third, the media must make choices about placement. Will they play the story up by putting it on the front page, the cover, or as the lead on the broadcast, or will they play the story down by burying it in the back pages or making it the "human interest" wrap-up at the end of the broadcast? Fourth, a decision must be reached about how to contextualize the story. In other words, what type of headline or lead-in should frame the story? What photographs should accompany the story? Should there be a side-bar, or accompanying interview from a different perspective? Finally, a decision must be made about whether or not to continue coverage. Should there be a follow-up report? The choices made by the media regarding each of these decisions are choices that elaborate their role as gatekeepers. They are also choices about how the issue will reach the public agenda.

A brief example will help illuminate the role of the media in regard to public controversy. In 1967 an event about a public issue occurred which has been referred to as the march of the Jeanette Rankin brigade. ABC News covered the event intensively, partly in order to conduct an experiment regarding the nature of journalism at that time. For some time, journalists had asserted that their role was merely to report the news as objectively as possible, that their function was to "hold a mirror to the world" to reflect what was happening. ABC decided to test that proposition.

In the case of the Jeanette Rankin Brigade, ABC produced a 16 minute news report of the event, the product of several days of investigation and the work of 17 reporters and camerapersons. In addition, they compared their coverage to that of the NBC Nightly News, the *New York Times*, the *Washington Post*, and the United Press International Wire Service. The lengthy ABC report revealed that a group of women, mostly middle-class and educated, from across the nation, mostly members of religious groups (YWCA, WSCS, church-women's groups) had planned to march at the Capitol and to deliver a petition to then majority leader Mike Mansfield requesting an end to the Vietnam War. Leading the march was to be Jeanette Rankin, then 87 and retired, but formerly the only female member of the House of Representative for many years and the only person to vote "no" regarding the U.S. participation in both World War I and World War II. ABC explained how the women were forced to alter their route for the march after government officials had invoked an obscure law prohibiting marches and demonstrations on the Capitol grounds, a law that had not been invoked during civil rights marches that had occurred earlier. ABC also presented interviews with a variety of the marchers, providing a human side to the story that showed the women as fairly ordinary people, not radical feminists or uninformed citizens. In addition, they covered both the march and the conference and rally held afterwards at a Washington hotel, noting that there was some division between the older, more conservative women and the younger, more radical women, but emphasizing the coalition-nature of the group.

When compared to the other news coverage of the event, the results were striking. David Brinkley gave the event 52 seconds on his broadcast and spoke exclusively about Jeanette Rankin and the petition she presented to her former colleague, Mike Mansfield, concluding with a quip that when he was 87 he hoped he'd just be able to walk, let alone march in support of a public cause. The *New York Times* assigned only three staff members to the story, who focused primarily on getting good, dramatic pictures of yet another demonstration against the war in Vietnam. In contrast, the *Washington Post* assigned nearly thirty people to the story, gave it several pages in the "Women's Section" of the paper, and emphasized the personal stories of the women involved. UPI gave it a couple of lines on the wire service, referring to Rankin as a "peacenik" and "aging hippie."

In the context of the times, the story of the Jeanette Rankin Brigade was just one piece in a large puzzle of news items about the Vietnam War. The issue was already on the public agenda. However, the disparate coverage accorded this event by various institutions of the media is a clear example of how both the importance of the issue and the identity of the advocate(s) can be influenced as the media perform their role as gatekeepers.

The context for the example just described leads us to a final consideration concerning the nature of contemporary rhetorical situations and the role of the media. The coverage of the Brigade was a fairly small and short message among many in the discussion of the war, and in this way it is somewhat typical of the form of public discussion as choreographed by the media. We are often confronted by a *multiplicity of messages that appear as fragments within a larger discussion of a public issue.*

The topic of public discussion in formal institutions and informal settings earlier in this chapter identified some forums that, because they were designed especially for public discussion, allow communication events to occur holistically. In these situations, advocates and audiences are physically present, and the event has a fairly defined beginning and end. Similarly, the message is whole. However, when we consider the use of media to transmit public discussion, we find that many times the media presents us with a multiplicity of excerpts of physically and historically real events and packages of staged and planned events. We, who view or read or listen, are the audience, but the advocates are multiple, sometimes obscure, and the messages are frequently fragmentary.

Michael McGee, a communications scholar who has commented on this phenomena of multiple message fragments, provided an interesting litany of the multiplicity of mediated public discussion about the issue of drug abuse in our society.[10] He described the news reports of basketball star Len Bias' death from a drug overdose, Nancy Reagan's "Just Say 'No'" public service announcements, an advertisement for beer that uses part of a music video showing a rock star singing about not being lonely tonight (lyrics that in context refer to cocaine abuse), a highly rated television show ("Miami Vice") that constantly illustrated the battle between a vice squad in Miami and the drug runners and pushers in Florida, and the news items that suggested that during the Iran/Contra affair an airplane used to deliver weapons to the "Freedom-Fighters" in Nicaragua was also used to deliver smuggled drugs to a U.S. military airport in the southern United States. His point was that the casual television viewer and newspaper reader was likely exposed to a multiplicity of message fragments that all bear on the issue of drug abuse. His observations, of course, could be extended to describe discussion of public issues generally.

Not only does the media provide us a constant stream of message fragments from which we the audience may have to construct a whole discussion of public issues, but many contemporary advocates use the media as a way to package their messages and attain the coverage needed to thrust an issue onto the public agenda. For example, both groups who have taken a stand on the abortion issue have produced films to support their positions. When Pro-Life groups produced "Silent Scream" as a documentary designed to convince viewers that abortion was wrong, Pro-Choice groups countered with "Response to Silent Scream" to convince viewers that women must be able to choose abortion as an option. Both films were made available to the media, and both were broadcast during prime time by the Public Broadcasting System. The films show a number of real and staged rhetorical situations, but they themselves function in a distinct rhetorical situation where the audience is the viewer, the message is the entire film, but the identity of the advocates becomes blurred. Is the director, the producer, the writer, the Pro-Life/Choice group, the characters in the film, or the broadcaster the advocate? The answer to this question is unclear. Consequently, the viewer who wants to analyze the discussion must be careful in evaluating the source of the message and, perhaps, give more attention to the content of the message, itself.

We will discuss methods for evaluating the multiplicity of messages, both in their whole and fragmentary forms later. For the present, however, it is essential that we remain aware that some contemporary rhetorical situations involve clearer delineations of who the advocates and audiences are than others. When we are confronted by mediated discussions of public issues, we will likely be confronted by messages that take a multiplicity of forms, may not be whole, and may not be attributable to a singular and obvious advocate.

Summary

Public discussion of public issues occurs in the context of situations that can be termed rhetorical situations. The essential components of any particular rhetorical situation are the exigence, audience, and constraints. Within a rhetorical situation, advocates present messages to audiences in the hopes of altering the situation. As discussion proceeds, the original advocate may become an audience and members of an audience may, in turn, send messages to the new audience. Sometimes advocates redefine the nature of the situation through their discussion. In contemporary society, public discussion occurs both formally in institutional situations and informally in a variety of forums. The most common exigencies are found in the structure of our society, the agendas of elite groups, or crisis situations. The media influences our understanding of public issues by covering both formal and informal discussions of public issues. Because of their role as gatekeepers, the media helps to set the public agenda. However, the public discussions that occur in institutional settings and the personal experiences brought to bear in informal discussions also contribute to the public agenda. When the media is used, either through the traditional operations of journalists or by the packaged persuasion of advocates, a multiplicity of messages are channeled through a complex rhetorical situation.

Notes

[1]Lloyd Bitzer, "The Rhetorical Situation," *Philosophy and Rhetoric* 1(1968):1-14.

[2]Robert J. Branham and W. Barnett Pearce, "Between Text and Context: Toward a Rhetoric of Contextual Reconstruction," *Quarterly Journal of Speech* 71(1985):19-36.

[3]Aristotle, *Rhetoric,* trans. W. Rhys Roberts (Cambridge: Modern Library Series, 1954), 1358b.

[4]W. Lance Bennett, *Public Opinion in American Politics* (New York: Harcourt Brace Jovanovich, 1980), pp. 112-115.

[5]M.E. McCombs and D.L. Shaw, "The Agenda-Setting Function of Mass Media," *Public Opinion Quarterly* 36(1972):176-87.

[6]A. Mazur, "Media Coverage and Public Opinion in Scientific Controversies," *Journal of Communication* 31(1981):106-19.

[7]David H. Weaver, "Media Agenda-Setting and Media Manipulation," *Mass Communication Yearbook 3* Eds. D. Charles Whitney and Ellen Wartella (Beverly Hills: Sage, 1982), 544.

[8]G. Lang and K. Lang, "Watergate: An Exploration of the Agenda-Building Process," *Mass Communication Yearbook 1* Ed. G. Cleveland Wilhoit (Beverly Hills: Sage, 1981), 447-68.

[9]R. Davidson and G. Parker, "Positive Support for Political Institutions: The Case of the Congress," *Western Politics Quarterly* 25(1972):600-12.

[10]Michael C. McGee, "Public Address and Culture Studies," Paper presented at Central States Speech Association Convention, April 1987, St. Louis, Missouri.

Suggested Readings

Aristotle, 1954. *Rhetoric*, Book I. Trans. Rhys Roberts. Cambridge, Massachusetts: Modern Library Series.

Becker, L.B., 1982. "The Mass Media and Citizen Assessment of Issue Importance: A Reflection on Agenda-Setting Research." *Communication Yearbook 3*. Eds. D. Charles Whitney and Ellen Wartella. Beverly Hills: Sage.

Bennett, W. Lance, 1980. *Public Opinion in American Politics*. New York: Harcourt, Brace and Jovanovich.

Bitzer, Lloyd, 1968. "The Rhetorical Situation." *Philosophy and Rhetoric,* 1:1-14.

Branham, Robert J. and W. Barnett Pearce, 1985. "Between Text and Context: Toward a Rhetoric of Contextual Reconstruction." *Quarterly Journal of Speech,* 71:19-36.

Lippman, Walter, 1922. *Public Opinion*. New York: Macmillan.

McCombs, M.E. and D.L. Shaw, 1972. "The Agenda-Setting Function of Mass Media." *Public Opinion Quarterly,* 36:176-87.

Weaver, David, 1984. "Media Agenda-Setting and Public Opinion." *Mass Communication Yearbook 8,* pp. 680-91. Ed. Robert N. Bostrum. Beverly Hills: Sage.

Chapter 3

The Anatomy of Controversy

Because public issues are situations that engender controversy, public discussion of those issues can be examined by examining the controversy. To do so, however, requires some understanding of how controversy proceeds. In other words we need to examine what typically happens when people engage in controversy. How do people disagree? On what grounds do they disagree? What sorts of things do they say when they disagree? What are the components of messages produced during public discussions? This chapter tries to answer these questions by exploring the anatomy of controversy. In general, we can understand controversy better by first determining the point at issue, or the disagreement, and second by identifying the arguments presented by the advocates on behalf of the various sides of the issue.

Locating the Issue

We have already defined an issue, in Chapter 1, as a situation with a likelihood of disagreement. Thus far we have referred to a variety of issues, from drunk driving to nuclear war, as if the noun that describes the subject matter was a reasonable statement of the issue. However, if we are to analyze public discussion of issues, we need to be able to describe not just the subject matter of the controversy, but the point at issue, the point of disagreement.

Anyone who has ever argued or quarreled with someone else has probably experienced the frustration that results when he or she is unable to determine what the point of disagreement between the two parties is. For example, two roommates may engage in argument about how their living arrangement should work. Margo may be the type of person who believes that everything has a place and everything should be kept in its place. Her roommate, Karen, may be the kind of person who finds a little mess perfectly livable and who, because she spends more time away from home at school, work, and social events, doesn't really notice when the house is messy. If we witnessed a discussion between these two concerning how the house should be kept, we would probably notice that they seem to be in agreement regarding some issues but in disagreement regarding others. The same phenomena of agreeing about some points and disagreeing about others occurs in public discussion. Thus it is helpful to begin analyzing a controversy by determining the point or points of disagreement.

Classical rhetoricians developed several systems for determining the point at issue. They referred to the point of disagreement as *stasis*, a Greek word that literally meant a point of stopping. In other words, they believed that when people argued, there was often a point at which the argument reached a point of stopping, a point at which one advocate said one thing and his or her opponent responded with a contradictory conclusion. Before the argument could proceed, or a decision could be made, the point at issue, or point of *stasis* needed to be resolved.

Cicero, a Roman statesman and rhetorician, provided one of the most complete accounts of *stasis* in his treatise, entitled *De Inventione*.[1] Cicero's book was concerned with describing methods by which an advocate could invent, or discover, arguments that could be used in a controversy. His discussion of *stasis* was geared toward legal arguments, in particular. Cicero himself was a prominent legal advocate. He described four points of *stasis*, or points at issue that were likely to arise in a legal proceeding. His description of *stasis* included the following:

1. **Fact:** What is?
2. **Definition:** What do we call what is?
3. **Quality:** What were the circumstances that may justify what is?
4. **Procedure:** What is the proper procedure for resolving the conflict?

Cicero's system of *stasis* is more meaningful if we consider an example. Consider a situation in which a college student believes that someone has been using her car without her knowledge or permission. Kathy, the owner of the car, walks out to the car one day, finds that what used to be a full tank of gas is now down to half-full, notices beer cans and empty potato chip bags in the back seat that were not there when she returned from a trip home the previous weekend. She quickly concludes that her car has been stolen since it is no longer in the same space on the lot where she parked it. After notifying the campus police of the apparent crime, her friend Jennifer rushes in to say that she saw Bob, a mutual friend, driving Kathy's car downtown the night before. Just to make the story interesting, let's assume that Kathy and Bob have just ended a romance and are not feeling very friendly toward each other. Consequently, Kathy notifies the local police to explain that Bob is probably the thief. Within hours the local police pick up Bob and charge him with theft of an automobile. If the case went to court, disagreement might occur on each of the points suggested by Cicero.

To have a legal case at all, the fact that the car was missing would need to be established. The prosecution would need to present evidence that the car was missing. Kathy's description of the missing gasoline, that suggested the car had been driven, and Jennifer's testimony that she had seen Bob driving the car in question would be crucial to establishing the facts. Otherwise, Bob might merely deny that he had taken the car. Without a missing automobile, the suggestion that a crime had been committed would make little sense and the case might end there.

Even if it was established that the car was missing and that Bob was the driver of the missing car, the controversy might stop in its tracks if the advocates did not deal with the question of definition. Let's assume that Bob admits: "Yea, I took the car for a few hours last night. But I didn't *steal* it; I just *borrowed* it." Now the prosecution must prove that the act, the facts as described, should be defined as stealing rather than borrowing. Perhaps a legal definition could be invoked that explained the criteria for stealing as "taking property without the knowledge or permission of the owner of that property." Confronted with such a definition, let's assume Bob reluctantly concedes: "OK, if you want to call it stealing, I guess you can, but I had a good reason for taking the car."

At this point, Bob has admitted both the fact and definition, but has just turned the dispute to the third point of stasis, quality. Are there circumstances that justify the act as defined? In most legal settings, a defendant may be found innocent even if the facts are defined as an illegal act. The verdict, innocent by reason of insanity, is a case in point. Similarly, if someone commits a murder in self defense, they may be released. The recent case of Bernard Goetz, the subway vigilante in New York City, is an example of the successful use of the issue of quality in defense. But let us return to Bob. Let's assume that he explains that:

> My best friend had just broken up with his girlfriend and the same day flunked his C.P.A. exam. He was desperate. I was pretty depressed too on account of my relationship with Kathy going awry. But I was really worried about Kent, my friend, so I thought I should do something to cheer him up. Going to the bars didn't seem like a good idea; we were afraid we might run into Kent's old girlfriend. So I thought if we could just share a few beers and talk in private things would get better. Both our roommates were studying. The only option was to pick up some beer, drive out to People's Park, and share our misery for awhile. I knew Kathy had class that night; I don't have a car and neither does Kent. So I dropped by Kathy's and her roommate, Joan, let me in. I just picked up the keys from Kathy's room and took the car. But I brought it back. I didn't really think of it as *stealing*.

Bob has presented a description that suggests the circumstances were extenuating and, thereby, justified the act even though some people might call it stealing. For the controversy to go any further, the prosecution would have to counter Bob's explanation. Let's assume the prosecution does so by calling Kent to testify. Kent explains that he wasn't that depressed, certainly not desperate, and anyway they could have walked to the Bottle Store and the park, even though it would have been kind of a long trek. (You may be wondering what kind of friend Kent is at this point, but stick with the story.)

As a consequence of Kent's testimony, Bob still has one more out, one more point of controversy that he might raise in an attempt to save himself. Knowing what Cicero had written, Bob might say: "Well, all that's been said so far sounds pretty bad, but I don't think we should be having this trial in the first place. The car was parked in a University lot, that's where I returned it to, we're all University students . . . This is a matter for the campus police, not the city police, so I want a new trial." This statement turns the controversy away from one about facts, definitions, and quality to one about procedure.

The rather lengthy example just described moved through each of the points of stasis described by Cicero. In real court proceedings, it is not uncommon for fewer than all four of the points of controversy to be called into question. A defendant may admit one or more of the points and base his or her defense on only one of the points. However, the value of Cicero's system of analysis is that it alerts us to the possible points of controversy and recognizes that advocates must determine the point of controversy in order to know which arguments to present in order to win the case.

A similar understanding of stasis, or the possible points of controversy, is helpful for understanding controversy about public issues. Typically, the possible points of issue in controversies about public issues have been described as follows:

1. **Fact:** What is and how do we define it?
2. **Value:** Of what value or importance is it?
3. **Policy:** What course of action should we take toward it?

We will examine each of these possible points of controversy in turn.

Issues of fact involve disagreement about what is — both how something should be described and how something should be defined. Ordinarily, we may think of facts as noncontroversial. Facts are often perceived as constant, verifiable statements about reality, as opposed to opinions, which are perceived as subjective statements about reality. Consequently, people may explain that they want to base a decision on the facts and may claim that they are less interested in opinions. However, even limited familiarity with the history of ideas reveals that what is accepted as a fact at one time and place may differ from what is accepted as a fact at another time and place. For example, the "fact" that the earth was flat was replaced by the "fact" that the earth was round, which was in turn replaced by the "fact" that the earth was pear-shaped. Such revisions of the facts occur frequently and suggest that, although there may really exist a factual reality, people are constantly involved in searching for, inventing, and modifying their conceptions of that factual reality. Such revisions are particularly noticeable in public controversy.

Sometimes factual questions provide the center for public controversy. For the better part of this century, the debate between creationists and evolutionists has centered on the factual question of how life began. A famous moment in this controversy occurred in 1925 in Dayton, Tennessee, when a young biology teacher by the name of John T. Scopes was charged with teaching evolution in violation of Tennessee statute. Although there was no disagreement about the fact that Scopes had taught Darwin's theory of evolution, Clarence Darrow, Attorney for Scopes, and William Jennings Bryan, representing the State of Tennessee, offered a variety of arguments concerning whether evolution or creation was the more accepted and accurate depiction of the fact of human existence. At the conclusion of the trial, Scopes was convicted for violating the law, but public opinion clearly questioned the factual validity of that law.

Typically factual issues involve questions regarding the appropriate description of a situation as well as questions about how that situation should be defined, or classified. For example, in 1986 and 1987 an issue that received much media coverage was airline safety. Initially, the question was simply: Is air travel safe? Answers to this question required both description and definition. Discussion of the issue focused on a host of descriptions of the situation—reports of recent plane crashes and near-misses, testimony by pilots who suggested that airplane maintenance was not always up to par, and statements by the U.S. Department of Transportation regarding the number and types of safety violations accumulated by various airlines. Embedded in such descriptions was a definition of safety. What constitutes safety was a second area of disagreement about the situation. Is "unsafe" determined by a particular number of casualties, or by a particular standard for equipment, or by some other measure? Official spokespersons for various airlines presented an alternative description of the situation and definition of safety. They pointed out that far fewer people died from air accidents than from automobile accidents and that, while some equipment might be in disrepair, there were enough "backup" systems to ensure safe air travel. As this example suggests, just because we assume that verifiable facts exist does not mean that facts are not controversial. In public controversy, questions about the facts depend heavily on how reality is described and defined.

While some controversies center solely on factual issues, other controversies may center on another issue but include disagreement about the facts. In the 1970s, consumer advocates argued that a number of common foods and food additives should be more heavily regulated, or even banned, by the federal Food and Drug Administration. Although the ensuing controversy centered on a policy issue, a considerable amount of disagreement concerned factual issues. Among the arguments of consumer advocates were a number of claims regarding the health risks of various food additives. For example, they presented studies showing that the sodium nitrites and nitrates in bacon and some other cured meats combined with amino acids common in the human body to produce carcinogens, cancer-causing agents. Similarly, they presented evidence that red dye #2, then used to color red M&Ms among other products, was carcinogenic. Likewise, studies of the effects of saccharine on rats had demonstrated that this additive caused tumorous growths. Opponents, both inside and outside the food industry, questioned the consumer advocates' description of the situation. Opponents pointed out, for example, that people had been eating bacon for years without ill effects, despite what the laboratory studies suggested. Similarly, they explained that the rats who developed tumors from saccharine had not ingested the substance in diet drinks but had been subjected to the painting of intense amounts of saccharine on their skin. Moreover, they argued that ordinary humans would have to drink several cases of diet drink every week for some time to simulate the experience of the rats. Thus, the opponents questioned the validity of describing the foods and additives as dangerous. The factual issue—whether or not these additives were unhealthy—was a matter of dispute. Eventually, red dye #2 was banned, and drinks containing saccharine were required to bear a warning label. Bacon, with its sodium nitrates, however, is still available in your local grocery store. The policy decisions regarding these products surely depended to some extent on the resolution of factual issues like those just described. However, such decisions probably also depended on resolution of value issues and, ultimately, policy issues.

Value issues concern the desirability and/or importance of something. Essentially, advocates who disagree about values disagree about whether something is good or bad. There is a sense in which we could think of the value issue as a particular type of definitional question that concerns what is defined as good or bad. But issues of value need not depend on prior issues of fact. Although frequently issues of value arise in connection with factual issues, it is not unusual for advocates to disagree about an issue of value apart from any particular factual description.

Advocates may simply disagree over whether a particular idea, principal, or circumstance is valuable. Value issues often occur when opposing values conflict, when opposing advocates work from differing perspectives regarding what is valuable. Such disputes are most apparent when advocates from different cultural, political, or religious backgrounds collide. In the late 1980s, for example, several court cases were brought against members of the Christian Science church. The controversy concerned whether or not members who allowed children to die by denying them medical attention should be found guilty of child neglect and abuse. Among the issues in dispute was a value issue—is the preservation of human life an absolute value? Christian Scientists declared that God, rather than human beings, held the power of life and death. Therefore, they argued that the use of human medicine, rather than God's medicine, was not valuable. Their position is undeniably a minority position because it reflects a rejection of a value held by many in our culture.

Similar examples emerge when advocates from different political cultures engage in public discussion. For example, much international diplomacy on the part of the United States during the 1970s and 1980s has manifested concern for the individual rights of people throughout the world. The political culture of the United States places much value on the individual. However, other political cultures, particularly Marxists societies, do not share the same enchantment with the individual. Thus they may present arguments as to why individual rights are not so important. Instead, they argue that the community, the collective, is most important and most valuable.

More typical, within a given culture, are disputes in which the value issue turns on disagreement over which of two or more values is most important. For example, advocates may disagree about which principle of justice—protection of individual civil liberties or maintenance of law and order—is more important.

Although value issues are sometimes the focal point of controversy, more often issues of value arise in connection to an already resolved factual situation and an as yet to be resolved policy question. Consider, for example, policy questions that concern consumer safety. One such controversy is that of motorcycle safety. For some time, the factual issue of whether or not death and injury from motorcycle accidents is related to whether or not motorcycle riders wear helmets has been noncontroversial. There is widespread agreement that wearing a helmet protects the rider and not wearing a helmet increases the likelihood of serious injury for riders who are involved in accidents. However, agreement about what policy such facts support is not so readily secured. Some argue that given the safety risks, governments should require riders to wear helmets. Their arguments center on the value of human life. In short, they argue that if helmets can save lives then helmets should be required. Opponents, however, argue that such requirements violate the rights of riders to determine how they wish to pursue their sport and use their mode of transportation. These opposing advocates uphold a value of individual liberty and human choice that conflicts with the value toward human life maintained by others. Their argument is that requirements for helmets are undesirable because they would violate principles of human choice. As this example suggests, issues of value may follow agreement about factual issues and render the factual question irrelevant. It may not matter if both sides agree that injuries result from a lack of helmets or that requiring helmets would reduce death and suffering if the advocates disagree about what value is most important.

In addition to issues of fact and issues of value, often public disagreements revolve around issues of policy. In other words, advocates may disagree about what course of action should be taken. Even if advocates agree about the facts and share a similar value orientation, they may disagree about what should be done. For example, an entire community may agree that there is a serious problem of drinking and driving and they may share a value for preserving human life, but they may disagree on how life may be better preserved. Some may argue that stiffer penalties should be applied to convicted drunk drivers; others may argue that more resources should be devoted to prevention of drunk driving by educational and other public service campaigns; still others may argue that our society should return to prohibition as a national policy in order to eliminate the very possibility of drunk driving. Similarly, in the 1980s there was much agreement concerning the problem of terrorism and the value of protecting the lives of American citizens who were subject to terrorist actions. Controversy centered on what course of action should be taken toward terrorists. In its simplest terms, the issue was should we negotiate with terrorists or not? Thus, the various sides of the issue may break down according to the various solutions offered in response to an agreed problem or objective.

Such disagreements about policy, however, usually can be traced to disagreements about facts and/or values. The contemporary discussion of abortion illustrates the conflict in facts and values that underlies many policy disputes. At base, the question is whether abortion should be legal or illegal, a question of what our policy toward abortion should be. Opponents of legalized abortion argue that abortion is murder and, because human life is sacred, such murder should not be condoned. Proponents of legalized abortion often disagree with both the opponent's description of the facts and their interpretation of the value. Proponents point out that the fetus may not yet be a human life; therefore, removal of the fetus cannot be defined as murder. Furthermore, proponents note that the value of human life is not absolute. They claim that if the fetus develops into an unwanted child who is severely handicapped or subjected to abuse then that life ceases to be as valuable as opponents suggest. In addition, proponents argue that the life (and quality of life) of the pregnant woman must be balanced against the potential life of the fetus. Within the context of such balancing, how the value should be applied is a matter of dispute. On their own behalf, proponents support a second value—the value of individual rights to choose that allow the woman to choose how she will deal with her own body. Opponents, in turn, disagree about application of the value of choice. They point out that abortion violates the right of the unborn child to choose life over death. Proponents counter such a charge by returning to the factual issue of whether or not the fetus should be defined as a person who has rights. As this abbreviated summary of the abortion controversy suggests, policy disputes often incorporate disagreement about both facts and values.

Despite their relationship with factual and value issues, policy issues can be viewed as distinctive because they move beyond questions of what is and how valuable it is to questions of what should be done about situations. Communication scholars have identified a number of sub-issues, or distinct points of potential controversy, that are common to policy issues. A standard list of sub-issues was provided by Lee Hultzen.[2] Hultzen, following the example of classical rhetoricians like Cicero, identified four common points of controversy within policy disputes:

1. *Ill*: Is there an ill in the present state of affairs?
2. *Reformability*: Is the ill curable? Is it caused by a reformable condition?
3. *Remedy*: Will the proposed remedy actually cure the ill?
4. *Cost*: Will the cure cost too much?

Both competing facts and competing values might be brought to bear in regard to any of these four sub-issues. According to Hultzen, when advocates discuss what course of action should be taken, they encounter the possibility of disagreement about any and all of the four sub-issues. A brief example should illustrate his analytical system.

Consider the controversy regarding whether or not smoking should be prohibited in public places. When communities first began to consider local ordinances to this effect, much discussion centered around a sub-issue of ill. Advocates claimed that "side-stream smoke," the exhaled smoke from smokers and the smoke from the burning cigarette, was harmful to nonsmokers who breathed the polluted air. Opponents, of course, challenged this claim, arguing that although smoking might be harmful to the smoker the evidence regarding its harm to nonsmokers in the vicinity was shaky at best. Questions regarding the number of nonsmokers who were affected and the extent of the health hazard were common. In some localities a consensus regarding harm to nonsmokers was reached; in other communities such a consensus has yet to be reached.

In addition to the question of ill, a second question regarding reformability was also raised. Opponents argued that although nonsmokers sometimes contracted lung disease, emphysema, and other health problems associated with smoking, it was unclear whether these deleterious health effects were the result of smoke or other environmental contaminants. They pointed out that a host of other factors (e.g., asbestos dust from the interiors of buildings, particulate matter from aerosol sprays, and even emissions and airborne residues from common household cleaners) might be the cause of lung-related health problems. Advocates often countered with the argument that even if there were other factors causing the problem, it was sensible to reduce the risk as much as possible by eliminating one cause, namely smoking. These disagreements about the cause of the ill exemplify what Hultzen meant by the sub-issue of reformability.

Questions concerning the cause of the ill naturally lead to questions regarding whether or not a particular proposal will solve the problem. For if we are unsure of the cause of the problem, it is difficult to predict whether a given course of action will solve the problem by eradicating its cause. Hence, opponents of public smoking ordinances could argue that just prohibiting smoking in public areas would improve hardly anyone's health. They could point to studies of the health effects of side-stream smoke, noting that the greatest ills were suffered by people whose family members smoked. The implication was that these innocent victims, if they had been hurt by smoke at all, were hurt at home, not in public places. Accordingly, suspending smoking privileges in public would not guarantee a completely smoke-free environment, because the problem and its cause would still persist in private places like the home. Again, advocates could counter by arguing that any dent that could be made in the problem would be appreciated, even if some part of the problem remained after enactment of their proposal.

But even where agreement concerning the nature and extent of the ill, the possibility of reform by proper identification of the cause, and the likelihood of remedy were reached, the possibility for disagreement still existed. If the cost of such a proposal was considered too high, then the disadvantages might be perceived to outweigh the gain obtained by curing the ill. As Hultzen pointed out, cost is a final sub-issue for any dispute over policy. In the present example, opponents of a ban on smoking could argue that such a prohibition was an infringement on the rights of smokers (both their right to pursue happiness and their right to choose how to deal with their own bodies, even if their choices spelled a future health disaster). Advocates could, and often have, countered that such prohibitions are not a violation of smokers' rights. They point out that nearly all laws constrain human behavior in one way or another (e.g., we do not allow people to drive on either side of the road they choose so that they can be happy or act out an unfettered right to choose) and, consequently, the cost of refraining from smoking in public is a very small one indeed. On the other hand, opponents attempt to magnify the loss of rights and point out that particularly when such a loss is compared to the minimal gains that a smoking ban would produce, it is just not worth the other obvious costs (e.g., the cost of enforcement, posting signs, etc.).

As the foregoing illustration suggests, the four sub-issues of policy issues are distinctive but often rely on considerations of additional factual and value issues. The question of ill, for example, concerns a factual issue insofar as the nature and extent of the problem (the description of the problem) is a source of disagreement. The question of reformability may likewise entail a factual disagreement concerning the cause of the problem. Value issues are most likely to arise in arguments about cost and ill. For a situation to be defined as an ill or another to be considered a cost, certain values must be embraced that allow participants to determine what is positive and what is negative. And, certainly when the gains are compared to the costs, arguments about values (what is more and less important or valuable) are likely to be operative.

Identifying the type of issue about which advocates disagree is a way to begin analyzing controversy from a communications, or rhetorical, perspective. Instead of searching for the origin of the controversy or the essence of some topic, the analyst may begin with what is said about the situation by one or more sides in the controversy and chart out the points at which disagreement exists. As the preceding discussion suggests, depending on which points are centers of disagreement, the analyst may expect to hear different topics discussed. When only one side of a public issue is presented, it may be helpful to determine which issue or issues are the center of attention and which are not. Such investigation can alert the analyst to the potential points of disagreement by opponents as well as to the function of the discourse under study.

Although any of the issues may arise at any time during public controversies, some are more likely in some places and times than in others. In Chapter 2, various institutions for formal advocacy were identified. Some of these institutions, for example legislative bodies and quasi-judicial forums, are designed to deal primarily with policy issues. Even so, depending on the particular controversy and time, other types of issues may become the center of attention. Consider, for example, the U.S. Congress. Congress debates and passes both resolutions and bills. While resolutions express what the Congress thinks is worthwhile and typically center on issues of value, bills lay out a course of action that will be implemented and thereby center on issues of policy. Moreover, Congressional hearings are often arranged to determine whether a problem exists and the probable cause prior to formulation of proposals to cope with the problem. These hearings focus on issues of fact. Appeals courts, on the other hand, are typically concerned both with resolving legal disputes from lower courts and interpreting the law and its application, often providing additional definitions. As such they frequently center on issues of fact, particularly the sub-issue of definition. However, as numerous opponents of unpopular Supreme Court decisions will testify, sometimes appellate courts are actually debating about issues of policy, determining what courses of action government bodies, particularly government agencies like the police, should take.

The role of the media in public controversy was also noted in Chapter 2. Because the media often provide a forum for advocates in disagreement, all types of issues may be discussed in the media. However, one type of issue is uniquely discussed by the media. News reports, despite journalistic creeds that emphasize objectivity, are always engaged in describing situations. As a consequence, news reports are often concerned with issues of fact by presenting viewers the facts through the eyes of the journalist. Investigative reporting, in particular, suggests a perspective on the facts that may lay the groundwork for future disputes about issues of policy. A famous, if unsympathetic, review of the engagement of controversial issues by the media was launched by former Vice President Spiro Agnew in 1969. Speaking for the Nixon administration, Agnew pointed out various sources of bias among television journalists and warned the public of the power of the Fourth Estate to determine what was accepted as fact and to inculcate particular values in the public sphere by their choice and development of particular news stories. Thus, even where controversy does not immediately suggest itself, it may be productive to examine discourse to determine the potential points of disagreement, to uncover the type of issue that is being engaged.

In order to determine the type of issues raised in public controversy, a sensitivity to arguments (claims and their support) advanced by advocates is necessary. If an analyst is to understand and criticize discussion of public issues or if a citizen hopes to participate in public discussion, then identification of arguments is a needed skill. As the discussion of issues has implied, the way advocates deal with issues is to present arguments in support or attack of the issues. Therefore, our discussion of the anatomy of controversy must proceed by examination of what constitutes an argument and how the constituents of an argument can be identified.

Identifying the Arguments

Our discussion so far has referred to arguments, claims, assertions, and so forth as if these speech acts were obvious and easily recognized. To some extent that is true. Most people are able to recognize when they are engaged in an argument, when they need to make arguments, and when others present arguments. In public discussions, whenever an issue is disputed, we expect and usually do hear a number of arguments. To identify these arguments in order to analyze and evaluate them, it is helpful to have a more technical definition of an argument. For the philosopher and the logician, an argument is often defined as the combination of premises that lead to a conclusion. For the ordinary citizen, an argument is generally viewed as the same as a reason. In other words, when advocates present arguments, they present reasons that justify their positions.

Although there exists an extensive body of literature from philosophy regarding the types of premises and conclusions that form arguments, we will concentrate on one particular scheme for recognizing arguments. This scheme is applicable to most arguments but is especially adapted to the types of arguments ordinary people make, present, attack, and defend in everyday situations that involve dispute. The scheme was developed by a philosopher, Steven Toulmin, who found that many other descriptions of argument were not particularly helpful in describing everyday argument.

The Toulmin model of argument is a spatial diagram of the parts of an argument—a diagram that literally lays out the various components that come into play when an advocate gives a reason for his or her position. The model appears as follows:[3]

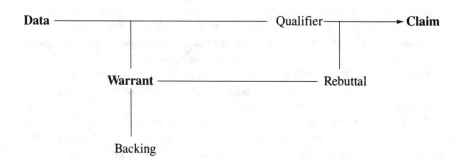

The three primary components of Toulmin's model are written in bold letters, with the three secondary elements written in regular letters. Initially, it is helpful to understand all six elements of an argument, but for our purposes, we will concentrate on only the three primary elements. However, before going into detail regarding **claim, data, and warrant,** an explanation of the complete model is in order.

The **claim** is the conclusion that the advocate offers an audience. Put another way, the claim is the assertion that an advocate offers for an audience's assent. Statements like "smoking is harmful," "wearing a seat belt can save your life," "we should choose the human race over the nuclear race," and so on generally act as claims.

Data is evidence or explanations provided in support of the claim. If an advocate offers statistics that show a cause-effect relationship between smoking and heart disease in support of the claim that smoking is harmful, those statistics act as data. Likewise, if an advocate shows film footage of the after-effects of the nuclear explosion at Hiroshima to elaborate her claim that we should choose the human race over the nuclear race, then that film footage acts as data.

The **warrant** is a bridge between the data and the claim. The statement(s), belief(s), or other connection(s) that is(are) necessary to buy the claim on the basis of the data act(s) as a warrant for the argument. For example, if studies show that smoking causes heart disease, we may reasonably conclude that smoking is harmful because we (1) believe that the studies are valid and (2) define heart disease as a harm. Our belief about the credibility of the studies and our definition of harm both act as warrants for the argument. Similarly, if we agree with the claim that we should choose the human race over the nuclear race on the basis of data that shows what the effects of a nuclear explosion at Hiroshima were, then we probably are warranting the argument by believing that (1) the effects of nuclear explosions are horrible, (2) the nuclear race increases the likelihood of more nuclear explosions and their ensuing horrible effects, and (3) there are no positive effects of nuclear explosions that outweigh the negative effects we have observed.

The **qualifier** of an argument indicates the strength of a claim given its supporting data and warrant. Terms like "probably," "usually," "certainly," and "always," are typical examples of qualifiers. Thus, an advocate may argue that "smoking is *always* harmful," if he or she has data that shows a cause-effect relationship between smoking and health hazards. On the other hand, if the evidence, or data, points only to a correlation between smoking and health hazards, then the claim might be modified to read, "smoking is *probably* harmful." The qualifier, then, is a modifier within the claim that indicates the strength of that claim.

Backing is additional data, or evidence, that is presented to bolster the warrant. If an advocate presented the credentials of the scientists who conducted the studies of smoking and heart disease and described the statistical methods used in order to prove that the study was a reliable and good one, then backing would have been provided.

The **rebuttal** is an explanation, or simple statement, specifying when a claim would not follow from the data presented. In other words, the rebuttal is almost a counter-warrant, an explanation of why the data does not naturally lead to a claim, a description of what an audience would need to believe if they rejected the claim based on the data provided.

A brief example should clarify the six parts of Toulmin's model. Consider the following argument:

> *Consumer Reports* lists the new Toyota Tercel as the "best buy" among subcompact cars. Because I think *Consumer Reports* is one of the most reputable sources for consumer information, I think I should probably purchase

a Tercel when I buy my new car. The only thing that might change my mind
is that I've heard *Consumer Reports* hasn't been as diligent in their testing
of subcompact cars in recent years.

This argument could be laid out according to Toulmin's model as follows:

Data	**Qualifier**	**Claim**
Consumer Reports says the Toyota Tercel is the "best buy" among subcompact cars.	Probably	I will buy a Tercel.

Warrant	**Rebuttal**
I think *Consumer Reports* is a reputable source for consumer information.	Unless it's true that *Consumer Reports* was not diligent in their tests of subcompacts.

(Backing)
My experience has been
good with products rec-
ommended by *Consumer
Reports.*

As the diagram indicates, the data from *Consumer Reports* leads to the claim
because of the warrant that explains why the data supports the claim. The rebuttal
takes issue with that warrant by specifying at least one condition under which
the data would not lead to the claim. The qualifier, "probably," indicates the strength
of the claim and thereby recognizes the impact of the rebuttal. In the original
argument, no backing was provided; therefore the backing is indicated
parenthetically as a hypothetical statement that might be made if backing were
called for.

Even without the backing, the argument just diagrammed is somewhat unusual
because it is relatively complete. More often, especially in the heat of public
discussion, arguments are presented that lack one or more of the six elements
identified by Toulmin. A more natural statement of the preceding argument would
probably be the following:

I think I'll buy a Tercel because *Consumer Reports* listed it as the "best buy"
among new subcompact cars.

In this abbreviated form, the argument would be laid out as follows:

Data ————————————————————————→ **Claim**
Consumer Reports says   I think I will buy a
the Toyota Tercel is the   Tercel.
"best buy" among
subcompact cars.

        (Warrant) ——————— **(Rebuttal)**
        I think *Consumer Reports*   Unless it's true that
        is a reputable source for   *Consumer Reports* was
        consumer information.   not diligent in their tests
                                          of subcompacts.

        (Backing)
        My experience has been
        good with products rec-
        ommended by *Consumer
        Reports.*

Again, please note that the warrant, rebuttal and backing appear in parentheses because they are not actually phrased in the original statement. Or, to use an even more familiar example, consider the argument that: "You'd better be good 'cause Santa Claus is comin' to town." Diagrammed the argument might look as follows:

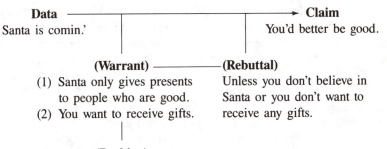

Data ————————————————————————→ **Claim**
Santa is comin'.   You'd better be good.

        (Warrant) ——————— **(Rebuttal)**
        (1) Santa only gives presents   Unless you don't believe in
            to people who are good.   Santa or you don't want to
        (2) You want to receive gifts.   receive any gifts.

        (Backing)
        Your parents told you about
        Santa and you believe them.

The frequency with which one or more parts of an argument are omitted during controversies holds several important implications both for the analysis of public discussion and the use of Toulmin's model. First, when an analyst examines what is said in order to locate the arguments, it is important to recognize that many arguments will be incomplete. The analyst may find multiple statements that act as data, but only a few statements that act as claims, and perhaps no statements that act as rebuttals. In other situations, the analyst may find a plenitude of claims but relatively little data presented in support of those claims. Such findings may assist an analyst in explaining why a particular advocate's message was or was not effective for a particular audience. This method of evaluation will be pursued in greater depth in the next chapter.

Secondly, the omission of some parts of the argument presents an obvious quandary for the analyst. If some parts are missing, how does the analyst know what to fill in parenthetically? If no warrant is presented by an advocate, how does the analyst know what the warrant is? This question of what should be filled in to complete the argument points out an important characteristic of public persuasion that was first recognized by the Greek rhetorician, Aristotle.

In his treatise on rhetoric, Aristotle observed that orators often did not provide their audiences with the complete chain of reasoning, the complete list of all their premises for a given conclusion. Aristotle named such abbreviated forms of arguments *enthymemes*.[4] In addition to observing the existence of enthymemes, Aristotle explained why enthymemes were useful in public discussion. To begin with, he noted that public discussion could proceed more efficiently if advocates left out those details already known and understood by the audience. In short, the advocates could get on to the dispute at hand by omitting statements that were already a part of the audience's frame of reference. In the case of the warning about Santa, for example, few people need to hear the complete explanation. Probably more important, however, was a second explanation by Aristotle concerning the value of enthymemes. He argued that enthymemes, by allowing the audience to fill in the missing parts, involved the audience in the adversarial process. By participating in constructing the argument, even if subconsciously or unconsciously, the audience was in fact persuading themselves.

If audiences are encouraged to fill in various parts of an argument, then it is likely that various individuals within an audience may fill out the argument somewhat differently. For example, if an advocate makes a claim that terrorism is a problem, but leaves the audience to supply the data, then some audience members may recall their viewing of the famous hijacking of a Pan American flight, while others may recall the story of Leon Klinghoffer who was killed by terrorists who held the oceanliner, Achille Lorre, hostage. Still others may supply images and knowledge of the actions of nation-states, from the Soviet Union in Afghanistan to Israel in the occupied territories, as a means of constructing the data needed to fill out the argument. As this illustration suggests, the data supplied by any particular audience member may actually alter the definition of the claim. In the present case depending on the data supplied, the claim might refer to state terrorism or individual acts of terror. Because multiple constructions are possible, the claim may gain assent from audience members who, if the data had been explicit, might have differed in their acceptance of the claim. The same could be said for other missing parts of the argument supplied by audience members. Different people are likely to supply different warrants, rebuttals, backing, and so on.

The propensity of individual audience members to fill out the missing parts of an argument differently suggests the responsibility of an analyst to be flexible in his or her construction of the implicit parts of an argument. Toulmin's components of an argument operate heuristically, as an aid in analysis, for the analyst. In other words, the parts alert the analyst as to what types of thoughts, statements, beliefs, and so on may be necessary to complete an argument, without determining precisely which ideas must be supplied to complete the argument. In general, a variety of potential data, warrants, and so forth may be supplied for arguments that explicitly state only some parts.

Given the variety of possibilities for each part of the argument, it is helpful to review familiar types of claims, warrants, and data — the three primary constituents of Toulmin's model. Two communication scholars, Wayne Brockriede and Douglas Ehninger, have elaborated Toulmin's model by explaining the different types of claims and warrants that are commonly laid out when the model is applied to everyday argument.[5] In regard to types of claims, they identify four: designative, definitive, evaluative, and advocative.

The four types of claims identified by Brockriede and Ehninger correspond to the four points of stasis recognized by Classical scholars such as Cicero. *Designative claims* assert what is by answering a question of fact. If an advocate argues that nuclear testing is done to assure the efficiency of technological weapons, then she is making a designative claim. *Definitive claims* assert how some situation, idea, or fact(s) should be classified, or defined. If an advocate argues that in contemporary society a checking account is a personal necessity, then he is making a definitive claim. He is defining a checking account as a necessity. *Evaluative claims* assert the value or importance of some idea, situation, or fact(s). If an advocate claims that apartheid practices are immoral, then she is measuring a situation by a standard of value, in this case the value of morality. *Advocative claims* assert what policy should, or should not, be adopted or followed. If an advocate claims that banks should provide free checking, then he is making an advocative claim.

In addition to describing four types of claims, Brockriede and Ehninger also describe three familiar types of warrants, or bridges between data and claims. Using Aristotle's description of the three means of persuasion as a benchmark, Brockriede and Ehninger classify warrants as substantive, authoritative, and motivational. Before explaining these three types of warrants, it is helpful to recall the Aristotelian categories on which they were developed.

According to Aristotle, the ancient orator had at his disposal three means of persuasion: logos, ethos, and pathos.[6] *Logos* referred to the arguments themselves that might convince an audience through their power of reason. In short, if the justification made sense and was reasonable, it should appeal to a rational audience. *Ethos*, on the other hand, referred to the persuasive power of the orator's personal character. Regardless of whether or not the arguments were convincing, Aristotle asserted that if an advocate was perceived as trustworthy — as a man of good sense, good character, and good will—then the audience might be swayed to accept his point of view. Finally, Aristotle suggested that the audience's state of mind might well affect their acceptance or rejection of a particular argument. He termed *pathos* the persuasive power of the audience's frame of mind, and noted that an advocate would do well both to recognize the state of mind of the audience and to attempt to shape the state of mind in order to assume the most productive reception of his arguments.

Brockriede and Ehninger's three types of warrants illustrate a contemporary adaptation of Aristotle's three sources of persuasive power. *Substantive warrants* are those connectors between data and claim that express some type of reasoning pattern. Statements of cause and effect, generalization, analogy, and so forth express a logical relationship that may explain why a particular claim follows from a particular bit of data. For example, if an advocate argues that health maintenance organizations (HMOs) will reduce the quality of medical care in the United States because that is what happened when such organizations were introduced in Britain, then the warrant that must be supplied is a substantive one that asserts Britain and the United States are comparable cases. In general, substantive warrants are any warrants that express a reasonable, or sensible, relationship.

Authoritative warrants, on the other hand, establish the link between data and claim by showing why the data is trustworthy. Authoritative warrants establish the authority, or credibility, of the source of the data. For example, if an advocate argues that all advertising for tobacco products should be banned because the American Medical Association has made such a recommendation, then the claim is believable based on the explicit data only if the audience believes in the authority of the AMA.

Motivational warrants, in contrast, connect the data to the claim on the basis of some psychological state, emotional configuration, or inner need of the audience. The needs or emotions that ground motivational warrants may be either positive or negative. For example, an advocate who claims that we should march for economic justice and provides as data the incredible feeling of unity among the marchers may be hooking into a warrant that emphasizes our need to feel at one with the group, to feel unified. On the other hand, advocates who support a claim that baby seals should be protected from hunters by showing the audience gory pictures of adorable animals being slaughtered may call up a warrant from the audience that expresses their desire not to participate in brutal acts.

Just as it is possible to enumerate different types of claims and different types of warrants, so it is possible to identify familiar types of data. Although anything that an audience will accept as evidence or support for a claim may act as data, communication scholars have long recognized three predominant types of data: *testimony, statistics,* and *examples*. Each type of data may take a variety of forms. For example, testimony may consist of a quotation from a revered source or may be presented live or on a tape recording in the form of an interview. Examples may be brief or extended, may be personal anecdotes or hypothetical illustrations.

Examples are almost always presented in the narrative form of a story. When public discussion occurs as talk, examples may be elaborated linguistically; when public discussion is presented by way of films, televised reports, or other audio-visual media, examples may be presented directly and dramatically as the camera and microphone follow a particular incident and show particular characters and scenes. Similarly, statistics may be presented verbally or graphically. Hence, a pie chart or computer graphic may present statistics as data as surely as a speaker may say "unemployment among youths is 20% higher than among the general population."

By identifying the type of data used to support a claim, an analyst may better be able to determine the particular warrant that is necessary to bridge the gap between data and claim. For example, if testimony is used to support a claim, then the warrant will surely need to include a statement that reflects trust in the source of that testimony. This idea that different types of data generally entail different sorts of warrants will be explored in the following chapter.

At this point, however, it should be clear that Toulmin's model may be used to identify the various parts of an argument. By specifying which statements by an advocate act as claims, data, and warrants, an analyst may uncover which parts of the argument are missing, not stated explicitly, and therefore must be filled in by the audience. Furthermore, the three primary parts of an argument may be classified according to which type(s) of data, warrant, and claim are used. Thus, an analyst can produce a fairly detailed description of an argument presented by an advocate.

Integrating the Issues with the Arguments

The discussion of the parts of an argument in the preceding section was oriented to a single argument. The examples presented typically treated an argument as having a single claim, a single datum, and a single warrant. While such a treatment is helpful when first learning what the parts of an argument are, actual messages presented in the midst of public controversy rarely follow such a neat and simple pattern. More often, advocates present multiple arguments in support of their position. Moreover, any single claim presented by an advocate may be supported by a multiplicity of data and require a collection of warrants for its acceptance. Therefore, a method for describing an entire persuasive message is necessary. Toulmin's model can be adapted to provide such a method.

Ordinarily an advocate's complete message will contain a thesis, or *main claim*. Typically, that main claim will correspond to one of the types of issues discussed in the first section of this chapter. For example, during a discussion of nuclear weapons testing in 1985, former National Security Advisor Paul Warnke presented a thesis, or main claim, that the United States should agree with the Soviet Union to ban nuclear testing. Warnke's adversary, then National Security Advisor Richard

Pearle claimed just the opposite—that the United States should not halt nuclear testing.

The thesis, or main claim, of an advocate's message is frequently supported by a number of main ideas, or sub-claims. In the nuclear testing debate, for example, Pearle presented several sub-claims. First, he claimed that because tests were necessary to assure the safety and efficiency of our weapons, those tests should not be banned. Second, he argued that because the Soviets could not be trusted to abide by such a ban, the United States could not afford to halt testing. Similarly, Warnke presented several sub-claims in support of his main claim.

Because sub-claims act as data for the main claim, each sub-claim requires one or more warrants in order for the main claim to be accepted. For example, Pearl's sub-claim that testing was necessary to assure the safety and efficiency of the weapons stockpile depends on warrants like the following:

>   Warrant 1:   The U.S. needs reliable weapons.
>   Warrant 2:   We don't want weapons that are unsafe.
>   Warrant 3:   It doesn't make sense to eliminate a procedure that assures
>   safety and reliability.

Notice that the first two warrants are both motivational warrants, while the third is a substantive warrant based on a cause-effect relationship that identifies testing as the cause of safety and reliability effects.

However, even when these warrants are supplied, we can see that opposing advocates or unfriendly audiences might not be satisfied. This is because the sub-claim that acts as data for the main claim is itself a claim that may need data for its support. Thus, Pearle's opponent, Warnke, questioned Pearle's argument concerning safety and reliability on two counts. First, Warnke asked if nuclear explosions were necessary to test for safety. Warnke asserted that the safety of weapons was determined by nonnuclear devices. This assertion takes direct issue with Pearle's sub-claim that testing is necessary to assure safety and suggests the need for Pearle to support that sub-claim with data. Second, Warnke pointed out that more than half of all tests are done to aid in the development of new weapons, rather than for the purpose of guaranteeing the safety and reliability of old weapons. Again, Pearle needed to provide data to support his sub-claim. If such data had been forthcoming, it would have required warrant(s) for a complete layout of the sub-claim presented in support of the main claim. Furthermore, if that data had been disputed, then it would assume the role of a claim that, in turn, required supporting data and warrant(s).

The main claim, any sub-claims, as well as supporting data and warrants may be diagrammed according to Toulmin's model as a way of describing an extended message. Such a diagram might look like the following:

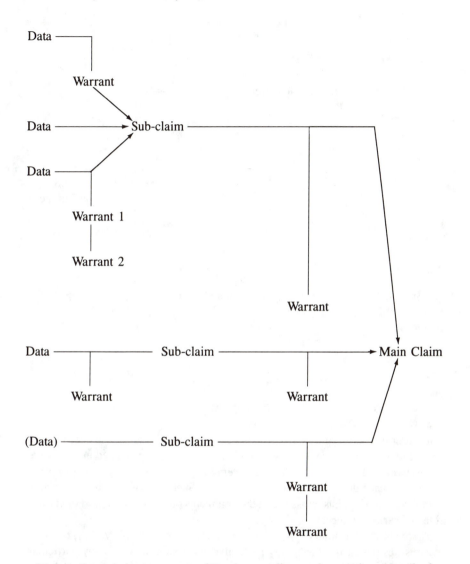

We can diagram the arguments of Pearle regarding nuclear testing accordingly. Such a diagram helps to show the relationships among the statements that constitute an advocate's message by showing which statements act as claims, which act as data, and which act as warrants. In addition, as the parenthetical parts suggest, such a diagram alerts the analyst to those parts of an argument that an audience must fill in. Once the parts of the message are laid out they may be categorized according to the type of warrant(s), data, and claim provided by the advocate. Because the various types of claims correspond to the various types of issues, the analyst may then determine what the points of controversy are.

Pearle's Argument

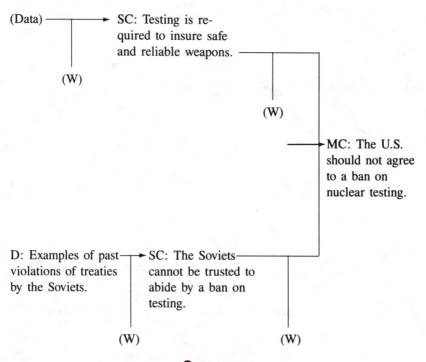

Summary

In order to analyze public discussion of controversial issues, it is necessary to be able to describe the controversy as well as the messages presented in the course of discussion. The nature of the controversy can be identified by analyzing the statements made during the course of discussion. Such analysis requires describing both the point, or points, at issue and the arguments presented in support of various sides of various issues.

There are three primary types of issues: fact, value, and policy. Any, or all of these issues may arise during any particular discussion or within any particular message. However, some are more common to particular institutions or during particular stages of public debate. Arguments can be laid out according to Toulmin's model. The parts of an argument can be categorized to provide further specificity for the description. Frequently, some parts of an argument are not explicit and await completion by the audience. Generally, advocates present messages that contain multiple claim-data-warrant patterns. Thus, diagramming the arguments may entail identifying a main claim that is supported by sub-claims that are, in turn, supported by data and warrants.

The arguments that advocates present act as reasons for their positions. The following four chapters (Chapters 4-7) explain various standards for assessing those reasons, or arguments. However, before such assessment can be made, the analyst of public discourse must be able to identify the arguments, their components, and the points at issue to which they relate.

Notes

[1]Cicero, *De Inventione,* trans. H.M. Hubbell (Cambridge, Massachusetts: Harvard University Press, 1949), pp. 21-29.

[2]Lee Hultzen, "Status in Deliberative Analysis," in *The Rhetorical Idiom,* ed. Donald Bryant (New York: Russell and Russell, 1966), pp. 97-123.

[3]Steven Toulmin, *The Uses of Argument* (Cambridge: Cambridge University Press, 1969), especially pp. 94-107. See also, Steven Toulmin, Richard Reike and Allan Janik, *An Introduction to Reasoning,* 2nd ed. (New York: Macmillan, 1984), especially pp. 23-78.

[4]Aristotle, *Rhetoric,* trans. Rhys Roberts (Cambridge: Modern Library Series, 1954), 1354a-1355a.

[5]Wayne Brockreide and Douglas Ehninger, "Toulmin on Argument: An Interpretation and Application," *Quarterly Journal of Speech* 46 (1960):44-53.

[6]Aristotle, 1356a.

Suggested Readings

Aristotle, 1954. *Rhetoric.* Trans. Rhys Roberts. Cambridge: Modern Library Series.

Bitzer, Lloyd F., 1959. "Aristotle's Enthymeme Revisited." *Quarterly Journal of Speech,* 45:399-408.

Brockreide, Wayne and Douglas Ehninger, 1960. "Toulmin on Argument: An Interpretation and Application." *Quarterly Journal of Speech,* 46:44-53.

Cicero, 1949. *De Inventione.* Trans. H.M. Hubbell. Cambridge: Harvard University Press.

Hultzen, Lee, 1966. "Status in Deliberative Analysis." *The Rhetorical Idiom.* Ed. Donald Bryant. New York: Russell and Russell.

Toulmin, Steven, 1969. *The Uses of Argument.* Cambridge: Cambridge University Press.

Chapter 4

Good Reasons Fit the Audience

In the last chapter, several methods and categories were explained to assist in describing the messages presented by advocates during controversy. That description reflects the notion that when advocates present messages about controversial issues they are explaining or justifying their positions on the issue by providing arguments or reasons. While description of these reasons or arguments is crucial to an analyst of public discourse, description alone provides an incomplete analysis. In this chapter and in Chapters 5-7, various methods for assessing or evaluating those arguments will be investigated. This chapter will discuss in some detail the first standard for evaluating such reasons: *Good reasons should fit the audience.*

To determine whether or not a reason fits a particular audience, the analyst must be able to describe the particular audience to whom an advocate's reasons are directed. What an audience knows, believes, feels, and values will determine how that audience will react to an advocate's message. This is a lesson most people learn at an early age. Jean Piaget, a French psychologist who has studied extensively the intellectual, emotional, and linguistic development of children, has pointed out that children begin adapting their talk to an audience around age 7.[1] The ability to take into account one's audience is often associated both with effective communication and general social maturity. Not surprisingly, effective advocates tend also to adapt their messages to the nature of their audiences.

This chapter begins by exploring the general nature of audiences — those aspects of an audience that are likely to affect their reception of public messages. Following that discussion, the characteristics of reasons are discussed in relation to the characteristics of audiences in order to provide the ground for determining if reasons fit the audience.

Audiences Respond Holistically to Arguments

The question of how people make decisions, how they come to accept some reasons and reject others, has been a subject of study for centuries. In the Classical world, the rational capacity of human beings was often emphasized even though the importance of human passion was frequently recognized. In his dialogue, *Phaedrus*, Plato discussed the nature of the soul.[2] He described the soul as divided into three parts represented by two horses and a charioteer. The two horses represented the passions, one goodness and virtue, the other lust and unrestrained desire. The charioteer represented reason who could reign in the passions. In Plato's story, he described how these three entities worked in regard to love. The dark passions pursued love relentlessly, as opposed to those passions that stood in awe of the beauty of love. Only by the skillful efforts of the charioteer, reason, could the passions be tamed and guided on a path that would lead to true intimacy. Plato's story was presented in the context of a discussion regarding the proper study and practice of rhetoric and thus provided direction for his discussion of the importance of knowing the nature of the souls to whom a message was directed. As is clear from his story, audiences are susceptible to appeals to the passions, but likely to temper their passionate responses with a reliance on reason.

Like Plato, Aristotle also recognized the passionate nature of human beings while emphasizing their rational capacities. Consequently, his suggestions regarding public persuasion centered on how to produce reasonable arguments, but included discussion of the importance of an audience's frame of mind, or state of passion. In short, he argued that the emotional state of a listener would influence his reception of an argument. For example, if a listener was angered because she felt slighted by someone, she might be more susceptible to an argument that developed a claim about that person's lack of responsibility.

While the Classical view emphasized rationality, it recognized that human beings also respond passionately. That holistic conception, of reason and emotion working together, is still useful for explaining and predicting how a particular audience will respond to a particular message. But before dealing with reason and emotion in more detail, it is helpful to explore the efforts by some to emphasize one of these characteristics over the other. At various points in history, emphasis has been given to either reason or emotion as the key to understanding how people respond to persuasive messages. Certainly the Classical viewpoint encouraged an emphasis on reason. Thus, various scholars, particularly analytical philosophers have concentrated on completing one of Aristotle's projects, namely determining a system by which logical conclusions may be inferred from established principles. In this vein, the standards of logic have been applied to reasons offered by advocates in order to determine whether or not those reasons are sensible. In general, such perspectives aim toward two determinations. First, they question whether or not the premises for an argument are true. Using the language from Chapter 2, the data and warrants would be compared to reality to see if they are true. Second, the logical perspective questions whether the reasoning used to reach the conclusion is valid, or free from logical error.

Although the logical perspective has been applied for centuries, it has long been recognized that such a perspective frequently does not account totally for the persuasiveness of everyday arguments.[3] Two philosophers in the twentieth century particularly, Stephen Toulmin and Chaim Perelman, have made this point. They have both pointed out that the rules of formal logic are more easily applied to mathematical proofs than to ordinary language usage. Moreover, even sound arguments sometimes fail to persuade. Consider, for example, the smoker who agrees with the argument that continuing to smoke will probably result in his death, but who responds by explaining that he just enjoys smoking and therefore plans to continue to smoke. In addition, people are sometimes persuaded to agree with positions not because those positions are logical, but because they are congruent with a person's needs or wants.

The importance of an audience's needs, wants, or motivations has been studied by psychologists with the same vigor as an audience's rational facilities have been studied by logicians. Particularly during the twentieth century with the advent of mass media that promoted mass persuasion and extensive advertising, motivation research has blossomed as a way to account for audience reactions to a variety of persuasive appeals. Throughout the history of the study of argument, various thinkers have emphasized the emotional, or passionate, side of human nature in their attempts to explain why some arguments are effective and others are ineffective. During the eighteenth century, for example, many British scholars who studied persuasion left the investigation of reason to logicians and concentrated instead on how arguments were presented such that those arguments impacted the imagination, aroused the passions, and guided the will to action.[4] Contemporary marketing research has often followed a similar tack.

As with the emphasis on logic, however, the emphasis on emotions has often provided only a partial explanation for how people decide as they do. Just as audiences may not always act according to reason, they do not always act simply on their emotions. For example, despite the suggestions of many a television commercial that a particular product is associated with happiness, sexiness, or the American way, few consumers will buy that brand solely for such reasons. A certain degree of sensibleness is expected in a persuasive message as well. Thus, consumers will often explain that they are not really affected by advertising, that they make their buying decisions according to the facts rather than according to the clever emotional ploys of advertising. There is a certain reasoned skepticism that people often employ when confronted with emotional appeals.

Whether or not the split between rational and emotional faculties is an accurate depiction of human nature is a subject of controversy. From the Classical treatises on the soul to contemporary studies of psychology, there have been competing schools of thought regarding whether or not the soul, the mind, and even the brain should be divided into constituent elements or treated as a unitary phenomenon. During the eighteenth century, faculty psychology subdivided the human mind into many parts including the will, the appetite, the imagination, reason, and so forth. Years later, gestalt psychology, that treated the mind as a holistic entity, emerged as the dominant force. Contemporary studies of right brain (associated with creative abilities and the residence of feelings) and left brain (associated with intellectual abilities and the residence of reason) appear to support the division between reason and emotion. However, studies of audience responses to persuasive messages have suggested that such a division is not made when people are exposed to persuasive messages. Individuals may characterize themselves as operating primarily according to either reason or feelings; however, in controlled studies audiences trained in the difference between rational and emotional appeals were unable to distinguish one from the other.[5]

Depending on which explanation of the human mind, or soul, has held sway at a particular point in time, students of argument and persuasion have often emphasized either a logical approach toward reason-giving that evaluates the rationality of reasons or a psychological approach toward reason-giving that evaluates the motivational power of reasons. The durability of both approaches, along with the common sense observations of thinkers from Aristotle to John Dewey, suggests that both factors must be taken into account when evaluating whether or not a particular argument fits a particular audience. Thus, in general, reasons can be said to be good if they fit *both* what the audience thinks is reasonable and what the audience feels or needs. Each of these factors will be considered in turn, even though the distinction may be an artificial one that, while helpful for purposes of dividing our discussion, may not reflect how people actually experience the reception of messages.

Before considering how an advocate's arguments may play on an audience's reason and emotion, another characteristic of how people make up their minds deserves mention. Contemporary psychologists have devoted considerable resources to the study of this problem. One dominant strain of thought has posited that, regardless of whether people are responding intellectually or emotionally, one factor guides their responses. They have posited the idea that people strive to be consistent.

Cognitive psychologists have spent considerable time attempting to describe how people rationalize, or make sense of the mental contents of their minds. Common to a group of theories, aimed particularly toward explaining how people change their attitudes and opinions, is the assumption that people strive to maintain consistency. The drive toward consistency has been demonstrated through experimental studies as well. In general, consistency theories posit that contradictions are uncomfortable for people. As a consequence, when people are confronted by an inconsistency, or made aware that they are holding two contradictory positions, those people will try to adjust their attitudes, opinions, beliefs, and even actions so as to eliminate the inconsistency. Two notable theories within this tradition are Heider's balance theory and Festinger's cognitive dissonance theory.

Heider's balance theory provides a relatively simple, yet straightforward, explanation of the notion of our drive toward balance, or consistency.[6] He pointed out that if three attitudes or beliefs come into contact with one another, the person who holds these opinions strives to make them consistent. The three mental contents that are related can be diagrammed as a triangle. A brief example illustrates the theory. Imagine that you have a friend who is an expert on basketball; he played pro ball for a couple of years, was an All American in college, and continues to keep up with the game. Not only do you enjoy this friend's company, but you respect his knowledge and judgment regarding basketball. Your attitude toward this friend could be characterized as positive, indicated in the following diagram by a "+." Furthermore, imagine that you have been following one of the new expansion teams in the NBA and, based on your own knowledge of basketball, you have concluded that this new team is likely to be a winner. You think they drafted wisely, have a good coach, and have played solidly in the games you have watched. Again, your attitude would be positive. Finally let's assume that one day you meet your friend for lunch and decide to tell him how impressed you are with the new expansion team. To your surprise, he responds that he has just the opposite reaction to the new team. He thinks that most of their personnel are second-rate at best, that the few good players they have don't coalesce well into a playing unit, and that their coach is a loser. Diagrammatically, the situation looks like the following.

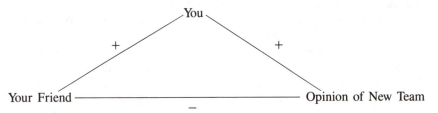

You are confronted with a problem, an inconsistency. You think your friend knows what he's talking about, but his opinion about the new team is at odds with your own opinion. According to Heider because such a state of inconsistency is uncomfortable, you will need to adjust one of your attitudes in order to bring the situation back into balance. In this case, you might either reduce your opinion of your friend's judgment about basketball or you could reevaluate your opinion of the new team. In the former case, if you decide that your friend really doesn't have good judgment about basketball, then you can ignore his negative evaluation of the new team and reside comfortably with your own positive opinion. On the other hand, if the latter alternative is chosen, you will maintain your positive opinion of your friend's judgment and adopt a view of the new team that is closer to his and different from your current positive judgment. The two diagrams below describe these two alternative ways of obtaining balance.

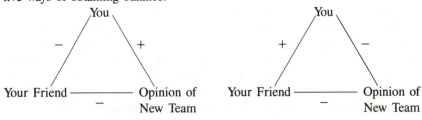

A second notable theory that illustrates the psychological drive toward consistency is an explanation advanced by Leon Festinger.[7] Although Festinger's development is different and more complex than Heider's, his theme is the same: that people strive to reduce dissonance, or inconsistency. Festinger conducted a series of famous experiments to validate his theory. The prototype of his experimentation involved the following procedure. Students were asked to participate in an experiment. When they arrived, they were asked to perform a tedious and boring task. The task involved turning a number of pegs that were placed in holes 1/4 of a turn. The students, or subjects, in the experiment were asked to turn the pegs repeatedly. Following completion of this boring task, one of Festinger's assistants, a confederate in the experiment, would ask the students if they would be willing to recruit other students to do the same task. Festinger's assistant would explain that the person who was supposed to do the recruiting had not shown up and, therefore, a substitute was needed. Half of the students were offered a substantial amount of money if they agreed to act as a recruiter. The other half were offered a minimal amount of money. In either case, the student was told by Festinger's assistant that they should tell prospective participants that the task was challenging, fun, or otherwise enjoyable. In short, the student subject was being asked to lie, to contradict his or her own experience with the task. Following this stage in the experiment, Festinger would interview the students about their participation, asking them what they thought of the experiment. Because the students thought the experiment began and ended with the turning of the pegs, their answers focused on their reactions to the peg-turning task. In these interviews, those students who had agreed to recruit other students with little monetary reward responded favorably to the task. They described the task as interesting. Students who had received substantial monetary awards, on the other hand, described the task as boring and uninteresting. Festinger's explanation for this difference relied on his theory of cognitive dissonance.

The explanation worked as follows. Both students, those who received substantial money and those who received minimal money, had been set up to experience dissonance. Their experience with the task had been one of boredom and tedium. Yet, they had agreed to present that experience to another student as interesting and challenging. Their lie was inconsistent with their experience, thereby creating dissonance in their own minds. According to Festinger's hypothesis, such dissonance would be uncomfortable. Therefore, the student would need to do something to reduce the dissonance, to rationalize the inconsistency. For those students who received substantial money, he explained, they could reduce their dissonance by explaining that they only lied because they were paid to do so. Thus they could respond truthfully that they thought the task was boring, but set aside their lie to prospective participants by attaching the lie to the monetary reward. This tactic was, of course, not available to those students who received very little monetary compensation. For them, dissonance could only be resolved by adjusting their attitude toward the task, by deciding that the task wasn't so boring after all.

Those students receiving the most money were least likely to change their attitude about the task. Those students receiving the least money were most likely to change their attitude about the task.

There are a variety of other theories that fall within the category of consistency theories. However, our purpose is less to review the psychological literature in this area than to make the point that people strive to be consistent. The inclination toward consistency provides a standard both for what an audience will accept as sensible and for what an audience will accept as congruent with their state of mind, or passions. In summary, then, audiences generally respond both with their hearts and their minds. In doing so, they strive toward consistency.

Arguments and Audiences:
The Persuasive Force of Arguments

The two constituents of an argument that support, or lead to a claim, may each be examined to determine if they are fitting for the audience. In general, both data and warrants should fit the audience. This is particularly true if the argument is made enthymematically, such that the audience must supply part, or all, of the data or warrant. However, even if the data and warrant are both explicit, an audience may reject, or qualify, them with a rebuttal if the data and warrant are not fitting.

In the last chapter, warrants were described as the bridges between data and claims and categorized into three types—substantive, authoritative, and motivational. By examining these types of warrants in greater detail, the relationships between warrants and an audience's reasoning and state of mind become clearer.

Both substantive and authoritative warrants work on an audience's assessment of the reasonableness of an argument. Motivational warrants, on the other hand, are more obviously related to an audience's passions, or state of mind, in regard to the argument. Despite these rough correlations, however, any particular warrant may incorporate both an appeal to reason and an appeal to emotion. A few examples should clarify the relationship.

Consider the argument that because Bob studied harder than Scott, Bob should get a better grade than Scott.[8] The argument can be diagrammed as follows:

Data ———————————————————▶ **Claim**
Bob studied harder than   Bob should get a better
Scott.   grade than Scott.

(Warrant)
The harder a person studies,
the better grades they will
get. **or** Students who study
hard get good grades.

The implicit warrant for this argument is a statement about the relation between studying and grades. If the generalization about that relationship is perceived as sensible by an audience, then the warrant works to support the argument because of its intellectual force, its appeal to what is reasonable. Strictly speaking, however, the warrant in the argument about studying does not really provide a valid argument because, by strict logical standards, it is not reasonable. This is so because the generalization refers to a correlation rather than a cause-effect relationship. Although it may be true that students who study hard get good grades, it may also be true that some students who do not study hard also get good grades. We all know some students who, because they are exceptionally bright, require very little effort to obtain good grades. In the present example, if Scott is one of those bright students, then just because Bob studied harder will not insure a better grade for Bob. This would most certainly be the case if, in addition, Bob was not a very talented student and therefore, regardless of how hard he studied, would probably not receive a good grade. The generalization, by expressing a correlation, indicates what generally occurs, what can generally be expected when students study hard, but is not predictive of the results for the particular individuals of Bob and Scott because there are multiple causes for the effect of good grades. Still, many people would accept the generalization as a sensible one and, therefore, accept the argument as legitimate on the grounds that it was sensible. For those who did accept the argument in that way, they would be supplying a substantive warrant, or a connection that was reasonable to them, for the argument.

This sensible generalization, of course, mirrors a more abstract, yet common, generalization that abounds in American society. One of our cultural warrants is that hard work pays off. A *cultural warrant* is simply a generalization that is accepted by a culture. Or, put another way, cultural warrants are those collections of statements that comprise what we ordinarily refer to as common sense. When an argument incorporates a warrant that expresses what is common sense, it is deriving its persuasive power from its appeal to our sense, or our reason.

However, common sense may not meet the logical standards for reasonableness furnished by centuries of study by logicians. Moreover, common sense may sometimes consist of blatantly contradictory statements as William Lewis, a professor of communication, has pointed out.[9] For example, common sense advises caution (Look before you leap.) at the same time it advises abandoning caution (He who hesitates is lost.). Similarly, "it may be home sweet home," but "a rolling stone gathers no moss." There are, of course, countless additional examples of contradictory common sense. What such contradictions suggest is that people accept such statements as sensible on grounds other than pure rationality.

If we return to the example of Bob and Scott, we can begin to explore what other grounds support our acceptance of generalizations as reasonable or sensible that, strictly speaking, may not be rational. Why is the warrant that students who study hard get good grades likely to strike people as sensible even though, as discussed previously, it may not be rational? The answer seems to be that the generalization appeals to our sense of fairness. It seems only fair that hard work should pay off, that studying should result in good grades. The allegiance we hold toward fairness, the value we place on fairness, helps explain why we might readily accept a warrant as sensible even though it does not meet the standards for logical reasoning. In short, audiences are motivated to accept as sensible those statements that reflect their values.

A second example should help to clarify the connection between substantive warrants that appeal to our reason and values. Consider the argument that Elizabeth Dole is worthy of our admiration because in 1988 she resigned her position as Secretary of the Department of Transportation in order to help her husband campaign for the Republican nomination for President. The argument could be diagrammed as follows:

Data —————————————————————→ **Claim**

E. Dole resigned her   E. Dole is worthy of our
position as Sec. of DOT in   admiration.
order to help her husband
campaign for the
nomination.   **(Warrant)**
                                         Women who support their
                                         husbands are worthy of
                                         respect. **or** Women should
                                         support their husbands.

The warrant for this argument, that women who support their husbands are worthy of admiration, is a generalization that may or may not make sense to an audience. If it does make sense,the audience likely subscribes to a set of values that place importance on the family and value a subordinate role, rather than a dominant one, for a wife. Such values incline an audience to accept the generalization regarding a woman's proper role as sensible. On the other hand, those who value individual achievement and place importance on the role of women outside the familial, or husband-wife, relationship might well reject this argument on the grounds that the warrant does not make sense. They would provide other generalizations regarding what actions are worthy of admiration based on their values. Unlike the value of fairness discussed earlier, which is widely accepted in American culture, the value of a woman supporting her husband and the more general cultural value regarding the family is less widely accepted. A variety of social changes that have occurred during the last twenty years have placed such values in a state of flux.

In cases where the substantive warrant draws its force from a value, such as with the argument concerning Elizabeth Dole, motivations come into play. Psychologists have theorized that people's values form the core of their personalities. The psychologist Milton Rokeach demonstrated this idea vividly with his model of personality theory.[10] Following is a diagram that illustrates the relations among values, beliefs, attitudes and opinions that Rokeach observed.

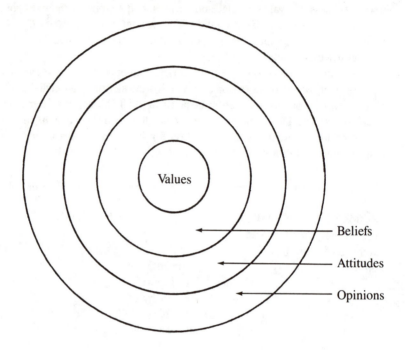

In the model, opinions and attitudes are surface characteristics of one's personality, while values lie at the core of a person's identity. Opinions about which political party is preferable and attitudes about whether or not taxes should be raised are more easily changed, for example, than values concerning freedom, democracy, individual liberty, and so forth. As this brief list of values suggests, values are frequently the product of social interaction, and as a consequence they are at least similar, if not identical, to the needs identified by other psychologists who deal with motivation theory.

Motivations, typically, are conceptualized as inner drives or needs that require satisfaction from some outside source.[11] In other words, people are assumed to experience some need, or feeling state, inside themselves, but that need or feeling is related to, or satisfied by, some force outside themselves. For example, the inner need of hunger is only recognized because we are able to satisfy it by eating (something outside ourselves identifies the feeling inside ourselves). Through the socialization process, people came to identify the variety of inner feeling states that they experience. Thus, from childhood on, people accumulate a vocabulary for describing their feelings, or inner needs, that help them distinguish between subtle differences in their state of mind. For example, generally feeling bad can be broken down into a variety of types of "bad" feelings—anger, disappointment, frustration, grief, and so on. Similarly, feeling "good" may range from joy to exhilaration to excitement and anticipation. These feeling states, although experienced naturally, are also learned. In the learning process, whereby people come to distinguish among different feelings, the state of mind is generally attached to some external force that either acts as the cause of that feeling or the potential satisfaction of that feeling.

The feelings, or motivations, that are experienced by people are often called upon to act as additional warrants for arguments that consist of substantive, or sensible, warrants. In addition, sometimes claims are supported primarily by these motivational warrants, even to the exclusion of any sensible warrant. If the motivational assumption is strong enough it may be sufficient to warrant the argument. Consider, for example, the claim that you should restrict your intake of red meat because a diet that includes large quantities of red meat often results in high cholesterol that can lead to an early heart attack. The "fact" that red meat, eaten in large quantities, leads to early heart attacks acts as data for the claim that you should restrict the amount of red meat you eat. The warrant for this claim is primarily a statement of motivation: you don't want to suffer an early heart attack. Put another way, the warrant is your need to stay alive and healthy. Although that need may make sense, the warrant derives its force primarily from a need to stay alive rather than from its logical appeal.

Such motivational warrants may also be culturally grounded. Because motivations are perceived as internal, but satisfied externally, our learning about motivations occurs socially. As a consequence, individual motivations may often result from, and mirror, cultural values. In the example concerning red meat, the warrant that concerned staying alive and healthy is a basic need that is probably common across cultures. However, it is possible to speculate about a possible culture or subculture that does not place value on staying alive. Imagine a culture in which the greatest value was viewed as dying. In death, people were considered to be released from the trials and tribulations of life on earth and allowed to enter a heavenly kingdom. If such a culture existed, its members might well not experience a need to stay alive and, therefore, might be unreceptive to the argument concerning diet.

If the argument is altered slightly, the importance of cultural values to motivational warrants becomes even clearer. Suppose the claim was the same, that you should restrict your intake of red meat. But suppose the data were changed to an explanation that the fat content of red meat causes people to gain weight and become obese. The motivational warrant could have nothing to do with health, but instead center on people's need to be thin. Contemporary American culture, of course, values body types that are slender, slim, and thin. We learn that "fat is ugly." However, a variety of western cultures throughout history have valued just the reverse. Corpulence was often viewed as a sign of wealth. Furthermore, a well-rounded body was often considered beautiful. Members of cultures that valued weight would not experience a need to be thin and, as a consequence, would not be convinced by the foregoing argument.

As the discussion thus far suggests, both substantive and motivational warrants may be heavily influenced by cultural values, or cultural warrants. The same may be said for the third type of warrant—authoritative warrants. Authoritative warrants come into play when the data, if believed, leads naturally to the conclusion. The data is believable because the source of the warrant is believable. An authoritative warrant may be accompanied by either, or both, a substantive and motivational warrant.

We can begin by examining an argument that rests exclusively on an authoritative warrant. Suppose an advocate claims that the Plymouth Voyager is the best mini-van on the market. When asked what data supports such a judgment, our advocate explains that *Consumer Reports* concluded that the Plymouth Voyager was the best mini-van in their 1986 study of new cars. The evidence seems to speak for itself. If a listener concurs with the claim on the basis of this data, then they must find *Consumer Reports* a believable, or reliable, source for information about automobiles.

In other arguments, an authoritative warrant may be accompanied by another type of warrant. For example, if an advocate argues that the United States should sell grain to the Soviets because studies from a variety of foreign policy analysts show that commerce with the Soviets increases the level of trust between the Soviet and United States government, then all three types of warrants come into play. First, a receptive listener would need to supply a substantive warrant that decisions about foreign sales of grain should be based on matters concerning international relations. Second, a receptive listener would need to supply a motivational warrant that voiced the desirability of trust, and increasing the level of trust, between the United States and the Soviet Union. Finally, and perhaps most important, the listener would need to supply an authoritative warrant that recognized the foreign policy analysts as knowledgeable and believable sources regarding the consequences of selling grain or other products to the Soviet Union.

Whenever an authoritative warrant is used, the force of the argument is carried by the audience's recognition of the source of the evidence as believable and reliable. If the source is deemed trustworthy, then it only makes sense to accept the argument. The reason why the source is considered trustworthy may well concern an audience's motivations. The audience may feel a need to trust someone, and if the source appears a fitting place for trust, then the authoritative warrant comes into play.

Who is trusted, which sources are deemed reliable and believable, varies across cultures. A dramatic example was furnished by Michel Foucault, a French philosopher and intellectual historian.[12] In the study of the treatment of madness by various cultures at various points in history, Foucault pointed out that at one time those who were mad were held in reverence and high esteem. People who hallucinated, had visions, and behaved in other ways that could be deemed peculiar were recognized as "seers," with mystical powers. Such persons might be called on to give advice to kings and other leaders of state. Of course, at other times, such folks were simply labelled "insane" and locked away in mental institutions. As Foucault's study suggests, whose opinion is trusted varies from place to place and time to time. Commentators on contemporary American culture have noted the faith that is placed in expertise and the trust accorded those experts who produce the facts. Whether they are scientists, professors, or journalists, those people who manage our information society are often deemed reliable and trustworthy sources.

As the discussion thus far suggests, the warrants for arguments are often complex. While some arguments may depend on either substantive, motivational, or authoritative warrants, others may depend on some combination of the three. Regardless of which type of warrant predominates, the force of the argument that comes from the warrant may play on either, or both, an audience's sense of what is reasonable as well as their sense of needs or feelings. The force of the data may often depend on an audience's assessment of the believability and trustworthiness of the source of that data. Furthermore, cultural values may undergird all three types of warrants, helping to determine what an audience considers sensible, what they understand as their driving motives, and whom they will trust and respect as sources.

Evaluating the Fit Between Arguments and Audiences

Simply laying out the arguments of an advocate provides an analyst of public discourse with a view of the contents of an advocate's reasons. As the preceding discussion suggests, such a layout reveals the parts of the argument furnished by an advocate and suggests the parts that must be supplied by an audience. The data and warrants for an argument may trigger either, or both, a reasonable and a passionate response in an audience. In order to determine if such arguments fit the audience, however, an analyst must move beyond merely laying out the argument.

The analyst must determine whether or not the data and warrants are consistent with an audience's way of thinking and emotional state of mind. To make such a judgment requires knowledge of what an audience accepts as sensible, what motivations are likely to be experienced by an audience, and what sources of evidence an audience is likely to trust. Because these components of an audience's frame of reference are likely to be based on an audience's values, knowledge of the set of values common to an audience is also helpful.

The following discussion reviews some basic descriptions of what contemporary American audiences take to be sensible, experience as motivations, accept as trustworthy sources, and share as cultural values. Many such lists exist from a variety of sources. While the descriptions included here have been used by rhetorical critics and communication analysts, they represent only a selection of those available. Moreover, because what is accepted as sensible, what is valued, who is trusted, and what needs are felt may vary from time to time and place to place, these descriptions may not always accurately depict the nature of the audience to whom arguments are addressed. Therefore, these descriptions should be taken as useful guidelines about contemporary American audiences rather than as rigid, unchanging characteristics of those audiences. More specific analyses of specific audiences should be consulted when such analyses are available. However, the following descriptions describe what appears to be the case generally for audiences involved in contemporary public discussions.

Patterns of Thinking Accepted as Sensible

First, we may consider what is accepted as reasonable for an audience. As mentioned earlier, logicians have developed a variety of axioms and rules for what constitutes rational thought. Many of these rules for reasoning appear to correspond to tacit knowledge, knowledge that people have without realizing that they have it, possessed by most human beings. Piaget pointed out that young adolescents intuitively understand some logical rules long before they learn those rules through formal education.[13] For example, youngsters seem to understand intuitively that if A=B then B=A long before they learn the commutative property of numbers in math or algebra classes. Other rules for reasoning are learned, primarily through the educational system, but also simply by being members of western culture. Regardless of whether or not the patterns of reasoning, or patterns of thinking, are innate or learned, four patterns seem to predominate. People seem to find reasonable connections that derive from similarity, classification, division, and causation. Put another way, people often think in terms of similarities, opposites, categories, or cause-effect conditions.

Arguments based on *similarity* base their conclusions, or claims, on data that may be described as either examples or comparisons. In the case of examples, an audience is asked to grasp the similarity between the examples furnished by the advocate and the particular case about which the advocate is making a claim. For example, if an advocate claims that our food supply is contaminated by a variety of toxic chemicals, she may support her claim with several examples. She may refer to tests of tomatoes, oranges, and grapefruits that revealed each of these products contained significant levels of pesticide residues that have been deemed toxic. Based on these examples, an audience might conclude that her claim is sensible because other foods are assumed to be similar to those that were tested. Because the foods are similar (we eat them all, we grow them in similar ways, they are handled and processed in similar ways, etc.), her claim appears to be a reasonable one. Thus, an audience could easily imagine lemons and limes being contaminated as well.

Arguments based on analogies follow a similar pattern of thinking. The audience is asked to grasp a similarity between two apparently different phenomena in order to conclude that the characteristics common to one are also common to the other.

For example, during a discussion of apartheid in South Africa, Jesse Jackson claimed that the United States should not wait on the government of South Africa to eliminate apartheid practices but should apply economic pressure in order to quicken the pace of social change.[14] One of his sub-claims was that Botha, the leader of South Africa, would probably not change on his own because the history of Pharaohs and dictators was not one of social change. This argument required the audience to supply a substantive warrant that noted the similarity between P.W. Botha and the ancient rulers of Egypt. If those ancient rulers exploited workers and resisted social change, then Botha would probably also continue to exploit workers and resist social change. If the audience accepted the alleged similarity between Botha and the ancient Pharoahs, then that similarity made Jackson's claim a sensible one.

A second familiar pattern of reasoning is based on *classification*. In arguments based on classification, the claim appears sensible because the data and warrant suggest that the case being discussed in the claim belongs to a category, or class, that exhibits certain characteristics. Therefore, the particular case in the claim can also be expected to exhibit those characteristics. Perhaps the most famous example of such a reasoning pattern is the one typically given to describe the categorical syllogism, a deductive form of argument that consists of a major premise, a minor precise, and a conclusion. The example runs as follows:

> All men are mortal.
> Socrates is a man.
> Therefore, Socrates is mortal.

The argument makes sense because if Socrates belongs to a class, or category (men), then he must share the characteristics of that class (i.e., be mortal). A clear example of such reasoning in the context of public discussion has emerged in the public debate about abortion. Right to Life groups argue that because abortion is murder, abortion should be illegal. Their argument depends on classifying, or categorizing, abortion as murder. If such a classification is recognized and shared by the audience, then the argument makes perfect sense.

Arguments based on classification also occur when something is classified as not belonging to a particular group. In such instances, the particular phenomena is claimed not to belong to a particular class because that phenomena does not exhibit the particular characteristics common to that class. In the discussion regarding apartheid, referred to earlier, Jackson argued that a famous Black activist who had been imprisoned for many years, Nelson Mandela, should be released from prison because he was a political prisoner. Jackson's opponent in the discussion, the Reverend Jerry Falwell, countered by arguing that Mandela was not a political prisoner but a terrorist. Falwell explained that Mandela had been caught with an arsenal of grenades and guns and in interviews had voiced his commitment to violent overthrow of the South African government. Falwell's argument was based on a principle of classification that classified political prisoners as being nonviolent. His description of Mandela as a terrorist was based on a principle of classification that defined terrorists as exhibiting violent tendencies.

A third familiar pattern of reasoning is based on *division*. Whereas reasoning based on classification plays on the category to which a phenomenon belongs by emphasizing the similarities that suggest a class or type, reasoning based on division plays on the mutually exclusive categories that exist by emphasizing the dissimilarities between phenomena. The old cliche that "either you're a part of the solution or you're a part of the problem" is illustrative of the pattern of thinking that rests on division. Just such a pattern has frequently been invoked during discussions of public issues. For example, activists on issues from environmental concern to illegal drug abuse have attempted to mobilize more individual action by suggesting that if a person is not actively engaged in protecting the environment or fighting drug abuse then they too are culpable. Why? Because you're either part of the problem or part of the solution.

Such patterns of thinking simplify the world, or part of it, into two categories, each of which exhibits different characteristics. Although such divisions may not always be logical because sometimes there is middle ground, the pattern of thinking is compelling because by simplifying the situation we are encouraged to believe that we can exert some control over it. For example, in the discussion regarding South Africa, Falwell claimed that those inside South Africa who advocated the elimination of Apartheid were inspired by Communism. Part of Falwell's evidence for this claim was his explanation that Communism thrives on social unrest and activists in South Africa were promoting social unrest. Implicit in his argument was the assumption that people are inspired by either Communism or Democracy. Those inspired by Communism foment social unrest, while those inspired by Democracy do not. Therefore, because the activists in South Africa were encouraging social unrest, they must be inspired by Communism rather than Democracy. Of course, some receivers of Falwell's message might reject his claim because they disagreed with his division between Communism and Democracy. However, those who accepted his claim accepted his division as sensible.

Finally, a fourth familiar pattern of reasoning, or thinking sensibly, is based on *causation*. By strict logical standards, causation establishes some condition as invariably leading to some consequence. Such connections are often stated in the form of "if-then" statements. For example, free market economists have long asserted that if the price of a product rises, then demand for that product will fall. However, that economic principle has often been modified with the phrase, "other things being equal." This modifying phrase recognizes that other factors may also affect the results. So, for example, if the price of water goes up, then demand for water will go down, unless other factors cause people to maintain their demand for water. By strict logical standards, these other factors must always be taken into account. However, audience's sometimes take as sensible the simple if-then connection without regard for other factors. That familiar phrase of common sense, "where there's smoke there's fire," is a case in point.

When causation is used loosely, without taking other factors into account, arguments may be based on variations of causality. Such variations are usually referred to as reasoning by sign or reasoning by correlation. With the example of smoke and fire introduced earlier, for example, smoke can be said to be a sign of fire, but not necessarily a cause of fire. Smoke often appears when fire breaks out, hence there seems to be a correlation between smoke and fire, but smoke does not necessarily cause fire.

These exceptions to the rule of causality and the difficulty of establishing a causal link, however, do not necessarily diminish the persuasive force of patterns of argument that invoke an if-then connection. Just as there may be exceptions to rules of classification, or middle ground between divisions, or differences among those things that share a number of similarities, there may be other factors that weaken causal connections. However, like the other patterns of thinking, reasoning by cause, sign, and correlation can be compelling because it provides an audience a way to order an otherwise disordered world. Causation provides an immediate explanation for why, a place to lay blame or responsibility.

In the discussion of apartheid, for example, Jackson argued ultimately that the United States should disinvest, or withdraw investments, from South Africa in order to pressure the South African government into discarding their policy of apartheid. Underlying Jackson's argument was the assumption that if the United States punishes South Africa by withdrawing investments, then South Africa would succumb to the wishes of the United States. That assumption invokes an if-then warrant, that if punishment is used, then the punisher can modify the behavior of the one being punished. Such a warrant makes common sense to many people, even though others will recognize that the result does not always, or even necessarily, follow from the prior condition.

As the foregoing discussion suggests, the four patterns of thinking are distinct in the type of principles, or generalizations, on which they depend. These patterns can meet the strict standards for logical thought. However, they sometimes can work to persuade an audience even if strict standards are not met. The patterns are compelling because they provide a way for people to make sense of, and simplify, their worlds. Hence, the analyst of public discourse should be able to identify which patterns an advocate is invoking in order to determine if the pattern will fit the sensibilities of an audience. The following chart summarizes the four patterns and indicates the types of statements that generally accompany each. The various exceptions to patterns of similarity, classification, division, and causality that can be made when an audience, or opposing advocate, objects to an advocate's arguments will be discussed in more detail in Chapter 6. For now, we are concerned primarily with determining what patterns are likely to be followed when an audience agrees with an argument because they think it makes sense.

Four Familiar Patterns of Thinking

	Type of Argument	Typical Language Used
Similarity	by example, by analogy	X is like Y.
Classification	by genus, by definition	All X is Y. No X is Y.
Division	according to dilemma	Either X is Y Or X is Z.
Cause	by cause, by sign, by correlation	If X, then Y. When X, then Y.

Needs as Motivational Factors

Just as there are common patterns of thinking that are invoked when people are asked to use their good sense to accept an argument, so there are common motivations that serve as the basis for appeals to an audience's passions. Motivation researchers and psychologists have attempted to describe the inner needs, motives, or states of mind that are common among human beings. As discussed earlier, these motivations, although experienced individually as internal states, are often learned through the socialization process. Thus, it is possible to examine a culture to determine what motives seems to predominate insofar as they are referred to consistently in persuasive messages. This technique has been used extensively to study what motivates contemporary Americans.

One study of this type was done by Vance Packard, who concentrated on the research used by marketing, advertising, and public relations professionals as guides for how to sell products.[15] The motivation research that Packard summarized was grounded on an assumption somewhat different than that proposed in this book. Motivation researchers have typically viewed motivations as operating separately, at a deeper level, than the intellectual warrants that cause audiences to believe an argument makes sense. Even so, Packard's findings are relevant as they identify not only what a body of research has characterized as the inner motives of Americans, but also because these motives have been the persistent center of attention for an overwhelming amount of contemporary advertising and persuasion. As a consequence, even if these motives were not experienced by Americans at one time, their persistent exposure to messages that presume these to be common motives has probably played a socializing role in teaching Americans what their motives ought to be. Thus, Packard's list of eight hidden needs of American consumers provides a handy list of motives for the analyst of public discourse.

Packard described each of these needs in relation to consumer product advertising. Such description is convenient for understanding what each need refers to, but our discussion will also refer to examples that bear on public issues as well as on private merchandising efforts.

Packard's Eight Hidden Needs

1. Emotional Security
2. Reassurance of Worth
3. Ego Gratification
4. Love Objects
5. Sense of Power
6. Roots
7. Immortality
8. Creative Outlets

The need for *emotional security* is a need to feel free from fear or anxiety, the need not to worry about impending disaster or bad surprises. In commercial advertising, this need is appealed to, for example, in the marketing of deodorant. Whether it is a slogan, like "the need to be Sure," or a dramatic example of an up-and-coming executive who apparently offends her coworkers with body odor as she bends over them at a conference table or squeezes into a crowded elevator, the motive that much deodorant advertising appeals to is one of emotional security. In public discussions, such needs may be invoked when advocates refer to the impact of a particular policy on the comfortable or secure aspects of the daily lives of individuals. For example, if an advocate argues that allowing women to participate in military combat would ultimately lead to romantic relationships between male and female soldiers that would finally disrupt a number of American families, then the need for emotional security has likely been evoked for some audience members. Or, similarly, when opponents of gun control devise scenarios that demonstrate why an ordinary citizen might want to keep a gun at home (to protect the safety and welfare of their family), the need for emotional security is invoked.

The need for *reassurance of worth* is characterized by people's concern for feeling valuable, for feeling that what they do is a positive contribution to someone. Commercial efforts to encourage a housewife or househusband to eliminate "ring around the collar" or to feed their children the peanut butter that will make them grow strong and tall play on the need to do something worthwhile. Public advocacy that urges citizens to volunteer their time to programs designed to feed and house the homeless or to contribute their dollars to send grain to those starving in third world countries similarly aim toward motives that direct people to engage in behavior that will reassure them of their own worth.

The need for *ego gratification* centers on people's need to think of themselves as special, unique individuals who form the center of attention. Commercial advertisements that demonstrate how a product or service is adapted just for "you" typically work on the need for ego gratification. When individuals are featured over the products, the person is made to feel central. In public discussions, too, the message may be personalized, demonstrating how policies or programs enhance the individual's sense of self. For example, socialized medicine may be promoted on the basis that every person is special and worthy of quality medical care, regardless of his or her economic station in life.

The need for *love objects* plays a role in both commercial advertising and public issue discussion. Many animal rights activists aim parts of their messages toward the audience's need for love objects. Their pictures of cuddly baby seals, adorable puppies, or warm and fuzzy kittens provide viewers and readers with love objects that they can protect by supporting particular legislative agendas or contributing funds. Similarly, campaigns aimed toward assisting the underprivileged frequently offer photographs of, and letters from, the young children or elderly people that audience members are encouraged to "adopt" by contributing to charitable organizations that attempt to provide assistance.

The need for a *sense of power* concerns an audience's desire to change or influence, the world in which they live. In commercial advertisements, the need for power is often presented blatantly by reference to the acceleration power of certain vehicles, the horsepower of certain engines, or the status that a particular brand of jeans will confer on the wearer. In public discourse, appeals to "the people" often aim toward an audience's need for power. A prototypical example occurred in a speech delivered by Spiro Agnew in 1969. The speech, "On Televised News," concentrated on the theme that the news media, particularly broadcast journalists, were wielding excessive power that was undermining traditional American governmental institutions. Agnew's arguments consistently referred to the need for "the people" (particularly the "Silent Majority") to recapture their power from the biased news media, whom he portrayed as behaving like a fourth branch of government without oversight. Agnew encouraged the viewing audience to satisfy their need for power by holding broadcasters accountable for their selection of news and to assert their power by openly criticizing various journalistic practices of the media managers.

The need for *roots* concerns people's need to feel a part of a community, to know and appreciate their social and even geographic origins. One type of persuasion that regularly calls upon the need for roots are the funding drives of alumnae organizations. Upon graduation from college and for years afterwards, alumnae are exhorted to support their "home" institutions by contributing money that will insure that future generations will experience the same pride about their school that the alumnae felt during their tenure there. Frequently alumnae organizations will offer contributors visible reminders of their roots in return for contributions. Thus, copies of the college newspaper, bumper stickers with the school's name and mascot, decals, mugs, and so on are offered as incentives for satisfying the need for roots. Public discussions also invoke the need for roots. Audiences may be exhorted to support certain trade policies because they will protect American products. After all, we all have "pride in America," our roots. Similarly, religious or ethnic group membership may be mentioned as a reason to support a particular policy. By doing so, the audience presumably will demonstrate their identification with that group and thereby satisfy their need for roots.

The need for *immortality*, of course, concerns our fear of death. When advertisers claim, for example, that a certain brand of yogurt has kept some people alive well beyond age 100, they are making the same appeal to immortality that public advocates use when they argue that by enacting laws that require lower speed limits lives will be saved. Similarly, when advocates call on audiences to follow a course of action in order to honor the dead, as Lincoln did in the Gettysburg Address, their argument finds some measure of force in the audience's need for immortality, the need to keep the dreams of those who died alive.

Finally, the need for *creative outlets* recognizes the desire of people to add a little something that is their own to the world, not because it proves their worth, but because it expresses their unique creativity. The marketing of products from "homemade" pizzas to "home" permanents works on the need for creative outlets. In regard to public issues, the same need may be invoked. In 1988, a public controversy regarding the censorship of art broke out in the city of Chicago. A young artist, whose work was on display at the School of the Chicago Art Institute, was condemned by a number of city aldermen because one of his paintings depicted the late Mayor Washington of Chicago in women's bikini underwear. Several of the aldermen went so far as to confiscate the art work. In the ensuing discussion, defenders of the artist claimed that artists should not be censored, that the flourishing of art required unrestricted pursuit of creativity. Their arguments thus affirmed the need for creative outlets.

Packard's list of needs is doubtless not exhaustive. Other writers have identified additional needs, and careful reflection might well reveal needs that have yet to appear on any researcher's list. However, the foregoing list provides at least a starting point for analysts of public discourse. By using Packard's eight needs heuristically, as an aid in analysis, the analyst may systematically dissect a message to see which motivations are triggered by particular arguments. As with what is sensible, what is motivating may vary from audience to audience. Thus when information concerning the motives of the particular audience is available, that information should be consulted.

Whom We Trust and the Credibility of Data

Just as scholars have attempted to identify sensible patterns of thinking and common motivations, so they have tried to determine the factors that predict whether or not a source of evidence will be accorded trust and legitimacy. Social scientists have focused much attention on the factors that determine the credibility, or believability, of a speaking subject. Their studies have focused primarily on the backgrounds and tactics of advocates who are perceived by audiences as credible. Although the lists of characteristics devised by these researchers include a variety of contemporary concepts, such as charisma and dynamic delivery, their work grows out of a line of study with a rich intellectual tradition. Aristotle's discussion of ethos was concerned with the same question: what characteristics make an orator, or advocate, trustworthy for an audience? This topic will be discussed later in Chapter 7. Our interest here is not so much with the trustworthiness of an advocate as with the trustworthiness of the advocate's sources of data. Hence our concern at this point is why an audience is likely to believe data from some sources and reject data from other sources.

In their study of the nature of and standards for assessing evidence, Newman and Newman, two scholars of argument, described various indices of the credibility of evidence.[16] They outlined 14 principles whereby the credibility of evidence may be assessed. Although some of these principles may not be applied by all audiences, their consistency with American legal practice and much common sense makes them a fair representation of which sources will likely be accepted and which will not. The following chart summarizes the 14 principles suggested by Newman and Newman:

Newman and Newman's Indices of Credibility for Evidence

Situational Tests

1. *Tension.* The lower the tension associated with an event, the higher the credibility of reports about it.
2. *Accessibility.* The more accessible the situation being reported on, both to the reporters and their audience, the more credible the report.
3. *Freedom to Report.* The more freedom a witness has to report things as he sees them, the greater his credibility.

Documentary Tests

4. *Authenticity.* The greater the presumption of authenticity, the higher the credibility of a document.
5. *Internal Consistency.* The higher the internal consistency of an author, the more credible his testimony.
6. *Carefulness of Generalization.* The more careful the generalizations of a writer, the higher the credibility of his testimony.
7. *Reluctance.* The greater the damage of his own testimony to a witness, the more credible it is.

Characteristics of the Writer

8. *Expertise.* The greater the relevant expertise of an author, the higher his credibility.
9. *Objectivity.* The greater the objectivity of an author, the more credible his testimony.

10. *Accuracy Record.* The more accurate the description and prediction record of a source, the higher the credibility of his testimony in general.

Tests of Primary Authorities

11. *Eyewitness Principle.* The greater a witness' personal observation of a matter to which he testifies, the higher his credibility.

12. *Contemporaneity.* The more contemporaneous the report of a witness, the more credible his testimony.

Tests of Secondary Sources

13. *Selection of Primary Sources.* The more discerning a writer's selection of primary sources, the more credible his testimony.

14. *Accuracy of Citation.* The more accurate the citations of a writer, the more credible his testimony.

Newman and Newman's guidelines are fairly self-explanatory; however, a few examples should demonstrate their importance to the force of an argument. Consider, for example, data quoted from the *Washington Post* versus data quoted from *The National Enquirer.* Experience will alert most audiences that the *Post* has a record for accurate reporting and that the pictures which accompany stories are generally authentic. The *Enquirer,* on the other hand, has a reputation for sensationalism, a record of inaccuracy, and many people suspect that the photographs published there are "doctored" in some way. A number of court cases have been filed by celebrities making such claims. Regardless of whether or not the *Enquirer* is actually that inaccurate, public perceptions are likely to cause rejection of the publication as a credible source on matters of public importance.

Public perceptions regarding the expertise and objectivity of a source of data play a similarly important role in according a source of evidence authoritativeness. Audiences are simply more likely to accept the assessment of independent consumer research organizations about the safety and performance of certain products than they are to accept the assessment of a celebrity who has no special expertise or of a corporate official who, although she may be an expert, has a personal interest in persuading consumers that her company's product is superior.

Principles like reluctance and the eyewitness principle also frequently play an important role in public controversy. Following the Iran/Contra Affair, some public discussion concerned how the government could avoid similar situations in the future. The testimony of people like Oliver North, who were eyewitnesses of the operations, was frequently used as data for claims regarding the nature of the problem. When questions arose about conflicting testimony, people frequently appeared to grant more trust to those who had the most to lose from their testimony.

Similar examples could be recounted for the other principles as well. Newman and Newman's guidelines suggest a systematic way to determine whether or not audiences will accept, or supply, the authoritative warrants necessary to move from data that seems to speak for itself to the claims that advocates offer an audience.

American Values as Cultural Warrants

Earlier in this chapter, the importance of cultural warrants was discussed. The values of a culture influence which logical connections will be accepted as sensible, which motivations will be recognized as compelling, and which standards will be applied to determine the trustworthiness of sources of data. Thus, the analyst of public discourse should be aware of the dominant values accepted by the culture within which an audience lives.

A variety of fascinating studies of American culture have been conducted by scholars. Probably the most notable project of this type was conducted by a French social philosopher, Alexis de Tocqueville, in the 1830s and reported in his work, *Democracy in America*. Over a century later, five contemporary scholars undertook a similar project and reported their findings in the bestseller, *Habits of the Heart*, referred to earlier in this text in Chapter 1. Both works pointed toward a number of uniquely American ideals, including our allegiance to individualism, our commitment to religious values, and our discomfort with the isolation and lack of community that accompanies the value placed on self-reliance.

Consistent with the findings of de Tocqueville and Bellah, et. al., but focusing on the values revealed in the public addresses featured during a variety of public discussions, two communication scholars have devised a list of standard American values. Edward D. Steele and W. Charles Redding compiled a list of sixteen standard American values.[17]

Steele and Redding's Standard American Values

1. Puritan and Pioneer Morality
2. The Value of the Individual
3. Achievement and Success
4. Change and Progress
5. Ethical Equality and Equal Opportunity
6. Effort and Optimism
7. Efficiency, Practicality, and Pragmatism
8. Rejection of Authority
9. Science and Secular Rationality
10. Sociality
11. Material Comfort
12. Quantification
13. External Conformity
14. Humor
15. Generosity and Considerateness
16. Patriotism

The value of *Puritan and pioneer morality* reflects a collection of virtues that were espoused by those who founded the United States. Honesty, simplicity, cooperation, self-discipline, courage, orderliness, personal responsibility, and humility are revered as characteristics of "good" people. The tendency of Americans to pass moral judgment based on these qualities is apparent in sources as diverse as history books and Hollywood films. Our heroes tend to exhibit the moral values of the Puritans and pioneers, whereas our villains violate those moral standards by demonstrating qualities such as deception, irresponsibility, and cowardice.

The *value of the individual* concerns the autonomy, uniqueness, and worth of every single person. From the Constitution to the Bill of Rights to contemporary interpretations of the law from the Supreme Court, individual rights and privileges are accorded high status. This value is apparent in well known cultural standards, such as the dictum that "it is better to let twelve guilty men go free than to jail one innocent man." Why? The answer lies in the value we place on the individual. A single wrongful conviction, unjustified death, and so forth is considered tragic because each individual is important. Human interest stories that often dominate the pages of newspapers and magazines similarly assert the value of the individual as they concentrate on "some*one* you should get to know" or the individual achievements and successes of some*one*.

Achievement and success characterize the means by which Americans attain status in society. Unlike other cultures, where a person's status might be determined by birthright, American culture has offered opportunity for advancement through achievement. The American dream revolves around the notion that "the tired,the poor, the wretched refuse yearning to be free" may, through the hard work and virtues of a Puritan and pioneer morality, seek their fortune. Success is measured by one's achievements. If someone fails to achieve success, that failure is more likely to be attributed to their lack of energy or ambition than to their circumstances. The achiever is valued; the nonachiever is not.

This country was founded during the eighteenth century when thinkers of the Age of Enlightenment believed that humankind had the power to mold life on earth in the image of life in heaven through scientific advancement combined with the application of humane values. Partially as a result of that influence, *change and progress* have established themselves as dominant cultural values. Americans strive to become better and better until they can become the "best that they can be," the creed of progress. Change, probably because it is necessary although not sufficient for progress, is highly valued as an end in itself. Americans change jobs, change Presidents, change investments, and even change their looks with the hope that progress will be served.

Common to the values of Puritan and Pioneer morality, the individual, and achievement and success is the theme that anyone can make it in our society. Everyone is assumed to have the potential for success. Everyone is accorded individual rights. Anyone can change. The reason circumstances are irrelevant is because equality is assumed to exist. Thus *ethical equality and equal opportunity* are valued as the means for assuring the equality that is so necessary to implementation and attainment of the American dream. A number of public institutions and public policies, ranging from free public education to anti-discrimination laws are founded on the principle and value of equality. For example, "if you cannot afford a lawyer, one will be appointed for you," because everyone should have an equal opportunity under the law.

Effort and optimism, of course, accompany our faith in change and progress and our commitment to Puritan and Pioneer morality. By working hard, we are told, we can achieve success. The pessimist is dismissed as being too negative, while the virtues of positive thinking are extolled. Our heroes, whether they are Hollywood characters like Rocky or corporate leaders like Lee Iacocco, display optimism even when they are the decided underdog. They beat the odds through simple hard work combined with a positive attitude. Hence, these qualities are valued.

Hard work alone, however, may not lead to achievement and success. The real success stories come from those who maintain a concern for *efficiency, practicality,* and *pragmatism*. "Eggheads" and "dreamers" don't get ahead. Success requires being practical, occasionally compromising the dream to act pragmatically, using your work time efficiently. Whether it is a sports team or a corporate team, the task must be accomplished efficiently which often requires practical thinking and discarding complicated theories or plans in favor of ideas that can be applied immediately to the "real" world. Those who do, those who "get the job done," are the practitioners. Those who think, but don't get the job done, may still be valued, but not as much as those who do.

From the overthrow of British rule by the colonists to contemporary suspicions regarding excessive interference by government agencies, Americans have tended to reflect an inclination toward *rejection of authority*. Power and those who wield it by virtue of their authority are regarded with caution. The homespun wisdom of common people is often accorded as much, and sometimes more, respect as the opinions of authorities. As Steele and Redding noted, even the American concept of peace is generally defined as the absence of some external authoritarian force.

The value placed on *science and secular rationality* is a natural accompaniment to values such as change and progress and effort and optimism. The notion that every problem has a cause that, if correctly identified, can be reversed to produce a solution reinforces Americans' faith in progress and general optimism. Historical events, such as the Industrial Revolution which helped to establish the United States as an economic power and the Manhattan Project which helped push the country into a position of military superiority, demonstrated scientific and technological capabilities and reinforced the value of science and secular rationality. Scientific setbacks, such as the tragic explosion of the Challenger Space Shuttle, assume an even more tragic presence than that related to the loss of life because we place such a high premium on our faith in science and our ability to solve problems rationally. Indeed, the solutions to many problems are postponed in the faith that science and secular rationality will eventually save us. Thus scientific solutions to problems as diverse as the threat of nuclear war and drug abuse often find favor among American audiences.

The value of *sociality* concerns the importance placed on "getting along," making contacts, being personable. Poll data, for instance, showed that even though many Americans disagreed with Ronald Reagan's policies and stands on issues, he was a popular president because people viewed him as a likable fellow. In short, Reagan was sociable. In the business world, too, sociability is valued. The sociable executive can make contacts, obtain invitations to join the "right" clubs, and thereby enhance business. Perhaps the Supreme Court even recognized the value placed on sociability when they ruled recently that women could not be excluded from a number of prestigious athletic and other private men's clubs because of the important role played by these organizations as a meeting ground for business leaders.

Material comfort is valued as a measure of achievement and success. The tangible rewards, or concrete manifestations, of the American dream have long been recognized as owning your own home, driving a late model car, and accumulating all the latest consumer goods. Presumably accumulation of such material goods makes Americans more comfortable, even though recent studies show that they create such comfort that Americans lack the proper exercise to maintain both physical and emotional health. The answer to such problems has not been to discard the easy chair or the television but to supplement it with other material goods like the exercise bike and the membership to a health club.

Steele and Redding pointed out that in a country characterized by tall mountains, endless plains, and wide open spaces, it was inevitable that people would place value on *quantification*. Simply put, "bigger is better." Two cars are better than one. As a survey of the garages of many wealthy citizens will show, three automobiles are even better than two, four better than three, and so on. The emphasis on quantification is played out in assessment of work as well. The best worker is often described as the one who can do the most, the farmer who produces the most corn, the auto worker who connects two parts faster than anyone else, the academic who writes the most books, and so forth. Quality is important, but quantity can be measured. For a society that values efficiency, such measurement assumes importance. If an advocate cannot quantify the damage of a particular program or estimate the benefits of another, her arguments may fall on deaf ears. Quantification is a way to demonstrate that practical, concrete matters are taken into account as opposed to the subjective, nonquantifiable assessments characteristic of more theoretical, less practical matters.

External conformity is valued as a way to demonstrate sociability and engender the cooperative spirit common to Puritan and pioneer morality. In addition, external conformity helps to verify that all Americans are equal. A superficial, but commercially lucrative, illustration of this value lies in the American fascination with changing fashions. The amount of money spent on purchasing the latest fashion when our old clothes are still perfectly good demonstrates the value we place on external conformity. Those who fail to conform are often described as "odd," "peculiar," or "eccentric." Perhaps the value placed on external conformity accounts in part for why it is so difficult for some to understand why a homeless person would prefer to sleep on the street than in a shelter. At base, the value given the individual promotes tolerance of even bizarre behavior, but the value given external conformity makes such behavior suspicious even when tolerated.

Humor, like external conformity, is a way that people demonstrate their sociability. Media professionals and political analysts, for example, claimed that a variety of events in the summer of 1988 that poked fun at presidential candidate, Michael Dukakis, were strokes of genius because those events showed that the candidate had a sense of humor. Dukakis' staff apparently recognized that Americans expected their political candidates to illustrate the value placed on humor as they organized "roasts" of the candidate.

The values placed on success and material comfort are, to some extent, balanced by the value placed on *generosity and considerateness*. Consistent with a Puritan and pioneer morality, Americans expect their neighbors to help out in times of crisis and their heroes to make generous contributions. Boy Scouts do good deeds and thereby display considerateness. Rudeness just isn't tolerated as long running syndicated columns like "Dear Abby," "Ann Landers," and "Miss Manners" persistently demonstrate. Only bad guys are "stingy," "tight," and "inconsiderate." The good guys always lend a helping hand. Generosity is expected from those who become successful. Even our rejection of authority is assisted by our faith in generosity. We may be suspicious of government authorities furnishing funds for all sorts of domestic programs and thereby putting a finger in the pie of how such programs will be run, but we welcome corporate and individual philanthropy as support for such programs regardless of the influence that such corporate sponsors may wield.

Finally, Americans value *patriotism*. Although our culture may be a mere collection of individuals, each individual is expected to display his or her pride in being an American. Our holidays and our history reinforce the value of patriotism. Noted sociologist, Robert Bellah, has pointed out that patriotism has been elevated to the status of civil religion in the United States.[18] Following the Christian tradition, the Washington Monument stands as a symbol of the "Father" of our country, the Lincoln Memorial represents our "saviour" during the most severe period of civil strife, and the eternal flame at Arlington Cemetery reminds us of the "holy ghost" of John F. Kennedy. Because patriotism is a cherished value, its existence in relation to particular policies is often taken for granted. For example, despite widespread reservations about and many objections to American involvement in Vietnam, young men who evaded military service by fleeing to Canada were frequently judged unpatriotic.

As this brief review of the standard American values suggested by Steele and Redding suggests, many of these values are consistent while others appear in conflict with one another. Like the studies by de Toqueville, Bellah, and others, Steele and Redding's list recognizes the tension between competing values common to American life. Such a list can be helpful for the analyst of public discourse as it indicates which values can form the basis for warrants that will appeal to an American audience. However, as with the other descriptions in this chapter, this list of values plays an analytical role that can be refined by analysis of the particular values shared by a particular audience. Some segments of the population may place a higher premium on some of these values as opposed to others.

Summary

In general, audiences respond both intellectually and passionately to the arguments presented during the course of public controversy. In addition, audiences strive to find consistency between the messages to which they are exposed and their internal states of passion and determinations of what makes sense. The warrants for arguments tend to be complex, often including components of all three types of warrants: substantive, motivational, and authoritative. All three types of warrants are influenced by cultural warrants that help members of a culture grasp what makes sense, what motives should be felt and acted upon, and what sources can be trusted. This chapter has provided a set of characteristics for what contemporary American audiences are likely to take as sensible, to recognize as motivational factors, and to accord credibility as sources of evidence. Perhaps most important are the standard American values that underlie what we know as common sense, what we feel as motivating needs, and whom we value as trustworthy sources. By investigating whether or not an advocate's arguments are consistent with the values shared by an audience, the analyst of public discourse can assess whether or not the reasons fit the audience.

Notes

[1] Jean Piaget, *Language and Thought of the Child,* trans. Marjorie Gabain, 3rd ed. (London: Routledge and Kegan Paul, 1959), pp. 19-25.

[2] Plato, *Phaedrus,* trans. W.C. Helmbold and W.G. Rabinowitz (Indianapolis: Bobbs-Merrill, 1956).

[3] For a representative discussion, see Michael Scriven, "Probative Logic: Review and Preview," in *Argumentation: Across the Lines of Discipline,* eds. Frans H. Van Eemeran, Rob Grootendorst, J. Anthony Blair, and Charles A. Willard (Providence: Foris, 1987), pp. 7-32; see also, E.M. Barth, "Logic to Some Purpose: Theses Against the Deductive-Nomological Paradigm in the Science of Logic," in *Argumentation,* pp. 33-46; and see, Ralph H. Johnson, "Logic Naturalized: Recovering a Tradition," in *Argumentation,* pp. 47-56. See also, Stephen Toulmin, *The Uses of Argument*

(Cambridge: Cambridge University Press, 1958) and Ch. Perelman and L. Olbrechts-Tyteca, *The New Rhetoric: A Treatise on Argumentation*, trans. John Wilkinson and Purcell Weaver (Notre Dame: University of Notre Dame Press, 1969).

[4] For a representative account of this type, see George Campbell, *The Philosophy of Rhetoric*, ed. Lloyd F. Bitzer (Carbondale: Southern Illinois University Press, 1963).

[5] George A. Sanborn, "The Unity of Persuasion," *Western Speech Journal* 19 (1955):175-83. See also, Randall C. Ruechelle, "An Experimental Study of Audience Recognition of Emotional and Intellectual Appeals in Persuasion," unpublished dissertation (University of Southern California, 1954).

[6] Fritz Heider, "Attitudes and Cognitive Organization," *Journal of Psychology* 21 (1946):107-112.

[7] Leon Festinger, *A Theory of Cognitive Dissonance* (Evanston: Row, Peterson, 1957). See also, Festinger, *Conflict, Decision, and Dissonance* (Stanford: Stanford University Press, 1964).

[8] This example is borrowed and adapted from Richard Rieke and Malcolm Sillars, *Argumentation and the Decision Making Process*, 2nd ed. (Glenview: Scott Foresman, 1984), 67-8.

[9] William F. Lewis, "Some Ideological Correlates of Common Sense Rhetoric," Paper presented at Central States Speech Association Convention, Schaumburg, Illinois, April 1988.

[10] Milton Rokeach, *Beliefs, Attitudes, and Values* (San Francisco: Jossey-Bass, 1968), especially pp. 156-178.

[11] For a synthesis of perspectives that lead to this conclusion, see Hugh Dalziel Duncan, *Communication and Social Order* (London: Oxford University Press, 1970).

[12] Michael Foucault, *Madness and Civilization*, trans. Richard Howard (New York: Vintage Books, 1973).

[13] Jean Piaget, *Six Psychological Studies*, trans. Anita Tenzer, ed. David Elkind (New York: Random House, 1967), pp. 48-54 and 92-98.

[14] "Jesse Jackson and Jerry Fallwell Debate South Africa," ABC Nightline with Ted Koppell, 9 September 1985.

[15] Vance Packard, *The Hidden Persuaders* (New York: Pocket Books, 1958), especially pp. 61-70.

[16] Robert P. Newman and Dale R. Newman, *Evidence* (New York: Houghton Mifflin, 1969), pp. 74-88, especially pp. 87-88.

[17] Edward D. Steele and W. Charles Redding, "The American Value System: Premises for Persuasion," *Western Journal of Speech Communication* 26 (1962):83-91.

[18] Robert N. Bellah, "Civil Religion in America," *Daedalus* (1967):1-21.

Suggested Readings

Bellah, Robert N., Richard Madsen, William M. Sullivan, Ann Swidler, and Steven M. Tipton, 1985. *Habits of the Heart*. Berkeley: University of California Press.

De Toqueville, Alexis, 1969. *Democracy in America*. Trans. George Lawrence. Ed. J. P. Mayer. New York: Doubleday, Anchor Books.

Fishbein, Martin, and Icek Ajzen, 1975. *Belief, Attitude, Intention and Behavior: An Introduction to Theory and Research*. Reading: Addison-Wesley.

Newman, Robert P. and Dale R. Newman, 1969. *Evidence.* New York: Houghton Mifflin.

Packard, Vance, 1958. *The Hidden Persuaders.* New York: Pocket Books.

Perelman, Chaim and L. Olbrechts-Tyteca, 1969. *The New Rhetoric.* Trans. John Wilkinson and Purcell Weaver. Notre Dame: University of Notre Dame Press.

Piaget, Jean, 1959. *Language and Thought of the Child.* Trans. Marjorie Gabain. London: Routledge and Kegan Paul.

Plato, 1956. *Phaedrus.* Trans. W.C. Helmbold and W.G. Rabinowitz. Indianapolis: Bobbs-Merrill.

Steele, Edward D. and W. Charles Redding, 1962. "The American Value System: Premises for Persuasion." *Western Journal of Speech Communication* 26:83-91.

Chapter 5

Good Reasons Structure the Audience's Response

In the last chapter, the nature of audiences was discussed as providing a standard for evaluating whether or not the reasons offered by an advocate fit the audience. This chapter concentrates on a second standard by which the reasons of advocates may be evaluated. In addition to fitting an audience, reasons should also mold the audience's expectations and beliefs. An effective advocate will incline an audience toward a particular conclusion and guide its response accordingly. While the content of arguments, discussed in the previous chapter, may contribute to the advocate's ability to guide an audience's response, the structure of arguments and the messages they comprise are equally, if not more, compelling. Thus, *an argument may be judged "good" if it strategically structures an audience's response*.

In this chapter, the importance of structure for an audience will be reviewed. Following that discussion, various schemata, or patterns, that can be applied to messages will be explained. By determining the structure of an entire message, or even a single argument, the analyst of public discourse can determine whether or not the advocate has strategically structured the audience's response.

The Nature of Structure and Symbolic Inducement

The importance of structure has been discussed by students of communication for centuries. Aristotle, for example, devoted Book III of the *Rhetoric* to a discussion of how persuasive orations should be organized and how stylistic devices could be engaged to serve persuasive ends. The notion that the structure of a message served strategic ends was put vividly by a Roman writer, probably Cicero, in the ancient treatise, *Ad Herrenium*. The author compared an orator's arrangement of his arguments for an audience to a military commander's arraying of soldiers for battle.[1] Just as a commander who left his flanks unprotected might be vulnerable, so an orator who misarranged her arguments might be vulnerable to attack from opponents and audiences alike.

The idea that choices about the order of a message can be significant is also verified by everyday experience. Most people learn through experience that the beginning of a conversation often sets the tone for what will happen later. Consider, for example, a conversation typical of many romances. Boy meets girl. Girl meets boy. A relationship develops. After some period of time, the relationship begins to follow familiar patterns. A routine develops. Our boy, Jack, gets in the habit of dropping by his girlfriend's house every Thursday evening after dinner. They go out at other times, but the Thursday evening get-together becomes a ritual. One Thursday evening Jack doesn't show. His girlfriend, Jill, passes it off at first. She thinks he's probably just been delayed. But as the evening grows, she begins to worry. Maybe he had an accident. Maybe he's in the hospital. By 10:00 p.m., Jill decides to call his home. His roommate only expresses confusion. "Yea," he says, "Jack left about 7:00; I thought he was coming over to your place." Jill begins to feel insecure. Maybe Jack didn't have an accident. Maybe he's out with another girl. Jill's righteous indignation begins to build. After all, she could have done something else this evening. But, no, she's spent the whole night waiting for Jack, and the inconsiderate bum didn't even call to say he wouldn't be there. 1:00 a.m. — a knock on the door — it's Jack.

How does Jill order her conversation. She could start by explaining that she doesn't like to be taken for granted, that he should have called, and questioning where he has been all this time. Or she could begin by expressing her relief at seeing him, follow with her disappointment that they hadn't been able to spend the evening together, and continue by inquiring where he's been. There are, of course, a number of other alternatives. However, of the two cited, the first is likely to elicit a defensive response from Jack. It is, after all, an attack. The latter message, on the other hand, first puts Jack at ease and then advances the questions about his whereabouts. The order of the message makes a difference in Jack's response.

The importance of order does not diminish when the message is a public one presented by an advocate on behalf of a public issue. Before recounting some examples of the impact structure can have in public controversy, some inquiry into why structure is so important is in order. In an attempt to explain how symbols work persuasively, a communications scholar, Richard Gregg, has described a variety of structures and their importance for human knowledge and human symbol use.[2] The discussion of the nature of structure that follows draws heavily on Gregg's work.

Studies in neurophysiology have revealed that the human brain works according to a structural model. In other words, the operations of the brain may be recognized by the firing patterns of the electro-chemicals in the brain. When a human is confronted by some stimulus, the brain reacts by firing a recognizable pattern. Such patterns have been illustrated in color photographs that show different parts of the brain in different colors. A vivid, but oversimplified, image of what happens is something like a string of Christmas tree lights. When a particular stimulus is encountered, the brain fires a pattern that could be conceived as a particular string of lights. Exposure to the same stimulus produces the same pattern. Another stimulus results in a different pattern, a different looking string of lights. Moreover, once one of these patterns is fired, subsequent firing of the same pattern becomes more likely. Exposure to just the beginning of a longer stimulus that produced a complicated pattern may be enough to trigger the whole pattern in the brain, even though the whole stimulus is not encountered. In short, the brain seems to work in structured or patterned ways.

Cognitive psychologists have also studied structure, the structure of the mind instead of the structure of the brain. Those scholars have devoted considerable time to the study of perception, the study of how people perceive the external phenomena in their environments. Normal, healthy people have been found to be able to perceive patterns. Abnormal, unhealthy people have a diminished capability to perceive patterns. One example of research that pointed in this direction involved an experiment that asked people to perform a relatively simple task. Subjects were given a box of yarn that included a variety of colors, weights, and textures and were asked to sort the yarn. Those who had been previously diagnosed as schizophrenic began by sorting the yarn according to one of the characteristics. But before they completed the task, they started over, sorting according to another characteristic. Eventually, these patients abandoned the task, apparently unable to complete any particular pattern. Subjects who had been diagnosed as healthy, on the other hand, completed the sort. Individual subjects varied in the characteristic they chose to structure or sort the box of yarn, but they always produced a completed structure. Thus the ability to perceive patterns has been associated with normal, healthy mental functioning.

Not only is the ability to perceive pattern or structure associated with mental health, but research indicates that this ability is developed regardless of formal training. Piaget pointed out that at very young ages, even before they accumulate a sufficient vocabulary to construct very complex sentences, children recognize the structure of the language common to their cultures.[3] A child with otherwise limited verbal skills, for example, will form syntactically correct sentences. The child has not been taught that sentences must include a subject and a verb, but nonetheless will construct sentences accordingly. Similarly, the child has not been taught the nature of direct objects, predicate adjectives, adverbs, and so on, but nevertheless constructs sentences as if she or he knew the rules of grammar. The implication is clearly that people perceive structural patterns naturally within their culture and that such perception of structural pattern is fundamental to the natural operation of the mind and brain.

Investigations of how people who are able to perceive patterns do so have revealed several principles or rules that characterize perception generally. First, people perceive *selectively*. In other words, from among the variety of stimuli that a person could focus on to find a pattern, the individual selects some characteristic or part to give order to the otherwise disordered and competing stimuli. The illustration concerning the box of yarn demonstrates this tendency to select a particular characteristic with which to start the pattern. Similarly, the varying interpretations that different people construct for what they see in the clouds or in inkblots illustrate the tendency toward selectivity.

Second, people tend to perceive whole rather than partial patterns. This tendency to complete a pattern is usually referred to as the principle of *closure*. This principle explains why, even when a part of the pattern is missing from the actual stimuli, people will perceive the entire pattern as being there. The principle of closure has been demonstrated with a variety of incomplete pictures in a variety of studies. For example, given pictures like the following and asked what was pictured, subjects typically respond with the answers, "a circle" and "a triangle." Yet, as close examination reveals, neither figure is complete.

Figure 1.   Figure 2.

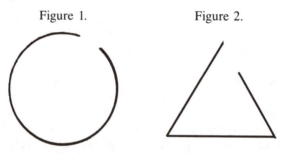

Everyday knowledge furnishes similar examples of the principle of closure at work. Consider the names that people give to the constellations. The big dipper and the bear are at best sketchy patterns among the stars that often leave gaping holes within the pattern. But our tendency to complete or close a pattern makes such names sensible descriptions of what we see. In a similar sense, people tend to feel uncomfortable if they cannot complete a pattern. Hayden's "Unfinished Symphony" leaves us with the same sort of lack of closure as any of those films from which people leave saying, "I can't believe they ended it there." In both cases, there is a lack of satisfaction that the pattern is left incomplete. Faced with such psychological discomfort, most people will attempt to complete the pattern. They may return to a prior musical phrase, play it silently in their heads, and finish the symphony. They may "decide" that the couple in the film did survive so as to end the story. Impatience regarding the completion of a pattern works in a similar way. The partner of a slow talker may finish the other person's sentences as a way of obtaining closure and moving on.

A third characteristic of perception is that once a structure is perceived, through whatever selection process and using whatever closure is necessary, people have an inclination to repeat that pattern of perception. As mentioned earlier in regard to brain patterns, once a pattern is fired and experienced, little stimuli is required to trigger the same pattern. In short, people seem inclined toward *repetition of pattern*. This tendency is illustrated by theories of cognitive processes such as the consistency theories discussed in the last chapter. Our tendency to believe things that are consistent with what we already believe and our discomfort with inconsistency demonstrates a preference for the already-experienced over the newly-experienced.

The principle of repeating patterns is also vividly illustrated by our typical reactions to those curious problems referred to as "brain teasers." Consider a familiar example. A ship comes into harbor, and the sailors take a brief shore leave. When they throw the rope ladder over the side, it is 7:00 p.m. The water is covering the bottom rung of the ladder. There are fifteen rungs on the ladder, and each is two feet from the other. The tide is coming in at one-half foot an hour. The sailors return at 1:00 a.m. How many rungs of the rope ladder are covered by water at that time? The answer is one, the same one that was covered when they disembarked. The boat (and the ladder), of course, rose with the incoming tide. The answer makes sense, but many people confronted with this problem will begin to make calculations, using the numbers provided in the story. Why? The beginning of the story sounds like one of those very familiar word-problems from math class. People begin to perceive the structure; because it fits a familiar pattern, they produce the familiar pattern and start to work on solving the problem mathematically, even though the problem calls for a different sort of solution or pattern of thinking.

Another familiar example illustrates the same point. Ask someone to spell "joke." Then ask them to spell "poke." Then ask them what they call the white of an egg. Whether the respondent is your younger sister or brother or your classmate, they will likely answer "yolk." Depending on their age, after a few seconds, they usually laugh and amend their answer to either "albumen" or "the white of an egg." The reason people are inclined to say the wrong answer, "yolk," is again this principle of repeating a pattern once the pattern is established inside their heads. The spelling exercise at the beginning establishes a pattern that is difficult for most people to break from long enough to say the right answer first.

The combination of the three principles of perception just discussed—selectivity, closure, and repetition—often accounts for perceptual errors. People often overlook real differences, or even mistakes, in the phenomena they encounter because their selective tendencies combined with their drive toward closure and inclination toward repetition encourages them to see what is not there or not to see what is there. A familiar example is furnished by the following sign.

Asked what the sign says, many people respond with "in the park." They ignore the extra "the," because the word doesn't fit the familiar pattern. To make a sensible, complete pattern requires overlooking that extra word. The principle of closure helps them define the word as "extra." Thus, they perceive the message selectively, ignoring that part which breaks the pattern.

Much humor works according to the same perceptual principles. Humorists make us laugh by somehow breaking the pattern, or changing the pattern that we expect to hear or see. Our funny bones are tickled by the break. If someone doesn't "get the joke," it is likely the result of his or her perceptual tendencies being so strong that they plug in the familiar pattern and overlook the pattern presented by the humorist. "The Far Side," a cartoon by Gary Larson, features just that sort of humor. Larson's jokes often play on changing the reader's perceptual frame. Familiar patterns are used, but animals play the role of humans and humans play the role of animals within that pattern. Interestingly, while many people think "The Far Side" is hilarious, a number of people say they fail to see the humor, they "don't get the joke." In the illustration below, the laughers laugh and chuckle, but others find the pattern so familiar that they fail to notice the reversal.

THE FAR SIDE By GARY LARSON

Suddenly, in the middle of the flock, the cook is goosed.

The Far Side. Copyright © 1987 Universal Press Syndicate. Reprinted with permission. All rights reserved.

Because our familiarity with a pattern may influence our selectivity, how we complete uncompleted patterns, and which patterns we tend to repeat, it is helpful to know what patterns are familiar to people. Gregg catalogued six patterns of human perception that appeared to be most familiar.[4] Using research from neurophysiology to linguistics, Gregg suggested that these six patterns were fundamental to human perception. Although sometimes invoked purposely, these patterns were often used unconsciously, or subconsciously. The six are listed in the following table.

Gregg's List of Six Patterns of Human Perception

1. Edging
2. Rhythm
3. Association
4. Classification
5. Abstraction
6. Hierarchy

Edging is the pattern that allows people to see, or perceive, one item as different, or distinct, from another. The human eye's capacity to distinguish between light and shadow allows us to find the edges, or borders, of things. Tests of perception that rely on pictures with varying degrees of light and shadow work with this pattern. Depending on where the edge is located, a person may see a skull or a woman sitting at the bureau in the same collection of light and shadow.

Rhythm is a pattern of vibrations. The ability to distinguish the intensity and sequence of the beat characterizes this perceptual pattern. People can tell when the vibrations increase in frequency and intensity and build to a climax. In other situations, the rhythm may be foregrounded and backgrounded so as to form a pattern. Ravel's musical work, "Bolero," used rhythm in just such a way, which may account for the decision to include it as background music for a particularly sensual scene in the movie, "10."

Association is the pattern of similarity. The ability to grasp the similarity between two distinct, edged, phenomena accounts for this pattern of perception. When people perceive a circle where an unclosed circle is presented, this pattern of association is being used. On those occasions when people notice the likeness between someone they just met and someone they used to know, association is coming into play.

Classification is a pattern that depends on association. Once similarities are grasped, people are able to group those things that are similar. Such grouping results in classification. The tendency of human beings to stereotype reflects this pattern of classification. A disordered world is made orderly by "putting things in their place," determining the group to which they belong.

Abstraction is a natural outgrowth of classification. Once a number of distinct phenomena have been grouped into a class, there is a tendency to label the class, to give a name to the type. The name, or label, is abstract as it refers to a collection of attributes rather than to a concrete phenomenon. As Gregg pointed out, once the skill of writing was developed in ancient civilizations, the ability to abstract was developed. By writing things down, the writer had a way of making those things stable, of keeping them in mind. Only by collecting a number of phenomena and keeping them stable long enough to ponder them, could a person begin to abstract their characteristics. General principles, or abstractions, thus were the product of the collection of individual cases.

Hierarchy refers to patterns that prioritize things. Hierarchy grows out of and completes the abstraction process. Once abstractions are made, the person looking at the patterns of classification can determine which groups are largest, most important, and so on. In other words, comparative judgments can be made on the basis of the abstractions that evolved from classifications. Gregg illustrates the point with the example of how lists are handled. By writing a list of "things to do," the list-maker stabilizes those things long enough to classify them. Some things will need to be done at home, others at work, and so on. The characteristics shared by various items on the list help the list-maker to categorize or classify the items. Once classified, the list-maker can make abstractions (e.g., "homework," "schoolwork," "workwork," etc.). Those abstractions can then be used to determine what needs to be done first, second, third, and so on.

The six patterns of perception identified by Gregg, then, help to fill out the detail of what is familiar, likely to be expected, and anticipated by people in regard to structure. These patterns and the three general principles of structure — selectivity, closure, and repetition — lay the ground for analyzing the structure of messages.

The Structure of Messages

As suggested earlier, communication scholars have been interested in the structure of messages for centuries. The Roman rhetorician and teacher, Quintilian, argued that an oration without order demonstrated the lack of a "fixed purpose or the least idea either of starting-point or goal."[5] Contemporary researchers have verified the link between arrangement and audience effect. Numerous studies have been conducted regarding the effects of arrangement on listeners' comprehension of ideas, agreement with the speaker's contentions, and assessment of the source's credibility.[6] These studies seem to confirm the general notion that structure is important to audiences as the data indicates that audiences comprehend better, are more likely to agree with a message, and are more likely to attribute credibility to the source of that message if the message is "organized."

But, what does it mean to say a message is "organized?" Surely it is impossible to construct a message, whether oral, written, or visual, that does not follow some order. By definition, something must be said first, and something else must follow. Even in a picture, something must be depicted somewhere and something else depicted elsewhere.

The principles of structure discussed in the previous section help to explain what an "organized" message does. First, if the order of a message is apparent, that structure may assist the selectivity of audiences by inclining them to perceive the structure in the way intended by the advocate, rather than allowing the audience to impose their own order on the message. Students typically distinguish between lecturers who are organized and those who are not precisely on this basis. Those lecturers who help them take notes, by specifying the main ideas and indicating what is important, are perceived as organized. Lecturers perceived as disorganized generally leave decisions about what the student should strive to remember in the hands and minds of their audience.

Secondly, the principle of closure suggests that organized messages will guide the audience's inclination to complete the form. Strategically structured messages will point the direction that the pattern should take as audiences strive to fill in the gaps. For example, when advocates use enthymemes that leave the claim open for construction by the audience, strategic structure will suggest a pattern likely to produce the claim that the advocate hopes will be supplied.

Thirdly, the principle of repetition suggests that strategically structured messages will follow familiar patterns. By triggering a pattern familiar to the audience, the advocate is more likely to be able to influence the audience's selectivity and choices regarding closure. If a familiar pattern is invoked, the advocate may not always need to be explicit about when one main idea has been concluded and the next is about to begin, because the pattern supplied by the advocate alerts listeners or viewers subconsciously as to the junctures and turns of the message. Gregg's list provides a general outline of patterns likely to be familiar to most audiences.

The idea that each of these principles can be used to assess the "strategic" value of structure is based on the notion that the form of a message can influence an audience, that the audience is open to a variety of alternative structural responses. This idea seems to be verified by the suggestions of scholars like those quoted earlier, but deserves additional elaboration. Kenneth Burke, who wrote extensively about the form of messages, provided a convenient definition of *form*. Burke defined form as "the creation of an appetite in the mind of the auditor, and the adequate satisfying of that appetite."[7] Because form is defined by its effect on auditors, Burke's definition is appropriate when discussing the strategic implications of structure. His explanation of how form works clearly is concerned with the psychological operation of form. In other words, his suggestion is that the form of a message sets up certain structural expectations within an audience. If the message goes on to satisfy those expectations, the audience feels closure and is psychologically satisfied. If not, the audience may be left aimlessly wondering and dissatisfied.

Burke followed his discussion of the psychology of form with a taxonomy of five types of form. The five types of form are *syllogistic progression*, *qualitative progression*, *conventional form*, *repetitive form*, and *incidental* or *minor forms*. [8] Syllogistic progressions move the audience from premises to conclusions in much the same way as a logical proof. In other words, the audience is led through a set of arguments that result in an intellectual agreement with the speaker. Qualitative progressions, on the other hand, move the audience from one state of mind, or psychological state, to another. To be effective, each successive state of mind must emerge naturally from the previous one, although the qualitative progression does not follow as rigid an order as the syllogistic progression demands. Repetitive form is the consistent maintaining of an idea through creative redundancy. Conventional form includes those patterns that have become traditional. Patterns of arrangement such as spatial, chronological, cause-effect, and so forth are clear examples of conventional form. Finally, incidental or minor forms are those small units of discourse that are immediately recognizable patterns, complete within themselves. Metaphors, paradoxes, rhetorical questions and the various figures of thought and figures of speech constitute excellent examples of incidental form.

An application and adaptation of Burke's taxonomy of form can provide a method for describing the arrangement of messages so as to highlight the effect of structure on the audience. The remainder of the discussion in this chapter will use Burke's terms for describing form; however, some alterations in the meaning and description of these forms will be used in order to adapt his taxonomy for the purpose of describing the communication that occurs during public controversy. A fundamental assumption guiding the remainder of this discussion is that structural characteristics abound at various levels within messages. Any particular argument, or reason, may exhibit a particular structure. In addition, the collection of reasons, or arguments that make up an extended message will display a certain structure. Finally, there may be a structure that characterizes an advocate's message, even when that message includes material that is not part of an argument. Therefore, Burke's terminology will be used to describe three levels of structure within a message — the large structure, the intermediate structure, and the small structure.

Large Structure

Perhaps the most durable advice regarding the organization of messages is that any message should have three parts: an introduction, a body, and a conclusion. From the Classical Age to the present, speakers and writers alike have been encouraged to follow this tri-partite pattern. Introductions are supposed to set the tone, establish the mood, introduce the topic, and otherwise warm up the audience for the body of the message that follows. The conclusion, on the other hand, wraps up the message by centering on the central idea, entering the advocate's final plea, leaving the audience with the main claim. Presumably, a well structured message will flow naturally from one part to another, providing a consistent and coherent pattern for the audience to follow.

The *large structure* of the message is the pattern that grounds the movement of a message from the introduction, through the body, to the conclusion. The two types of progressions identified by Burke, *syllogistic* and *qualitative*, provide useful categories for describing the large structure of a message. It is difficult to conceive of an effective message that does not progress, that does not attempt to move the audience from one level of understanding, belief, or action to another. Identifying the type of appetite or desire that is aroused initially and following the structure to see how that desire is satisfied provides clues as to the effects of the message. The rather cerebral character of the syllogistic progression is likely to produce effects different from those emanating from movement through a series of psychological states in the qualitative progression. The emphasis on order inherent in a perspective that describes the large structure of the message as a progression allows us to note the logical, intellectual progression of ideas and/or the psychological progression of feelings in the audience. Hence, our orientation toward structure is immediately wedded to the strategic, in terms of audience effects.

The differing natures of syllogistic and qualitative progressions, as well as their differing effects on an audience, are more easily understood with illustrations. Therefore, let us consider two famous persuasive speeches, each of which illustrates one of the progressions, and a contemporary video message concerning world hunger that overlays a syllogistic progression on a qualitative progression. The first is a speech given by Martin Luther King during the civil rights movement.[9] In 1963, during the largest ever civil rights march in Washington, D.C., King delivered his now famous "I Have a Dream" speech. The speech advocated a society free from racism and was one of a multitude of messages presented on behalf of legislative, judicial, and informal social action that would guarantee civil rights to all people in the United States.

King's "I Have a Dream" provides an excellent example of a qualitative progression that moves the audience through a series of psychological states. The speech began with a reference to Lincoln and the Emancipation Proclamation that likely put the audience into a state of nostalgic hope. That was followed immediately by a description of the Negro's state of being in 1963 that most likely shifted the audience to a mood of despair. From this despair arose hope as King moved into his famous promissory note metaphor in which he explained that all citizens, black and white, had been given a "check" promising equal rights. The audience then experienced injustice as they were told that the note had come back marked "insufficient funds." Immediately following, his statement that "we have come to cash this check" raised hope again. The speech continued through psychological states of urgency, determination or threat, caution, conciliation, determination, magnified injustice, satisfaction, increased hope, and unrestrained joy. If the list of psychological states were charted to indicate their progression with a focus on high, positive states and low, negative states, it would probably look like the graph below.

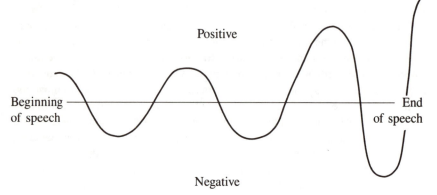

Hence the speech moved the audience through small ups and downs initially, following those with exaggerated lows and highs. The effect of the qualitative progression is one of inspiration as it ended with King's dream, the ultimate high.

In contrast to the qualitative progression exhibited in King's speech is the syllogistic progression followed by an advocate six years after King spoke. In 1969, then Vice President Spiro Agnew launched what is still regarded by many as the most pointed attack on broadcast journalism ever made. In November of 1969, the Nixon-Agnew administration had experienced increasing pressure from the media and citizens alike to end the war in Vietnam. Americans had viewed months of televised news that not only brought the barbarism of the war into their homes but also vividly portrayed demonstrations, riots, and other scenes of social unrest on the domestic front. In his now famous speech, "On Televised News," Agnew asked his audience to hold the media accountable to a standard of reporting that he believed was not being met.[10] He claimed that broadcast journalists were presenting an unfair account of events and over-editorializing in their reports of official government actions and policies. Worse yet, he warned that the media, described as unrepresentative of the views of ordinary Americans and unrestrained by any countervailing force, were wielding enormous power and influence. In short, his speech spearheaded the discussion of a new public issue regarding the power and proper role of the broadcast news media.

Agnew's "On Televised News" provides an excellent example of a syllogistic progression. Agnew began by asking two questions: "Are we demanding enough of our televised news presentations? And are the men of this medium demanding enough of themselves?" These questions likely instilled an appetite of inquiry that set the tone for a progression of arguments that eventually led the audience to an answer of "no" to both questions.

In his introduction, Agnew used an extended example of the television coverage of former President Nixon's address on Cambodia, broadcast about a week earlier, and a comparison of television treatment of Winston Churchill and John Kennedy to lead the audience into an initial negative answer. He then proceeded through a series of arguments in the body of the speech. Those included claims that television commentators are powerful, are an insulated elitist group, are biased, that the people would not tolerate similar concentrations of power in government, that democracy requires pluralistic views, that the First Amendment does not apply to televised commentary, and that the power of the media is dangerous. His final move was to suggest that the answer to the powerful, elitist, biased and dangerous press could only be achieved by media professionals demanding more of themselves and the people demanding that the media carry out this responsibility. His concluding remarks were comprised of a comparison of the television coverage of his speech with newspaper coverage of the speech that dramatized the nature of media and citizen control over the media. The major points of the speech acted as premises, which if accepted by the audience, led inevitably to the conclusion that the media does not demand enough of itself nor do the people demand that the media act responsibly.

The two speeches just reviewed follow very different progressions in their large structure. However, to say that King's speech follows a qualitative progression is not to suggest that his speech does not also invite some intellectual response from the audience. Similarly, characterizing Agnew's speech as following a syllogistic progression does not imply that his advocacy is devoid of an emotional appeal. Although one type of progression can be seen to predominate in each of these messages, structural components at other levels may follow patterns that compliment the large structure with intellectual or psychological thrusts that depart from the structure in the large. Some messages may actually follow both a syllogistic and qualitative progression simultaneously, accompanying each premise with a defined psychological state that finally lead to both an intellectual and emotional conclusion. However, generally, one or the other progression will dominate the large structure.

The large structure of other types of messages, for example print or film, may be examined similarly. A third, nonoratorical, example demonstrates a dominant qualitative progression that reinforces a simple syllogistic progression. The "We Are the World" videotape is a film account of the making of the record, "We Are the World," and a persuasive plea from many of the participants to the audience to help stop world hunger.[11] The title of the videotape is illustrative of the structure of its main claim. The videotape makes the argument that, because all of us are a part of the world, when one of us dies or goes hungry, that hurts all mankind. The only answer to the problem posed by world hunger, then, is to try to stop it so as to help humankind and thereby help ourselves. The progression of the argument is syllogistic. However, the large structure of the complete videotaped message is more characteristic of a qualitative progression.

The videotape begins with narrator Jane Fonda reminding viewers of the "historical" significance of so many celebrities from diverse perspectives joining together to cut a record designed to fight world hunger. Viewers are thus put into a serious, concerned, and even awesome state of mind. Fonda then raises the audience's expectations and sense of anticipation as she explains that the viewers will soon see how such an effort was brought to completion. The video then shifts to actual production activities, beginning with the arrival of the "stars" at the studio and following the night-long production of most of the vocals. Throughout this sequence, hopes of a completed product are successively diminished as the "stars" encounter minor problems (e.g., Lauper's earrings jingle the mike, Dylan's voice cracks, Stevie Wonder works on the braille machine). The song is never completed as the video shifts to narration and interviews with the "stars" concerning the seriousness of world hunger. Following a series of individual pleas for "your help," the film returns to a completed version of "We Are the World," finally satisfying the expectations of the audience and lifting their spirits once again. Thus, the series of psychological states that the video evokes is characteristic of a qualitative progression even as the main claim of the video is structured in a syllogistic progression.

Intermediate Structure

The *intermediate structure* of a message refers to the pattern that is used to fill out the large structure and is generally characteristic of the body of the message. Usually advocates present their reasons, or arguments, in the body rather than in the introduction or conclusion. Although an advocate may mention the main claim initially, sub-claims are usually reserved for the body of the message. Just as these sub-claims work to support the main claim, so the intermediate structure of a message works to fill out the large structure of a message.

The categories of *conventional, repetitive,* and *incidental* forms can be used as a way of describing the intermediate structure of the message. *Conventional* forms are those patterns for arranging arguments that are so familiar that they have become conventions. Audiences are accustomed to hearing arguments that follow a pattern of problem-solution, cause-effect, criteria-satisfaction, chronology, and so forth. *Repetitive* forms merely enact a pattern of repetition, each time elaborating the theme in a different way, but retaining thematic unity. *Incidental* form occurs when an advocate uses a conventional form in an unconventional setting. For example, most people are familiar with the structural pattern of a sermon. The pattern is conventional in religious settings. However, the explicit norms of American society suggest a separation between church and state, and consequently audiences do not typically expect to hear the pattern of a sermon within a political speech. Yet, from time to time, political candidates and officials use just such a pattern. Communication scholars have labeled the use of the religious form in political discourse the "jeremiad."[12] For our purposes such a use of form would be characterized as the use of incidental form.

Any of these forms can be used to construct either a syllogistic or a qualitative progression. For example, a chronological sequence or a problem solution form may lead the audience through a syllogistic progression. To the effects of the syllogistic progression are added the effects of following a conventional form. Not only does the audience have a sense of moving through a logical sequence, but because the pattern is conventional the audience can anticipate successive intellectual moves with great confidence. Similarly, a message might use a repetitive form to make the same basic argument in regard to diverse examples, finally securing audience agreement with the central argument in the case specified by the speaker. Here, the force of repetition can assist in moving the audience through a syllogistic progression.

The forms can also be used to develop a qualitative progression. For example, the conventional form of a motivated sequence (the pattern associated with most sales pitches that includes five steps: capturing attention, establishing a need, satisfying the need, visualizing results, and calling for action) may move the audience through various states of need and discomfort to a state of satisfaction and optimism. Or repetitive form may take the audience through a series of high, positive states and low, negative states finally resulting in the state of mind the source desires from his or her receivers.

Again, reviewing some examples should clarify how these categories can be used to describe the intermediate structure of a message and its ensuing effects on an audience. Let us return to the speeches of King and Agnew and the music video.

In King's "I Have a Dream," the qualitative progression seems to be achieved through a pattern that is very close to the conventional form of a motivated sequence. The first half of the speech develops needs regarding the inequity, injustice, and betrayal experienced by the American Negro. At the midpoint, he encourages his audience to "continue to work" and to "not wallow in the valley of despair." Immediately thereafter he launches into his "I have a dream" sequence and follows that with his "let freedom ring" sequence, thereby visualizing the result of true equality and brotherhood. This motivated sequence pattern compliments and reinforces the qualitative progression and in and of itself adds to the inspirational effect.

In the case of Agnew's speech, the pattern that emerges in support of his syllogistic progression seems to be a conventional problem-solution order. His arguments regarding the power, elitism and bias of the television medium laid out the problem. His claims that the people would never tolerate such power in the hands of government and that the people and the commentators differ in their perception of the state of the world underscored the severity of the problem. His refutations of the applicability of the First Amendment and the innocuousness of television coverage dispelled any remaining doubts regarding the existence and urgency of the problem. Consequently, the only rational solution to this problem was suggested by a return to his initial question. In other words, if the audience was not demanding enough of the media, then the solution was to demand more. His final comparison enacted the solution by guiding the audience along one potential path for demanding more of the news media. The nature of the problem solution order mirrored that of the question-answer form of the syllogistic progression. Hence the audience was led through a logically consistent and rational inquiry.

Again, nonoratorical messages may also be examined for their intermediate structure. In "We Are the World," repetitive form predominates. The music of the song is played in the background throughout the film. The lyrics are sung, numerous times in part, and in totality at the end. In addition, the words are character-generated on the screen. Thus, the theme of world hunger and the argument that something needs to be done about this problem are repeated throughout the film. In addition, the conventional form for a documentary film is used. There is narration, followed by actual film footage in chronological order, followed by interviews and more narration, followed by footage of the final product.

Small Structure

The *small structure* of a message concerns single units of a message, such as a single main idea, an individual argument, or even an opening or closing remark of an advocate. When we shift our focus to the small structure of the message, we can again use the categories of conventional, repetitive, and incidental forms. But to this list, should be added *minor forms*.

Within any single unit of a message, an advocate may use any of the forms that were associated with intermediate structure in the previous section. For example, the conventional form of a cause-effect relationship might characterize one main idea in a larger problem solution pattern that followed a syllogistic progression. Similarly, a time order could be evident in a narrative comprising one segment of a repetitive pattern used in a qualitative progression. Repetitive form, on the other hand, could be used as a form of emphasis in the punctuation for either a conventional or incidental pattern that moved in either a syllogistic or qualitative progression. Likewise, incidental forms may provide the pattern for any particular part of a message.

If we return to Burke's original conception of *minor forms* for examining structure in the small then we would look for metaphors, rhetorical questions and the like as comprising the structure of small units of speech. Ordinarily, these minor forms are termed figures of speech, or stylistic devices. However, critics within the rhetorical tradition have pointed out that these *figures of speech* are also *figures of thought*. Their point is simply that particular patterns of wording evoke particular patterns of thinking for listeners or readers. Minor forms, because of their structure, may evoke a specific pattern of thinking for the audience.

Two Belgian philosophers, Chaim Perelman and L. Olbrechts-Tyteca, have described various forms that single arguments may take.[13] Their descriptions can be summarized into three categories of minor forms. Borrowing their terminology, the minor forms of individual arguments can be divided into three types: *associative structures*, *disassociative structures*, and *quasi-logical structures*.

Associative structures are those patterns that encourage an audience to associative or draw some manner of comparison between two subjects. The two subjects might be very similar or significantly dissimilar, but the pattern of the argument encourages an audience to grasp similarity and dismiss dissimilarity. At base, any statement of the form "x is *like* y" uses associative structure. Thus, any statement that draws a direct comparison uses this type of minor form.

Among those stylistic devices or figures that incorporate associative structure, several are quite familiar. Frequently, however, the associative structure is not altogether obvious. Metaphors and analogies share the use of associative structure, but each stylistic device elaborates the association in a slightly different manner. Metaphors use terms that are apparently unrelated to a subject in order to make some characteristic of the subject vivid. In doing so, metaphors invite the audience to associate the characteristic(s) of one subject with another. Probably the classic metaphor is, "man is a wolf." This statement encourages the audience to associate the characteristic(s) of a wolf with man. Stated more directly, the pattern is simply "man is like a wolf." The metaphor works like an enthymeme in that the audience is asked to participate by supplying the characteristics of a wolf and drawing the comparison between wolves and men. The metaphor, by suggesting an association, triggers a pattern of thinking in which comparisons are chained out.

Analogies encourage another sort of associative thinking. An analogy follows the pattern of a ratio, or proportion. X is to V as Y is to Z. Usually analogies include the word, "like," in their statement of relationship. For example, the advocate who says that "giving more money to the state legislature is like giving more blood to a hemophiliac" is drawing an analogy. Like the metaphor, the analogy draws a comparison. But unlike the metaphor, the analogy draws the comparison more specifically by following the format of a ratio. A particular characteristic of a subject is associated with another subject. In the example above, the legislature is compared to a hemophiliac in a very precise way. What the audience is asked to conclude is that the legislature uses money the same way that a hemophiliac uses blood. This particular characteristic of a hemophiliac is associated with the legislature. Both analogies and metaphors are compelling minor forms in so far as they mirror the perceptual pattern of association that Gregg identified as a fundamental pattern.

Patterns of association may also be invoked nonverbally. Pictures that show two items next to one another often invite the viewer to "see" the similarity between the two. For example, an advertisement from a group whose mission is to save baby seals from slaughter showed a picture of a fish sandwich next to a picture of a baby seal, inviting the reader to associate the seal with the contents of the fish sandwich even though seal meat was not an ingredient of the sandwich. Other nonverbal symbols, like paralanguage, can also be used to invite association. During an address to the 1988 Democratic Convention, Senator Ted Kennedy used the tone of his voice to establish a rhythmic pattern for the line, "where was George?" By repeating the same rhythmic intonation for the question each time he mentioned a pressing and unsolved social problem, Kennedy encouraged the audience to associate George Bush, the Republican nominee for president, with failure.

Disassociative structures encourage a pattern of thinking exactly reverse of that encouraged by associative structures. The audience is encouraged to recognize opposites, to find the differences among the phenomena described by an advocate. Similar to disjunctive reasoning, disassociative structures tend to follow a pattern of language that uses "either/or" or "not this, but that." Among those familiar stylistic devices that illustrate disassociative structure, antithesis provides a clear case. Former president John Kennedy was notable in his use of antithesis. One of the most frequently quoted passages from his Inaugural Address is, "Ask not what your country can do for you, but what you can do for your country." Kennedy's famous plea is an example of antithesis and was the culmination of a pattern of disassociative structure that permeated his whole speech. Disassociative patterns are also presented visually. The logos that draw a red line diagonally through some known symbol, such as the "no smoking" logo, are illustrative.

The third type of argumentative structure identified by Perelman and Olbrechts-Tyteca that can be used to describe minor form is *quasi-logical* structure. Quasi-logical structure is similar to incidental form in that the pattern follows a pattern of familiar logical reasoning. Even if the argument is neither valid nor really logical, the pattern may encourage an audience to accept the argument because it mirrors a form that ordinarily would be associated with good sense. In other words, the form of the argument lures the audience into feeling as if they were thinking rationally regardless of whether the content of the argument meets standards for rationality. Anytime symbols are formatted to follow familiar mathematical formula, like $A+B=C$, quasi-logical structures are being presented. Such formatting occurs orally, in print, and even with pictures.

As with the other levels of structure, the small structure of King's and Agnew's speeches and the music video on world hunger can be examined according to the categories just discussed. Several forms are used to fill out the motivated sequence pattern of King's speech. The order of King's introductory comments followed an incidental form closely parallel to Lincoln's Gettysburg Address. His beginning, "Five score years ago, a great American . . . signed the Emancipation Proclamation," immediately called this form to mind. His explanation of the current segregation and exile of the Negro in the following two paragraphs mirrored Lincoln's explanation of the strife of civil war. His next statement, "So we have come here today to dramatize a shameful condition," completed the form with its parallelism to Lincoln's statement regarding the symbolic value of consecrating the battlefield of Gettysburg. This minor form assisted in establishing a need by elevating that need to symbolic, perhaps mythical, proportions and underscored the hope, despair, and determination elicited by the qualitative progression.

King's famous promissory note metaphor, that followed his introductory comments, further established the need for civil rights legislation. The power of the associative structure was that it offered a new way of thinking about the need. The metaphor moved the need from the heights of the symbolic to the everyday life of ordinary people, while maintaining the sequence of psychological states (hope, despair, and determination). Furthermore, the creative redundancy of following the statement of need established by the incidental form of the Gettysburg Address with the metaphor added emphasis to the need through the force of repetition.

Similarly, the repetitive forms of the "I have a dream" and "let freedom ring" sequences in the latter part of the speech not only provided a way of visualizing the results, but also magnified the psychological states of hope and joy through sheer repetition. Other forms could, of course, be identified in the small structure of the message, but the foregoing description illustrates how the small structure of King's address could be described.

As with the King speech, several other forms reinforce the intermediate and large structures in Agnew's attack on televised news. For example, an incidental minor form of rhetorical question was used repeatedly to develop the problem within the problem-solution pattern of the intermediate structure. As a transition into the first three sub-claims, Agnew asked the following rhetorical questions: "Now how is network news determined?" "Now what do Americans know of the men who wield this power?" "Do they allow their biases to influence the selection and presentation of news?" The question form reinforced the process of inquiry; the answers that immediately followed each question reinforced the tightness of his argument, the didactic character of his syllogistic progression. In addition, the use of this question-answer form in the problem part of the speech assisted the audience in anticipating the answer to the problem, itself. In other words, the minor form confirmed the probably subconscious supposition that a solution would follow. Thus the minor form of the small structure mirrored the problem-solution pattern of the intermediate structure that in turn mirrored the syllogistic progression of the structure of the large, consistently driving the audience toward an inevitable conclusion.

In "We Are the World," the main claim in the lyrics of the song follows a quasi-logical structure. Because we are all "one," problems for any one of us affect all of us. Associative structures are suggested by the pictures of people hugging. The stars from differing musical backgrounds are portrayed as one big family, so we are encouraged to think of all humanity as one big family. Disassociation is minimized throughout the video, while association is magnified and pressed into service for the main claim.

Summary

Structure is important to audiences because people perceive and make sense of the world around them by discerning or imposing pattern on external stimuli. The structure of an advocate's message may be examined from at least three perspectives. Taken as a whole, the large structure of a message can be described as following either a syllogistic or qualitative progression, or some combination of the two. By focusing on the body of the message, the intermediate structure can be revealed. The intermediate structure may follow conventional, repetitive, or incidental patterns. Finally, individual units and arguments within a message can be examined for the small structure that they invoke. The conventional, repetitive, and incidental patterns that comprise the small structure entail minor forms that will likely play on the appeal of associative, disassociative, or quasi-logical structures.

The principles of structure, discussed earlier in this chapter, furnish guidelines for assessing the effectiveness of the structure an advocate follows within a message. Audiences will perceive structure selectively, attempt to fill out patterns that are somehow incomplete, and be inclined to repeat familiar patterns. Gregg identified six patterns that are particularly fundamental. The structure of an advocate's message may be examined to determine how an audience will likely respond and whether the patterns invoked are familiar and likely to lead the audience to an appropriate process of closure.

Notes

[1]*Ad Herrenium,* trans. Harry Caplan, (Cambridge: Harvard University Press), III, ix, 18.

[2]Richard B. Gregg, *Symbolic Inducement and Knowing: A Study in the Foundations of Rhetoric* (Columbia: University of South Carolina Press, 1984).

[3]Jean Piaget, *Language and Thought of the Child,* trans. Marjorie Gabain (New York: New American Library, 1974), pp. 25-68; see also, Piaget, *Structuralism,* trans. and ed. Channinah Maschler (New York: Harper and Row, 1971), pp. 74-96.

[4]Gregg, pp. 25-54.

[5]Quintilian, *Institutio Oratoria,* trans. H.E. Butler, (Cambridge: Harvard University Press), VII, i, 37.

[6]See, for example: Howard Gilkinson, Stanley F. Paulson and Donald Sikkink, "Effects of Order and Authority in an Argumentative Speech," *Quarterly Journal of Speech,* 40 (Apr. 1954), 183-92; Harold Sponberg, "The Relative Effectiveness of Climax and Anti-Climax Order in an Argumentative Speech," *Speech Monographs,* 13 (1946), 35-44; Raymond G. Smith, "An Experimental Study of the Effects of Speech Organization Upon the Attitudes of College Students," *Speech Monographs,* 18 (Nov. 1951), 292-301; Kenneth Beighley, "An Experimental Study of the Effect of Three Speech Variables on Listener Comprehension," *Speech Monographs,* 21 (Nov. 1954), 248-53; Halbert E. Gulley and David K. Berlo, "Effect of Intercellular and Intracellular Speech Structure on Attitude Change and Listening," *Speech Monographs,* 23 (Nov. 1956), 288-97; Harry Sharp, Jr. and Thomas McClung, "Effect of Organization on Speaker's Ethos," *Speech Monographs,* 33 (June 1966), 182-3; Ernest Thompson, "Some Effects of Message Structure on Listener's Comprehension," *Speech Monographs,* 34 (Mar. 1967), 51-7; Christopher Spicer and Ronald Bassett, "The Effect of Organization

on Learning from an Informative Message," *Southern States Speech Journal*, 41 (Spring 1976), 290-9; Charles R. Petrie, Jr., "Listening and Organization," *Central States Speech Journal*, 15 (Feb. 1964), 6-12; Arlee Johnson, "A Preliminary Investigation of the Relationship Between Message Organization and Listener Comprehension," *Central States Speech Journal*, 21 (Summar 1970), 104-7; John Parker, "Some Organizational Variables and Their Effect Upon Comprehension," *Journal of Communication*, 12 (Mar. 1962), 27-32; Mark Knapp and James C. McCroskey, "The Siamese Twins: Inventio and Dispositio," *Communication Quarterly*, 14 (April 1966), 17-8; R. Winterowd, "Beyond Style," *Philosophy and Rhetoric*, 5 (Spring 1972), 88-110.

[7] Kenneth Burke, *Counter-Statement*, (Berkeley: University of California Press, 1968), p. 31.

[8] Burke, pp. 123-83.

[9] All references to the King speech are based on Martin Luther King, "I Have A Dream," reprinted in Wil A. Linkugal, R.R. Allen, and Richard L. Johannessen, *Contemporary American Speeches*, 3rd ed., (Belmont, California: Wadsworth, 1972), pp. 289-93.

[10] All references to the Agnew speech essay are based on Spiro Agnew, "On Televised News," reprinted in Linkugal, Allen and Johannessen, *Contemporary American Speeches*, 3rd ed., pp. 191-200.

[11] All references to the music video are based on "We Are the World: the Video Event," United Support of Artists for Africa, 1985, RCA/Columbia Pictures Home Video, Burbank, California.

[12] For an explanation and application of this concept, see Richard L. Johannessen, "The Jeremiad and Jenkin Lloyd Jones," *Communication Monographs* 52 (1985): 156-72.

[13] Ch. Perelman and L. Olbrechts-Tyteca, *The New Rhetoric: A Treatise on Argumentation*, trans. John Wilkinson and Purcell Weaver (Notre Dame: University of Notre Dame Press, 1969), pp. 193-5, 350-410, 411-50.

Suggested Readings

Burke, Kenneth, 1968. *Counter-Statement*. Berkeley: University of California Press.

Gregg, Richard B., 1985. *Symbolic Inducement and Knowing: A Study in the Foundations of Rhetoric*. Columbia: University of South Carolina Press.

Piaget, Jean, 1971. *Structuralism*. Trans. and Ed. Channinah Maschler. New York: Harper and Row.

Chapter 6

Good Reasons Withstand Objection

By definition, a controversy involves at least two sides or competing interests. Often a multiplicity of divergent viewpoints are expressed during discussions of public issues. Formal situations for advocacy almost always offer the opportunity for expression of opposing points of view. Even informal situations usually include competing claims and interaction among opposing advocates. As a result, an advocate's arguments are often the object of attack by his or her opponents. Even when an opposing advocate is absent, however, an advocate's arguments may be assessed critically by the audience. Confronted with a problem or issue that has yet to be decided, audience members may approach an advocate's message with some degree of reasoned skepticism. Consequently, a third standard for evaluating arguments is a necessary addition to the notions advanced in the previous two chapters. For a reason to be classified as good, it should not only fit the audience and structure the audience's response, but it should also withstand objections by either opposing advocates or the audience itself. This chapter concerns the standard that *good reasons should withstand objection*. The basis for this third standard for evaluating an advocate's message is explained first in this chapter. Following that explanation, twenty potential lines of objection are defined and described.

The Probability of Refutation and the Universal Audience

The notion that discussion of public issues was a sort of intellectual battle in which opposing advocates attacked and defended arguments was common to the Classical conception of public argument. Cicero's discussion of stasis, reviewed in Chapter 3, was designed to alert opposing advocates to various areas where objections or disagreement might arise. In *De Inventione*, Cicero detailed a number of objections that could be raised as an advocate developed his position regarding the facts, the definition, the quality, or the procedure in question. In addition, he suggested various lines of defense that could be used by an advocate to answer possible lines of attack. For example, he pointed out that an advocate may elaborate on the issue of quality by indicating that the accused did not intend to do wrong. Denial of intent could be supported by showing that the act was the result of ignorance, accident or necessity.[1]

Cicero's discussion followed a rich tradition of study initiated by Greek philosophers, such as Aristotle, who were concerned with developing systematic ways to find and to evaluate arguments.[2] In both the *Rhetoric* and the *Topics*, Aristotle discussed systematic ways for finding arguments. His method suggested that an advocate familiarize himself with a list of *topics*, or cuewords, that would assist the advocate in coming up with things to say in support of his position. For the Greeks, topic literally meant place. Such topics or places had long been used as an aid to memory. If a speaker, particularly a bard or storyteller, wanted to remember certain details of a story, he was supposed to visualize a place that would contain the various details he needed to remember. By thinking of the scene of a battlefield, for example, the bard could recall the various details that should be woven into the story, such as the armor, the weapons, the wounded warrior, and so forth. Topics functioned in a similar way for the advocate. By reminding himself of a particular place or category, the advocate could remember a number of potential lines of development for an argument. For example, the topic of intention discussed by Cicero, might alert the advocate to a number of factors relevant to intention—knowledge, planning, forethought, and so on. Any of these factors could then be mentioned to support the advocate's claim that he did or did not intend to commit a particular act.

The Classical writers, like Aristotle and Cicero, tended to view the discovery of arguments as a different process from the evaluation or judgment of arguments. Thus topical systems were advanced as aids for discovering arguments, while the rules of logic were presumed to provide a systematic way to judge an argument. Even so, most of their treatises that concerned the rules of logic were designed to explain scientific demonstrations or philosophical disputations, rather than everyday public argument. As a consequence, their discussions of topics often served as a guideline for both finding things to say in support of a position and finding things to say when one attacked or raised objection to an opposing position during everyday arguments. Because the topics could be used to attack as well as to defend, they bore some resemblance to the standards for judging arguments that were explained in regard to logic.

Students of argument during the intellectual periods that followed the Classical age tended to combine the process of finding and judging arguments in even more direct ways. Thus, the guidelines of logic, the methods of finding the faulty reasoning in an argument, were often offered as a method for discovering what to say in response to an opponent's arguments. Moreover, contemporary advocates whether intercollegiate debaters or law school students are frequently offered lists of *fallacies*, or descriptions of various types of faulty reasoning, as topics that can be used for *refutation*, the process of disproving or attacking an opponent's arguments. Because the fallacies developed in the study of logic are often difficult to apply to ordinary language, they are typically adapted to everyday argument by reference to "informal logic." Their function is to provide a coherent list of potential weaknesses in arguments and to alert advocates to the objections that could be raised against an opponent's arguments.

The discussion of sources of objection that comprises most of the remainder of this chapter follows the tradition just outlined. In other words, by familiarizing herself with a set of topics that mirror a set of fallacies, the analyst of public discourse can determine whether or not an advocate's reasons will withstand objection. The lines of objection to be discussed resemble both traditional lists of topics and traditional discussions of informal fallacies. However, they remain true to neither subject of study. Instead, these lines of objection sometimes pass over distinctions that informal logic would wish to make, and at other times possess a concern for reasoning that topical systems would likely deemphasize in favor of lines of argument that are less content free. However, the lines of objection presented here do represent objections that are fairly typical in the course of discussions regarding public issues.

Before proceeding on to the list of typical objections, a few additional words about the importance of this standard for evaluating arguments are in order. The case for the necessity of taking the audience into account has already been made in Chapter 4. However, in our discussion of the need for arguments to fit the audience, emphasis was placed on the audience's psychological need to find the argument consistent with their frame of reference. Even our discussion of substantive or intellectual warrants centered on an audience's perception of an argument as sensible based on their familiar patterns of thinking concerning what was sensible. To leave the discussion at that point ignores the assumption of that generalization regarding audiences, namely that people try to act sensibly.

The idea that different people strive toward and manifest different degrees of concern regarding what is reasonable or sensible seems self evident. However, the concern with rationality across time, the emphasis placed on critical thinking within educational systems, and the proclamations of many ordinary people that they try to make decisions "wisely," suggest that at least part of an audience's response to an advocative message will depend on their confidence that the advocate is not providing them with foolish reasons. Consequently, it is necessary for the analyst of public discourse to go beyond determining if reasons fit the audience to assess whether or not the reasons fit the critical standards of an audience that is doing its best to evaluate the arguments critically.

The Belgian philosophers Perelman and Olbrechts-Tyteca made a similar point in their treatise on contemporary argumentation.[3] In their discussion of the nature of the audience, they described the various audiences to whom an advocate must appeal. Of course, any message will be directed toward some particular, concrete audience. This particular, concrete audience may be fairly limited, as when the message is directed to twenty-five people who are physically present to hear the advocate's arguments, or quite broad, as when the message is directed to the general reader, each of whom may read the message at a different time and place. Similarly, an advocate's message may be directed to multiple audiences simultaneously. Lincoln's Gettysburg Address, for example, found an immediate audience on the battlefield at Gettysburg but was also distributed in print throughout the nation shortly after its delivery. In addition, the message found a historical audience as it continued to be presented to generations of Americans throughout the twentieth century.

Perelman and Olbrechts-Tyteca explained that when an advocate visualized his or her particular audience, certain characteristics unique to that particular group of people would emerge and act as constraints on the choice of arguments that would be effective. In addition, however, they asserted that every advocate faced a group they referred to as the *universal audience*. The universal audience has a single characteristic. It represents the rational human being acting in the most logical manner. In short, the universal audience can be conceived as that collection of the best minds operating in the most logical fashion. The universal audience, then, is an ideal image, an image of the most reasonable audience imaginable.

The concept of the universal audience is useful as a basis for introducing the potential lines of objection that follow. When an analyst attempts to determine if an argument can withstand objection, he or she cannot be sure what objections will actually be raised by the actual audience toward the particular argument. However, the analyst can imagine the types of objections that would be raised by an ideal audience, that is an audience that was trying to be reasonable and respond to the message with reasoned skepticism. Thus the lines of objection that follow do not necessarily need to be raised by an opposing advocate in order for an analyst to apply them. Instead, because they are the type of objection that an ideal audience might raise, these objections serve as standards for an analyst concerned with the effectiveness of any particular argument.

The notion that these lines of objection might be used to refute or disprove an advocate's argument was suggested earlier. Such refutation does not ordinarily occur in a vacuum. Instead, when an opposing advocate raises objections to an argument, that argument is generally defended by the original advocate. Also, when the audience takes on the role of opposing advocate and is the party to raise the objection, the advocate may attempt to answer the objection. When an advocate is absent, as when an argument is presented in print or through some other mediated channel, the audience may both raise the objection and consider whether there is a reasonable answer to that objection. This would certainly be the case if the ideal image of a universal audience was operative.

The analyst of public discourse, then, acts like a universal audience when applying the standard that good reasons should withstand objections. Any particular objection acts like the rebuttal in Toulmin's scheme for laying out the argument. The analyst then attempts to determine whether or not there exists a reasonable defense against the line of objection. If so, the argument can be said to withstand objection. If not, the argument can be said not to withstand objection. If none of the potential lines of objection appear to apply to the argument, then the argument also may be judged to withstand objections.

The twenty lines of objection that follow are grouped into three categories. Because, as discussed in Chapter 3, arguments consist of data and warrants that support claims, both the data and the warrants may be the source of objections. Thus, the first two categories review characteristic objections to evidence and to reasoning. The third category reviews typical objections that are made to the procedure by which the argument is made. These objections center on the symbols — verbal and nonverbal — used to make the argument as well as the form and manner of presentation of the argument. With all three categories, the objection is a rebuttal of the claim. The grounds for that rebuttal, however, vary according to the source of the objection.

Objections to Data

There are eight typical objections that arise from the nature of the data used by an advocate. The first three objections — insufficient evidence, irrelevant evidence, and suppressed evidence — refer to the data generally, regardless of what type of data it is. The remaining five objections are related specifically to a particular type of data — testimony, statistics, or examples.

(1) **Insufficient Evidence** is an objection based on the lack of data to support a claim. This objection is most obvious when an advocate presents a claim without providing any data to support it. If it is a claim that most reasonable people would not accept without proof, then the advocate is subject to a charge of providing insufficient evidence. For example, many charitable organizations solicit donations to assist the hungry and claim that if you donate money you can be sure that it will go where it is needed. However, without any data to support that claim, the argument may not be convincing. Particularly for an audience who knows that many charitable organization spend a majority of their funds on administrative costs rather than on products or services for the needy, the claim is objectionable without additional data. This objection can be applied by asking: Is there evidence to support the claim? Charges of insufficient evidence may also be made in terms of the quality of the evidence presented. However, such charges are treated separately here and discussed in detail in the last five types of objection listed in this category.

(2) **Irrelevant Evidence** is an objection that concerns whether the evidence presented relates to the claim. Often data is provided, but the data does not appear to be relevant to a claim. Quotations may be used, examples may be recounted, or statistics may be presented, but if they do not relate to the claim, the objection of insufficient evidence is appropriate. For example, in 1952 Richard Nixon, then

Republican candidate for Vice President, appeared on national television to respond to charges that he had been the beneficiary of a campaign fund that was potentially illegal and probably unethical. In his speech, now known as the "Checkers Speech," Nixon claimed that there was nothing ethically wrong with his use of the fund. In support of that claim, he quoted the judgment of a prestigious law firm who had concluded that there was no question as to the legality of the fund.[4] The data was relevant to the legal charge, but not necessarily relevant to the ethical charge. Consequently, as several commentators noted after the speech, Nixon was open to an objection regarding the relevance of his data.

(3) **Suppressed Evidence** is an objection to the choice of data that the advocate presents in support of a claim. If an advocate omits any mention of relevant evidence that is contradictory to his or her claim, he or she is guilty of suppressing evidence. A classic example of suppressed evidence is the argument by a member of the Department of Defense that the department needs a larger amount of funding because of the escalating costs of equipment. In support of such an argument during the late 1970s and early 1980s, advocates frequently provided evidence of the rising costs of large equipment such as tanks and airplanes. However, evidence of the outrageous costs of ordinary items like hammers and toilet seats was suppressed. When Congressional leaders learned that the department was paying $500.00 for a hammer that could be purchased at most hardware stores for $15.00, the claims regarding the need for more money found objection. Similarly, much attention has been given to the level of knowledge of various government officials regarding illegal and unethical activities. As officials have claimed that they have acted with the highest regard for the law, people have questioned whether or not they were suppressing evidence by not revealing their knowledge of questionable activities by aides or others under their supervision. The inquiry concerning suppression of evidence, then, concerns the question of whether relevant but contradictory evidence is being withheld.

(4) **Unreliable Source** is an objection to testimonial data that questions whether the source of the data is likely to provide an accurate depiction of the facts. The basic question concerns whether the source is or was in a position to know what he or she is quoted as saying. For example, if an advocate quotes a movie star's characterization of the problem of the arms race, there is room to question the authority of that star's comments. While the actor may know much about movie-making, why should an audience assume any expert knowledge on foreign policy or weaponry?

Two variations on the charge of an unreliable source concern evidence that shows an idea to be true on the basis of either *tradition* or *popularity*. Just because something is traditional or popular does not mean that it is right or accurate. For example, while it may be traditional to exclude women from combat, it is not necessarily right. Therefore, relying only on tradition as the authority or source for determining whether women should serve in combat may not be sensible. Similarly, just because an idea is popular does not verify that it is accurate data.

For some time the world was thought to be flat. The idea was quite popular. But popularity alone does not make data trustworthy.

(5) **Biased Source** is an objection to testimonial data on the grounds that the source is biased or has a special interest that may incline him or her to state the facts in a biased way. Although someone may be in a position to know the facts, they may present only one side of the story if they have a special interest in the outcome. Thus, even though a member of the military might be in a better position than a Hollywood star to know the facts about nuclear weapons, that person might have a vested interest in presenting only one perspective, a perspective favorable to the military establishment. Similarly, if an advocate quotes testimony regarding the health effects of tobacco from a research foundation funded by the Tobacco Institute, her evidence could be questioned because of a potentially biased source.

(6) **Unrepresentative Sample** is an objection to the nature of statistical evidence. Statistical data generally derives from sampling techniques that gather the numerical description of some phenomena from a sampling procedure and then extrapolate those numbers to characterize the entire population from which the sample was drawn. For example, if a statistician wanted to know the airworthiness of the nation's commercial air fleet, she might conduct tests on a portion, or sample, of the thousands of airplanes in use and then generalize from that sample to the total fleet. If ten percent of the 100 airplanes tested were found to be poorly maintained and to pose a safety hazard, then the results of that sample might be used to characterize the whole fleet. The statistic might be used by an advocate to suggest that ten percent of all the several thousand airplanes in service were poorly maintained and, therefore, posed a threat to safety. However, if the sample is unrepresentative, such a conclusion is objectionable. If the 100 planes tested in the sample were all built in 1952, for example, whereas only 20% of the total fleet was built prior to 1960, then the sample would not accurately represent the total of all airplanes. Or if the sample included planes from only one airline and if other airlines used different maintenance procedures, the sample could be challenged as unrepresentative. A recent example of such an objection occurred following release of a report on sexuality by Sherri Hite. Hite reported that a large percentage of women were dissatisfied with their relationships with men. In the ensuing public discussion about the nature of male-female relationships in contemporary society, a number of other researchers charged that Hite had used an unrepresentative sample to arrive at her figures, thereby casting doubt on the conclusions. A sample may be deemed unrepresentative if, in any way, it does not accurately reflect the characteristics of the whole population from which it is drawn. If a sample is too small to obtain enough subjects typical of the whole population, it may be unrepresentative. Similarly, if the collector of the cases draws the sample from an uncharacteristic source or at an uncharacteristic time or place, the sample may be unrepresentative.

(7) **Lack of Proportion** is another objection that is characteristically associated with statistical evidence. The notion of proportion concerns establishing the

appropriate ratios between things. When statistics or statements are exaggerated they typically exhibit a lack of proportion. Following the first Tylenol disaster, when tampering with the popular pain-killer resulted in several deaths, a second incidence of tampering was discovered. Many news reports of the second incident illustrated a case of exaggeration, or lack of proportion, in that they suggested that the same problem was occurring again. In fact, in the second incident, the amounts of arsenic and other chemicals added to the drug were so small that a person would have needed to ingest nearly a whole bottle of Tylenol in order to suffer poisoning. The statistics had been exaggerated. Similar charges of statistical exaggeration have been made by a number of opponents of increased regulation of a variety of consumer products. These opponents frequently point out that although the product in question does create a health problem when it is used in excessive quantities, it is unthinkable that anyone would use the product in such excess. Therefore, they claim that advocates are guilty of lack of proportion.

A similar lack of proportion arises when statistics are manipulated to understate some characterization. Just the opposite of exaggeration, statistics can be used to minimize a problem. For years, anti-nuclear power groups have charged advocates of nuclear energy with this sort of lack of proportion. They claim that nuclear advocates minimize the problem of safety by referring to statistics that indicate the likelihood of a nuclear accident is very small. They charge a lack of proportion on the grounds that when an accident does happen, even if it is only once in a lifetime, the results would be so large as to be catastrophic. In other words, they object to the choice of statistics used by advocates on the grounds that those statistics reveal a lack of proportion. Charges of "tokenism" illustrate a similar concern with lack of proportion. For example, advocates have sometimes supported their claims that there is no discrimination against women in Congress by pointing out that there are several female Congresswomen. Opposing advocates, however, point out that the ratio of women to men in Congress is minuscule compared to the ratio of women to men generally. These opposing advocates are pointing out a problem with lack of proportion.

(8) **Atypical Example** is an objection to exemplary data that questions whether an example is typical or representative of the class of phenomena being discussed. It has been said that in a country as large as the United States at least one example of anything can be found. It would, of course, be foolish to conclude that people eat fire on the basis of one example of a fire-eater. However, it is not unusual for people to conclude that many social problems, for example missing children, are widespread on the basis of one example. What is of concern here, is whether the example is typical. If even one child is snatched at a shopping center and brutally murdered, that situation, of course, merits concern and attention. However, opponents to a variety of policies aimed at protecting children from such actions have pointed out that the example is unusual, rare, that most children are not subject to the threat of brutal treatment by strangers. Moreover, if an advocate presents an example either verbally or nonverbally that is particularly bizarre, audiences

may object on the grounds that they don't know anyone to whom nor anyplace where such an incident has happened. Such objections are objections to the typicality of the example.

Summary of Objections to Data

1. Insufficient Evidence: Was evidence presented in support of the claim?
2. Irrelevant Evidence: Was the evidence presented relevant to the claim?
3. Suppressed Evidence: Was contradictory evidence withheld?
4. Unreliable Source: Was the source of the data in a position to know the facts?
5. Biased Source: Did the source of the data have a special interest that could have biased their presentation of the facts?
6. Unrepresentative Sample: Was the sample from which the statistics were drawn representative of the whole population that the statistics were used to characterize?
7. Lack of Proportion: Was the statistic or example exaggerated or minimized so as to exaggerate or minimize the real situation?
8. Atypical Example: Was the example representative or characteristic of the phenomena being discussed?

Objections to Reasoning

In Chapter 4, four patterns of thinking or reasoning were discussed. They were categorical thinking, oppositional thinking, causal thinking, and thinking based on similarities. Most of the seven potential objections discussed in this section relate directly to one of those four patterns of thinking. However, the first two relate to reasoning or lack of reasoning in general.

(9) **Question Begging** is an objection to an advocate's reasons on the grounds that the advocate doesn't really offer reasons. In its simplest form, question begging occurs when an advocate claims that something should be done because something should be done, that something is valuable because something is valuable, that some circumstance exists because some circumstance exists. Such argument or lack of argument is reminiscent of the type of arguments made by very young children. Asked to justify their behavior, young children confronted with the question of why they did something often reply, "because." Unfortunately older advocates often use the same sort of "because-because" pattern of argumentation. I can recall an incident in college where I questioned the justification for a "late fee" that I had been assessed. The answer I received was, "because that's the policy." I pressed by asking why such a policy was implemented. The answer was,

"because that's the way we do things here." And so on. Anyone with similar conversational experience knows the frustration attendant to question begging.

(10) **Inconsistency** is a source for objection with effects almost as frustrating as question begging. An advocate is inconsistent when he or she seems to make claims or offer data that contradict one another. During the 1970s many advocates who supported the employment of women in nontraditional fields accused their opponents of inconsistency. For example, they noted that opponents of nontraditional employment of women argued that women were needed to work in the home and to take care of the children. These same opponents also argued that the nontraditional jobs were too strenuous for women. Advocates of nontraditional work pointed out an inconsistency in that their opponents seemed to think it alright for women to lift a twenty-pound child at home but unthinkable for those same women to lift a twenty-pound sack at work. Another typical example of inconsistency occurs in discussions where one side advocates federal funding of a particular program. Opponents sometimes make two inconsistent claims within the same message when they argue first that the program should not be funded because it is not meritorious and second that it should not be funded because someone else is already funding a similar program to take care of the problem. Either it is a problem or it is not; it is inconsistent to maintain that the problem does not exist but to support other efforts to deal with the nonexistent problem.

(11) **Questionable Cause** is an objection to a causal relationship suggested by an advocate. Among the most notable is the charge that an advocate has identified a correlation, but not a cause. Stated in the Latin phrase used to describe this fallacy, the objection is *post hoc ergo propter hoc*. The phrase literally means after this therefore because of this. In simple terms, if an advocate argued that pregnancy was caused by drinking milk because after several women drank milk they became pregnant, he would be committing a *post hoc* error. The problem with such reasoning should be evident. Even so, such reasoning often appears during discussions of public issues. In 1985, for example, a political official claimed on national television that Congress' decision to cut off aid to the Contras was the cause of an alleged invasion into Honduras by the Nicaraguan Sandinistas. His evidence was simply that several days before the invasion, Congress had voted down a bill to supply aid to the Contras. Because the vote took place before the invasion, he concluded that the vote caused the invasion. His argument, of course, was just as objectionable as the earlier argument about pregnancy.

(12) **Slippery Slope** is an objection to causal reasoning as well. With slippery slope, an objection is raised on the grounds that so many causal connections are required to lead to the conclusion proposed by the advocate that there is likely to be a mistake somewhere in the reasoning process. A popular item of graffiti reads: "The more you study the more you know. The more you know the more you forget. The more you forget the less you know. The less you know the less you forget. So why study?" Amusing, but not very sensible. In the 1960s, during the discussion of the new health insurance system of Medicare for the elderly,

a similar mistake of slippery slope was made by some opponents of the Medicare program. They argued that if the government took responsibility for health insurance for the elderly, the result would be government meddling in free enterprise and before long the whole country would have turned socialistic. An even more familiar example of slippery slope from the same time period was the theory used by some to justify U.S. involvement in Vietnam. These advocates argued that if Vietnam fell to the Communists, then Cambodia would fall to the Communists, then Laos and Thailand would fall, and before long all of Asia would be controlled by Communists. The same type of argument has been used by advocates in the 1980s to justify U.S. involvement in countries like Nicaragua and El Salvadore. In each case, the advocates propose such a lengthy chain of causal links that the probability of one of the links being weak, or multi-causal, is high, and the quality of the argument is thereby subject to question.

(13) **False Dilemma** is an objection to reasoning of the "either-or" variety. The objection usually arises when other alternatives besides the two posed by the advocate exist. As a result, the "either-or" situation posed by the advocate is called a false dilemma. For example, advocates of U.S. support for the Contras have argued that the United States is faced with only two alternatives. Either our government should fund the Contras to fight the reigning government in Nicaragua or we must abandon the possibility of a democratic form of government in Nicaragua. Because there is a third alternative, pursuing diplomatic negotiations as a method of influencing Nicaragua, their argument illustrates a false dilemma. A similar argument, subject to the same objection, has often been advanced in debates about energy use and environmental protection. Some advocates of alternative sources of energy argue that either we must abandon fossil fuels (coal, oil, natural gas) or we will ruin the environment with air pollution and acid rain. Because there are other alternatives, for example strengthened emission controls, the argument poses a false dilemma.

(14) **Questionable Classification** is an error in reasoning that occurs when an advocate inaccurately identifies a particular instance as belonging to a class and subsequently attributes some characteristic of the class to the particular instance or some characteristic of the particular instance to the class. For example, at one time the National Organization for Women (NOW) argued that divorced women should be provided employment rehabilitation so that they could successfully reenter the work force following their divorces. As data for their claim, they often recounted the tragic stories of former homemakers who, without marketable job skills, were forced to go on welfare to support their children. Their argument probably had some merit if the class of divorced women consisted only of homemakers who were not active members of the work force. However, the argument was vulnerable to objection on the grounds that some, probably a large percentage of, members of the class of divorced women were already gainfully employed, active members of the work force.

(15) **Questionable Analogy** is an objection to any sort of comparison that attempts to find similarity between dissimilar or incomparable instances. For example, some opponents of U.S. pressure on South Africa to stop their apartheid practices claim that because the U.S. has not disinvested in the Soviet Union, where various members of the population were subject to repression, the U.S. should not disinvest in South Africa, where the Black and colored population was subject to repression. These advocates, while attempting to draw an analogy between the situations in the Soviet Union and South Africa, have overlooked some important differences between the two countries that may make the comparison a faulty one. In the Soviet Union, minority groups are oppressed by the majority while in South Africa a majority group is oppressed by a minority. Of course, both situations are deplorable, but not necessarily comparable.

Objections to Intellectual Warrants

1. Question Begging: Is a reason or warrant provided to support the claim?
2. Inconsistency: Does the advocate present reasons (either data, warrants, or claims) that conflict with one another?
3. Questionable Cause: Is the cause cited linked to the effect as either a necessary or sufficient condition that must occur for the effect to occur?
4. Slippery Slope: Does the warrant require so many causal connections that at least one of the links in the causal chain is likely to be faulty?
5. False Dilemma: Are the alternatives suggested by the advocate really the only alternatives available?
6. Questionable Classification: Is the instance cited a representative member of the class to which it is attributed, and are the characteristics of the class attributable to the instance cited?
7. Questionable Analogy: Are the instances cited as similar comparable?

Objections to Procedure

Objections to procedure arise when an advocate obscures the argument by using verbal or nonverbal symbols that confuse the argument or by employing a reason that clouds the issue. The first three objections discussed in this category pertain directly to symbols. The last two objections are two frequent methods of clouding the issue that are not related directly to language or nonverbal symbols.

(16) **Confusing Language** is an obvious source of objection to procedure. When an advocate uses jargon, bureaucratise, acadamese, euphemisms, or weasel words, an opposing advocate or audience may be unable to penetrate what the advocate

means. As a consequence, they may be unable to evaluate the argument critically and to counter it effectively. Therefore, such arguments are subject to objection on the grounds that the argument may not proceed until the meaning is made clear. Obscure language, because of its confusing nature, may also make a good idea sound bad or a bad idea sound good. This too inhibits effective evaluation of the argument.

Jargon is language that is specialized to a particular field of discourse, such as the academy, the bureaucracy, the scientific community, and so on. Because jargon is typically understood only by members of the "in-group" that use it, almost like a secret language, it is inappropriate for most public discussions that include auditors outside the in-group. Consequently, when jargon is used objections may be raised. For example, following the explosion of Challenger, the space shuttle, public dispute regarding the safety of the space program ensued. During discussion of the cause of the explosion, an official of NASA (National Aeronautic and Space Administration) was questioned as to why he did not respond to misgivings expressed by engineers as to the safety of the shuttle. The official replied that he had been responsive by declaring a "Level 2 situation." In order to evaluate whether his claim that he was responsive was sound, the audience needed to be able to evaluate his evidence, a "Level 2 situation." However, because his language was composed of jargon, such a determination was not immediately possible. Thus, his argument was subject to objection.

Such jargon is often used to strip an idea of any emotional content so as to avoid other objections. When this happens, the language can also become a source of objection. For example, many Pro-Choice advocates describe an abortion as a simple medical procedure in which the "fetal matter is evacuated from the woman." Pro-Life advocates have long objected to such language on the grounds that it obscures what actually happens. According to these advocates, "fetal matter" is an "unborn child" and "evacuation" is "the dismemberment of that unborn child." They charge that, by using medical terminology for the procedure, the act of an abortion is made sterile and stripped of its emotional and moral consequences.

In some cases, language with particularly pleasant connotations is substituted for language with particularly unpleasant connotations in order to obscure what is being discussed in an argument. Such substitutions of language are generally called *euphemisms*. Unlike jargon, many euphemisms are commonly understood, yet they may still strip some of the meaning from the idea being discussed. For example, most people know that "pork" is really dead pig meat and that "restrooms" are rarely used for rest. But people prefer the euphemistic language because of its more pleasant connotations. However, like jargon, euphemistic language is sometimes used in less benign ways, as a source of confusion by which an advocate hopes to persuade an audience to support a view that they might otherwise find revolting. Probably the most infamous example of such language occurred during the Nazi Holocaust when death camps were referred to as "family relocation centers" and the genocide of millions of people was called "the final solution." Many peace advocates have accused advocates of nuclear weapons development of using such euphemistic language as well. They point out that "clean bombs" are devices that kill people and leave the buildings standing and that the "Peacekeeper" is a multi-warhead missile capable of killing millions and making the earth uninhabitable. Thus euphemistic language may be the source of objection on the grounds that such language obscures the argument.

(17) **Loaded Language** is an objection that arises when an advocate uses language that triggers such an intense emotional reaction in receivers that their rational response to the argument may become clouded. As will be discussed in some detail in Chapter 8, absolutely neutral language is difficult to come by. Most language exhibits some degree of bias because of the connotative, or associative, meaning of words. However, loaded language exhibits a strong degree of bias. Although language may be loaded either positively or negatively, it is generally the source of more objection when it is loaded in a particularly negative way. For example, a former Secretary of the Interior, James Watt, was particularly notable for his use of negatively loaded language. Shortly after his description of the inclusion of a handicapped person on a Presidential task force in 1984 as the inclusion of a "Crip," he was asked to resign his position. Similar incidents are not uncommon during discussions of controversial issues. Several years ago, a representative of Planned Parenthood was invited to debate a representative of a local Pro-Life group on the topic, "Resolved that the taking of human life by abortion is unnecessary and immoral." After seeking advice from this author, the Planned Parenthood representative was advised that before she accepted the invitation she should request that the wording of the topic be changed. In the form suggested, the topic exhibited loaded language. Abortion had already been defined as "the taking of human life," a negative definition that the Planned Parenthood representative would likely want to dispute. Thus, the loading of the language was a source of objection to procedure.

(18) **Equivocation** is an objection that may be raised when an advocate uses language inconsistently. If an advocate uses a word or phrase to mean one thing at one place in his or her message, but changes the meaning later, the resulting inconsistency may render the argument invalid. For example, advocates of drug testing sometimes craft messages in which they point out the danger of employee drug use by referring to the consequences of an addict who regularly ingests heroine or cocaine in order to persuade the audience that a problem exists. However, they sometimes follow that discussion of the problem with a description of drug tests designed to uncover the casual user of milder drugs along with the addict of "hard" drugs. In such a case, the advocate is guilty of equivocation, for at one stage of the message "drug-user" refers to a hardened addict who regularly ingests heroine or cocaine and at another stage "drug-user" refers to a casual user who occasionally uses marijuana or No-Doze. Such equivocation can, of course, cause confusion for an audience. The audience may agree that addicts should not be allowed to continue working, but may be reluctant to fire the casual user. Even if the audience seeks some method for dealing with the casual user, they may wish such a policy

to be different than the one applied to the addict. In any case, such equivocation may be the source of objection to the argument.

(19) **Straw Man** is an objection, not to the language, but to a procedure used by some advocates to cloud the issue. An advocate uses a straw man when he or she misrepresents opposing arguments in order to make them easier to attack. More specifically, an advocate may describe opposing arguments in a way that portrays them as particularly weak. Then the advocate continues by easily defeating these very weak arguments and finally claims victory. The tactic is called a straw man because it is as if the advocate constructed an argument so weak that it could be blown away just as a man made of straw could be blown away by a stiff breeze. Such a tactic is problematic because it may confuse the audience regarding what the arguments of the opposition really are. By building a fantasy argument and then defeating it, the advocate who uses straw men is interrupting the procedure of disputation and obscuring the audience's ability to make a decision based on the best available information. For example, during a discussion of the appropriate posture for the United States in Central America broadcast by the MacNeil-Lehrer News Hour, one advocate claimed that we should discontinue funding of the Contras because they had no chance of winning a military fight. The advocate's opponent responded that his partner in the discussion was soft on Communism and favored discontinuing funds because he didn't think the countries in Central America were important. He supported his argument by pointing out all the reasons why Central American countries were vital to American interests, then sat back and smiled. He had just constructed a straw man that had nothing to do with what his partner in the dialogue had said, but which was easy for him to refute. Such a tactic is objectionable because it obscures the issue, or adds confusion about the point in dispute.

(20) **Ad Hominem** attacks are probably the most common source of objection to procedure in public discussions. The ad hominem objection arises when an advocate departs from the issue and begins attacking his or her opposing advocate instead of the arguments provided by the opposing advocate. A notable example of ad hominem occurred during the discussion on South Africa between Jesse Jackson and Jerry Falwell that was mentioned in Chapter 4. Both advocates fell into ad hominem arguments. Late in the discussion, Jackson commented that it seemed little had changed because, he claimed, Falwell had opposed the Civil Rights Movement and claimed that Martin Luther King was Communist inspired, just as he was now opposing the disbandment of apartheid practices in South Africa and suggesting that people like Bishop Tutu and the World Council of Churches were Communist inspired. Falwell countered with his own ad hominem argument. He said people changed and argued that although he might have been a racist at one time that was no longer the case. Then in elaborating on his point he recalled that Jackson had allegedly engaged in questionable behavior when Jackson was young. Falwell recounted a story that Jackson had spit on a salad, pretending it was Italian dressing, and passed it out the window of a restaurant to a white family,

concluding that therefore Jackson had also once been a racist. Whether either accusation was true or false is irrelevant. What each advocate had done was to divert the attention of the audience away from the issue of U.S. policy toward South Africa and the arguments relevant to that issue, thus making rational judgment more difficult. The moderator of the discussion, Ted Koppel, intervened and ask both advocates to refrain from personal attacks and return to the issues.

1. Confusing Language: Is the language free from jargon or euphemisms that might obscure the content of the argument?
2. Loaded Language: Is the language free from extreme bias that might cloud the audience's thinking?
3. Equivocation: Are terms used consistently throughout the message?
4. Straw Man: Has the advocate accurately represented opposing arguments?
5. Ad Hominem: Is the advocate attacking the arguments rather than the personal character of his or her opponent?

Summary

The twenty possible lines of objection discussed in this chapter are not exhaustive. There are other lines of attack that are made by opposing advocates and other grounds for challenge that some audiences may generate. However, these twenty potential objections are typical and provide a basis for beginning to evaluate whether or not an advocate's reasons will withstand objection. These objections should be used for their heuristic value. Thus, the question of exactly which category an objection fits into should be secondary to the question of whether or not the argument being analyzed is open to an objection. By playing the role of the universal audience, the analyst of public discourse can use these lines of objection to evaluate the data, the intellectual warrants, and the procedure of advocates.

Notes

[1]Cicero, *De Inventione,* trans. H.M. Hubbell (Cambridge: Harvard University Press, 1949), especiallly pp. 31-32.
[2]For a discussion of the historical tradition of topical systems, see Eleonore Stump, "Introduction," *Boethius's De topicis diffentiis,* trans. Eleonore Stump (Ithaca: Cornell University Press, 1978), pp. 13-26. For discussions of Aristotle's topical systems, see William Grimaldi, "The Aristotelian Topics," *Traditio* 14 (1948): 1-16; see also, Donovan J. Ochs, "Aristotle's Concept of Formal Topics," *Speech Monographs* 46 (1969): 419-25.

[3]Chaim Perelman and L. Olbrechts-Tyteca, *The New Rhetoric,* trans. John Wilkinson and Purcell Weaver, (Notre Dame: University of Notre Dame Press, 1969), pp. 17-35.

[4]Richard M. Nixon, "The Checkers Speech," in *Great Speeches for Criticism and Analysis,* eds. Lloyd Rohler and Roger Cook (Greenwood: Alistair Press, 1988), pp. 137-144. For a brief review of commentary concerning the relevance of Nixon's evidence, see Martha Cooper, "Ethos, a Cloth Coat, and a Cocker Spaniel," in *Great Speeches,* especially pp. 157-58.

Suggested Readings

Kahane, Howard, 1984. *Logic and Contemporary Rhetoric,* 4th Ed. Belmont: Wadsworth.

Toulmin, Steven, Richard Rieke, and Allan Janik, 1984. *An Introduction to Reasoning,* 2nd Ed. New York: Macmillan.

Chapter 7

Good Reasons are Ethical

Ethical questions frequently arise in matters of public discussion. Most obvious are those instances in which a particular advocate's ethics are called into question. For example, if an aspiring political candidate, like Senator Joseph Biden in 1987, presents the words of others as if they were his own, he is accused of plagiarism and a lack of ethics. Similarly, if a public official's public statements appear inconsistent with his or her actions, ethics become an issue. For example, when members of the Reagan Administration followed their consistent warning of the dangers of dealing with terrorists by trading arms for hostages, their ethics were questioned by many both inside and outside of the United States. Perhaps most obvious are those situations in which advocates appear as unethical because their arguments seem to rest on false premises. Fabricating evidence, misquoting testimony, manipulating statistics in order to exaggerate claims, and downright lying provide fertile ground for charges of a lack of ethics. It is instances such as these that will be examined in this chapter. The theme is simply that *good reasons are also ethical reasons*. The chapter begins with an explanation of the ground for this fourth standard for evaluating public discourse and proceeds with explanations of several systems by which an analyst may make an assessment of ethics. In the last section of the chapter, the benefits of ethical argument for the advocate are discussed.

The Social Contract as Grounds for Ethical Considerations

To explain why good reasons must be ethical it is helpful to recall the fourth characteristic of rhetoric — rhetoric is a social transaction. It is this characteristic that accounts for the importance of ethics in public discussion. Thus, a reasonable starting point for exploring the ethical dimension of public discussion is a review of the nature of the transaction.

You may recall from Chapter 2 that rhetoric was described as a social transaction because at least two parties—advocate(s) and audience(s)—actively engage with one another in the course of public discussion. That engagement is characterized by a sense of commitment. When people make choices through discussion, they share commitments with others. There is almost a sense that something personal is involved. Such a sense of commitment is probably most easily understood by reflecting on private relationships.

Imagine yourself involved in a private relationship. You begin by going out with someone, spending time together, and sharing ideas and experiences. As the relationship progresses, you may begin to fantasize about it, imagining what your parents will think of your new friend, how your friends back home will respond to him or her, what color eyes your children will have if you get married and have children. At some point, it is altogether likely that you and your friend will actually talk about the relationship. Is this serious? Will you go out with only each other? Is there a future to your relationship? Will you become, or are you, committed to each other? Once you have talked about your level of commitment, chances are you will feel much freer to continue your fantasies about the future. There is something about talking about your decisions, bringing them into the open, that makes them seem more concrete, real, and durable. If, later on, you and your significant other break up, you may feel betrayed. You may hear yourself saying: "But this isn't fair; you said you loved me. We talked about it." This rather melodramatic example illustrates the stock we put in talk that generates a commitment. In other words, part of the nature of the social transaction that occurs when we make decisions through communication is a sense of commitment, a sense that when people say things, they really mean what they say, or what we think they said.

A similar sense of commitment and good faith accompanies public discourse. If an advocate argues in favor of a particular policy or takes a stand on a particular issue, we expect their statements to reflect what they really believe. We hear their statements, in a sense, as commitments. Consequently, if we find out later that the advocate changed his or her mind, or actually supports the other side of the issue, we feel a sense of betrayal similar to the betrayal we feel over personal matters like the one just described. For example, in 1964 many people were surprised and betrayed when, following a series of television commercials in which the U.S. Surgeon General explained that smoking was hazardous to your health and if you smoked you should kick the habit, they learned that the Surgeon General smoked two packs of cigarettes a day. More recently, journalists expressed outrage, disbelief, and a sense of betrayal when it was reported that the same airplanes that had transported aid to the Contras in Nicaragua had returned to the United States loaded with illegal drugs. Why? Because the administration that was sponsoring the aid was also conducting a campaign against drugs, pointing out the necessity to "just say no."

The general description of how social transactions produce commitments that, if violated, cause a sense of betrayal and a loss of good faith provides a useful context for a more specific discussion of the nature of the communicative transaction. The essence of the social transaction is that of a *social contract*. When people present arguments in order to secure the agreement of others concerning a public issue, an implicit commitment, or social contract, is made. The contract suggests that communication will be the method used to resolve the controversy. By extension, advocates and their audiences are agreeing not to use other means to resolve the problem. They are implying that brute force, power, coercion, dictatorial decision, and the like are being dismissed in favor of a resolution through communicative means. The existence of such an unstated social contract can be verified by examining what happens when the contract is broken.

The notion of a social contract is one familiar to students of politics. A fundamental example of social contracts is provided by a political system that depends on elections as the process for selecting officials. When an election is chosen as the means for determining who will hold office, certain expectations naturally arise. Various candidates are expected to respect the vote count. Those candidates who win are expected to take office and assume responsibility, while those who lose are expected to acknowledge the winner. Losing candidates are not expected to plot and carry out assassinations of the winner in order that they may seize power. Similarly, incumbent candidates who lose an election are not expected to refuse to relinquish power, to say: "Sorry, I didn't really mean it. Since I wasn't elected, the election is invalid. We'll just keep doing it until the voters get it right and elect me." The reason why these expectations are so clear and violation of them seems so obviously wrong is that the choice of elections as a method for selecting officials implied a social contract.

Another example of an implied social contract in the choice of means to an end was provided during the 1987 National Football League Strike. Following the strike, owners and management of the various football clubs were confronted with a problem. The owners had agreed that the rosters of teams could be expanded, that replacement players who had performed during the strike could be retained just in case the unionized players decided to reactivate the strike. Many owners and some coaches decided to use their new personnel option, expand their rosters, and keep a number of replacement players on the payroll. The Chicago Bears seemed to make a different choice. Coach Mike Ditka announced that he would take a vote during a team meeting of the regular players. The results of the vote were clear: the regular players voted *not* to retain the replacement players. A day after the vote, the Bears' organization announced that the roster would be expanded and several of the replacement players would be retained. Both the regular players and journalists observed that the vote apparently had been a sham. The social contract suggested by the vote, that the regular players would have a say in the decision, had been violated.

The workings of a social contract in the two examples just described mirror the workings of the social contract when people choose communication as the means for public decision making. Anything that violates expectations of how decisions are made through communication violates the social contract. Ethics enter into the analysis of public discourse when the sanctity of the social contract of communicative decision making is called into question. In other words, when strategies and tactics of advocacy are used that violate the social contract, those strategies can be labeled unethical.

In order to understand which communication practices are ethical and which are not, it is helpful to examine the characteristics of the social contract common to situations in which advocacy and argument are chosen as the preferred means for resolving disputes. The philosopher, Henry Johnstone, provides a useful description of the assumptions involved in such a social contract. Johnstone refers to those assumptions as "criteria for genuine argument."[1] There are three criteria:

1. The advocate must assume that the audience is beyond his or her control.
2. Advocates and audiences must be open-minded.
3. Advocates and audiences must both have an interest in the outcome of the argument.

Each of these characteristics deserves elaboration.

First, advocates must assume that audiences are beyond their control. This assumption grants legitimacy to the audience. In other words, audiences are assumed to have minds of their own, to be able to make choices. The idea of choice is clarified if we consider an idea suggested by Kenneth Burke. Burke argued that there are two kinds of processes common in the world: motion and action.[2] Motion goes on without conscious human intervention and is characteristic of natural processes. For example, trees drop acorns. The effects of sun, moisture, and the surrounding environment eventually result in the growth of new saplings from those acorns. The new sapling grows into a tree and eventually drops its own acorns to start new trees, and so on. Human beings experience motions also. Various bodily processes, like breathing, just sort of happen and continue to happen while the body is alive, without the need for any conscious intervention on the part of the particular human being. Action, on the other hand, requires choice, conscious human interaction. Humans can choose to hold their breath (usually motion takes over after a while, even in small children determined to throw a temper tantrum). According to Burke, it is these choices that humans are capable of making that explain, in part, how symbols take on meaning. By using symbols, humans exercise choice and thus create action where only motion may have existed before.

If we consider the idea of choice, then, we can understand the necessity of Johnstone's first assumption. Audiences, of course, have numerous choices regarding the advocate's management of symbols. At base, audiences may choose to, or not to, listen. Audiences can certainly choose the parts of a message to which they will attend and attribute meaning. But most importantly, audiences can choose how to respond to the advocate. They may dismiss his ideas, withhold judgment until a later date, or embrace the position of the advocate wholeheartedly. Johnstone claimed that when advocates do not recognize the capacity of choice in the audience and thereby dismiss the notion that the audience is autonomous, they are no longer arguing. Such advocates are, instead, manipulating, coercing, or engaging in propaganda.

Unfortunately, the idea that audiences are beyond the control of advocates is a difficult one to accept for most advocates. Advocates frequently confuse their power to influence with a more absolute power over the audience. Everyday talk about how to win arguments and influence others suggests that there are tactics or tricks that can be used to "pull one over" on the audience. Even well-meaning advocates sometimes forget that the audience is ultimately beyond their control. Our inclination to forget about the autonomy of an audience sometimes becomes painfully obvious. Consider, for example, the broken romance syndrome. One person in an intimate relationship decides to end the relationship. If the other person wishes to continue the romance, he or she may find numerous and varied reasons why the relationship is good and should continue. But, ultimately, if one party has decided to leave, no measure of effective communication is likely to reverse that decision. Ultimately, the person who is left is forced to confront the idea that the other is beyond his or her control. A broken heart is, among other things, evidence of the autonomy of others, their capacity to exercise choice on their own behalf.

By emphasizing the autonomy of the audience, Johnstone was not denying that advocates can influence audiences. Fundamental to his ethical perspective was the idea that what is most distinctly human is our capacity to persuade and be persuaded. But for Johnstone, persuasion involves the recognition and exercise of choice. He demonstrated his point with a vivid example. Imagine a robber who points a gun to your head and commands: "Give me your money or I'll shoot." If you respond immediately, without thinking, as if you have no choice, this is a clear example of coercion. But if you reflect, even for an instant, on the choice available (hand over the money or die), then you are responding to persuasion. Your choices in this instance are surely constrained to the point that the situation almost seems like a coercive one. If the robber had not pointed the gun, but had concealed his weapon and simply said, "Give me your money or I may hurt you," the range of choice would be wider. The move away from coercion would have been greater. Thus, Johnstone's point is that genuine argument recognizes the autonomy of the audience by maximizing the potential for choice.

The ethical implication of Johnstone's first criteria for genuine argument is that any time an advocate acts in ways that fail to recognize, or subvert, the autonomy of the audience the advocate is violating the social contract that was made when discourse was chosen as the means for resolving the dispute. What are the characteristics of reasons that violate the assumption of audience autonomy? Reasons that fail to provide adequate information, or conceal some known and relevant information, or use half-truths or exaggeration are some examples of reasons that violate this principle.

Johnstone's second criteria for genuine argument is closely related to the first. He argues that advocates must be open-minded because audiences can ignore, disbelieve, or refute the reasons offered. Because, as was pointed out in Chapter 2, audiences are potential advocates, Johnstone's claim can be expanded to include the requirement that audiences also must be open-minded. In the case of either advocate or audience, the necessity for an open mind arises from the risk that either party may have their reasons defeated. The assumption that either party may have their reasons defeated illustrates another facet of the social contract. In addition to assuming that all parties to the social contract made by public discussion are autonomous and can exercise choice, Johnstone assumes that entrance into the social contract implies that people are willing to risk their ideas and opinions. In other words, if people are serious about choosing discussion as the means for resolving disputes, they must recognize that the outcome of the discussion might lie in favor of their opponent rather than with them. To participate in the social contract, therefore, requires good faith and willingness to change one's mind.

As with the first criteria, the necessity of an open mind, or good faith, can be illustrated by referring to what happens when this expectation is violated. Everyone has probably experienced the feeling of betrayal that accompanies the belated recognition that a partner in argumentative conversation is unwilling to be moved. Perhaps our earliest experience with this phenomena is during that often awkward period between childhood and adulthood. A young person may decide that some rule established by their parents should be modified. A typical example might be the familiar rule concerning bedtime. A child, or adolescent, may initiate a conversation with their parents about why the time is too early. Maybe there is an argument about a television show that extends beyond "bedtime." Perhaps the next day is not a school day, so even if the young person "oversleeps" the next morning, the consequences will be minimal. If the parents engage in conversation about the matter, the young person (whether or not he or she realizes it) begins to sense that a social contract has been made. Whoever presents the best reasons will prevail. However, sometimes the parent fails to recognize that social contract. During the discussion, the parent may run out of objections to the proposal and have nothing left to offer as justification for their position. Yet the parents end the discussion with: "We're not going to discuss this anymore. Go to bed." The astute child immediately recognizes that the conversation that just finished really wasn't a conversation at all. The parents had made up their mind before the conversation started. The parents violated the social contract. The conversation had not proceeded with good faith. Of course, depending on the child, he or she may not have acted with good faith either. He or she may have been unwilling to take into account the parents' reasons.

Unfortunately, the problem of bad faith is not confined to the emergence from youth to adulthood. Recall the episode concerning the Chicago Bears during the NFL strike. Although an appearance of concern for opposing views was suggested, opposing views were not instrumental in the eventual decision. Anyone with experience working in a large organization or institution with various levels of management will also recognize the violation we are exploring. Much too frequently, workers, staff, ordinary personnel are asked to discuss a new policy or a problem with the promise that their input will make a difference in the outcome. Only later do these people find out that the decision had already been made. Communication may have occurred, but communication in which the parties maintained an open mind was not in evidence.

Some institutions for advocacy, for example the courts, modify the requirement for an open mind. In the judicial system, advocates are not expected to display an open mind, but are required to provide the best representation possible for their clients. Instead, a complex set of procedures are followed to insure that whoever makes the judgment, a formal judge or a jury, maintains an open mind. In the celebrated case of Robert Bork, nominated to serve on the Supreme Court, the fundamental concern surrounding his confirmation by the Senate was skepticism about his ability to maintain an open mind. Bork's eventual withdrawal as a nominee was in large part the result of his recognition that he was unlikely to change the minds of Senators who, as a result of Bork's prior public statements and writings, believed he would not maintain an open mind.

As with the first criteria, violation of the second criteria of maintaining an open mind suggests a violation of the social contract and a subversion of the choice inherent to public discussion as a preferred means for resolving disputes.

Johnstone's third criteria for genuine argument is that all parties to the discussion must have an interest in the outcome. His idea is that without mutual interest in the outcome, communication is being used for some purpose other than resolving problems. In some ways, this criteria is the foundation for the good faith requirement suggested by the second criteria. If one party does not have a stake in the outcome, there is no reason for that party to operate with an open mind, there is no motivation to be influenced. Similarly, the one party that does have a stake in the outcome may direct their efforts toward gaining the assent of the other without worrying about taking into account the other's concerns.

It is helpful to examine when the reverse of this assumption occurs in order to understand more clearly how the assumption is crucial to the social contract involved in public discussion. Consider, for example, a case of direct sales. Some sales strategies assume that only the salesperson has a stake in the outcome. If a vacuum cleaner is sold, it means that the saleswoman makes a commission. Customers may try to point out their stake in the outcome — they can't afford a new vacuum at this time, their old vacuum still works, the only problem they have is with one room in which they have shag carpeting. If the saleswoman operates according only to her own agenda, her customers will probably feel neglected and she will probably not make a sale. On the other hand, if she recognizes that both parties in the exchange have a stake in the outcome her talk will deal with the concerns of her customers and she will more likely make the sale. It is no surprise that most successful salespeople describe their success as resulting from a genuine like and regard for other people, a recognition that others have a stake in the outcome. The same principle works in reverse. If a customer asks for a demonstration of an appliance, a showing of a house, or a test drive in a new car, salespeople expect the person to have a stake in the outcome, to be seriously interested in buying the product. If the salesperson finds out later that the customer was just looking for a way to spend some time and was not interested at all in buying, the salesperson feels a sense of betrayal. The same principle of responsibility for the outcome on the part of both parties applies to public discussion. If there is not mutual interest in the outcome we are dealing with informative and one-directional communication at best, and not with public discussion. To engage in discussion without taking responsibility is to make the discussion a sham and to violate the social contract that has been established.

To summarize, then, part of viewing public discussion from a rhetorical perspective involves recognizing that when people choose communication as their preferred means for resolving public controversies, they are forging a social contract. In general terms, any actions that subvert communication by making continued argument less possible are a violation of that contract. More specifically, the social contract assumes the autonomy of the audience, the good faith of the participants, and mutual interest on the part of the participants. Any departures from these assumptions will probably constitute violations of the social contract. Violations of the social contract provide the ground for charging that arguments presented are unethical.

A clear example of public discussion that suffered from violation of Johnstone's criteria for genuine argument occurred during the 1950s.[3] Following World War II, the United States was eager to exploit its new found military superiority. The government was eager to explore the secrets of nuclear weaponry. To do so required nuclear testing and public acceptance of that testing. The Eisenhower Administration, therefore, engineered a public relations campaign known as "Atoms for Peace" to secure the approval of the citizenry. Part of that campaign was aimed at gaining the assent and support of residents of Utah and Nevada for nuclear testing in remote areas of those states. Pamphlets were distributed that extolled the virtues of atomic power, described the need for tests in terms of protecting national security, and declared that careful testing would cause "no danger" to those living near the test sites. In addition, two teams of public relations personnel were sent to these areas. One team operated openly, arguing the government's position, answering questions and demonstrating protective gear and radiation measuring devices. The other team was unknown to members of the community. They operated "underground"; their charge was to infiltrate the community, work as handymen, join local organizations, volunteer to teach Sunday School, and become accepted by the residents. Later when discussions of the issue were held, members of the second team argued in favor of testing as if they were just ordinary members of the community. The citizens eventually voted to allow the tests.

A Congressional inquiry into the program in 1979 revealed that throughout the discussion period, the Atomic Energy Commission, who had been in charge of the public relations campaign, had concealed information regarding the dangers of radiation and radioactive fallout. Hence, both the identity of some advocates and relevant information had been suppressed. By doing do, government officials had not allowed their audience to exercise real choice. The audience had made choices based on incomplete, if not inaccurate, information. The government had violated an assumption of the social contract by attempting to put the audience under their control. The government did not maintain an open mind during discussions. Their primary goal was to *assure* citizen approval. Moreover, by planting public relations personnel in the relevant communities, the government sought to minimize disagreement and maximize the potential for its own influence. This tactic, along with the suppression of relevant evidence denied residents an ability to act on their stake in the outcome. In short, government officials orchestrated the appearance of a social contract but systematically violated that social contract.

Standards for Evaluating the Ethics of Public Advocacy

In his book, *Ethics of Human Communication*, Richard Johannesen describes a variety of standards for evaluating ethics.[4] Among those perspectives aimed at ethical evaluation of political discourse, four themes are persistent: rationality, choice, democratic procedure, and democratic values. Rationality is important insofar as advocacy is aimed toward reasoned discussion by advocates and reasonable skepticism by audiences. Thus, the means for evaluating the soundness of evidence and reasoning discussed in the previous chapter may be used as tools for ethical analysis as well. Choice plays the same important role that was discussed in regard to the social contract explained in the prior section of this chapter. Democratic procedure enters into ethical considerations because of the importance of both the political system that allows for public discussion and the uniquely human capacity to persuade and be persuaded. In terms of our humanity and our political system, the means to confront opposing points of view are essential characteristics of ethical public discussion. Finally, our political system marks democratic values as crucial to ethical discussion. Democratic systems assume that public interest exists and consists of shared values that ground public decision making. As a consequence, ethical discussion should embody those shared values.

George Yoos, a contemporary philosopher, suggested four standards for evaluating the ethics of arguments or persuasive appeals.[5] Yoos' four standards seem to take into account the nature of the social contract as well as the four themes just described. He suggested that those interested in ethics examine discourse to determine how it deals with four factors: the A, R, E, and V, factors. A summary of those factors appears in the following chart:

Yoos' Four Ethical Standards

A-factor	Agreement	Are the participants seeking mutual agreement?
R-factor	Rationality	Is the audience's rational autonomy (right to disagree) recognized?
E-factor	Equality	Do all participants have equal opportunity to present and defend their positions?
V-factor	Value	Is community spirit in evidence? Do the ends of the audience have value for the advocate?

The A-factor, seeking mutual agreement, recognizes the importance of the social contract, that discussion is the means chosen to resolve the issue. The R-factor, the audience's rational autonomy, recognizes the importance of human choice as opposed to the repression of that choice through the use of tactics that impede its actualization. The E-factor, equality, suggests the risk that all parties take when they subject their viewpoints to discussion and implies the need for procedures that guarantee exercise of and respect for opposing points of view. Finally, the V-factor, value, suggests that the participants have a mutual interest in the outcome. In discussions of public issues, the suggestion is that common concerns, community interests, will ground the discussion.

Just as important as arriving at a list of ethical standards is an ability to use those standards in order to evaluate public discourse, in order to determine which discourse is ethical and which is not. Before examining particular messages or strategies, it is helpful to have some benchmark for deciding what is and what is not ethical. The standards supplied by Yoos move us in that direction. In other words, it is possible to examine how the talk about a public issue proceeds to see if the four factors are being taken into account.

When investigating the A-factor, situational factors, like those discussed in Chapter 2, come into play. The essential question being asked is: Are the participants seeking mutual agreement? In other words, does the controversy revolve around a public matter, a matter that entails community rather than private interests? Furthermore, does engagement in discussion reflect an interest in the outcome by all parties? If discussion centers on how a decision is to be implemented when, in fact, there is widespread disagreement as to what the decision may be, then discussion may be proceeding unethically. Similarly, if later revelations reveal that discussions were a sham and a decision had already been reached, then ethics should be questioned. If an advocate's statements are inconsistent with his actions, then questions regarding his stake in a mutual consensus are appropriate. The example of the Chicago Bears' discussion of replacement players is a case in point of violation of the A-factor.

The R-factor can be investigated by examining what is said to determine if the message(s) promote rational choice. The various strategic aspects of arguments already discussed in this book provide a clue as to what should be examined to determine the rationality of a message. Because claims are supported by data and warrants, both the nature of the data and the nature of the warrants are sensible places to evaluate the ethics of an argument. In the previous chapter, twenty potential objections to data and reasoning were reviewed. All of these objections mark aspects of data and warrants that could be judged unethical. For example, if an argument is supported by evidence that reflects an unrepresentative sample, then the advocate is guilty of violating the audience's rational autonomy by failing to provide adequate data from which the audience could make a rational decision. Similarly, if the argument requires a reasoning pattern that does not make sense, then the advocate is guilty of the same incursion on the audience's rationality.

Assessment of the E-factor involves examining both what is said and the procedure for discussion. Johnstone provided a useful concept for evaluating both what is said and the procedure by which it is said. He described something he called, "bilateral argument."[6] The advocate who uses bilateral argument operates by a standard akin to the Golden Rule. The advocate embodies the assumptions of the social contract by using no methods, devices, or strategies that he or she would not make available to his or her adversary or audience. Using the principle of bilaterality, an analyst of public discourse may examine the message and ask whether or not what was said would be allowed by the advocate if an adversary or an audience had made a comparable statement.

We can explore the workings of the ethical standard of bilaterality by reconsidering some of the aspects of argumentative messages already discussed in this book. Arguments that invoke common sense, even when that common sense is contradicted by other common sense, are probably not objectionable. Similarly, an advocate would probably not be disturbed if her audience or adversary chose to refer to common needs or values. Likewise, structuring a message in strategic ways would probably be considered a fair option for any participant in a discussion. However, many of the tactics discussed in the last chapter as grounds for objection probably do not fall within the domain of bilateral argument.

Consider, for example, the objection based on confusing language. Confusion, as a tactic, seems to violate Yoos' R-factor by dismissing the importance of the audience's rational autonomy. If the message or information presented is confusing, informed choice is difficult at best. Just as important, the analyst may ask: Would an advocate allow the audience to engage in confusion? At first sight, the question seems confusing. How would an audience engage in confusion? Contemplation of this question reveals a variety of subversive tactics. Audience members could ask the advocate a number of irrelevant questions. They could nod when they disagree and shake their heads when they do agree. The possibilities are fascinating. Johnstone, himself, comments on the difference between bilateral communication in the classroom, where a teacher addresses her class in such a way as to suggest that the students might make statements just as credible as her own, versus unilateral classroom techniques such as authoritative lectures that withhold the same devices of presentation from her students. We can extend Johnstone's example by considering how a teacher would react if students directed their energy toward confusing the teacher whenever they communicated with her. For a teacher, this is a frightening fantasy. Such a fantasy seems to demonstrate why we could designate confusion as an unethical tactic. Neither party to the discussion would probably be willing to grant the other side use of that tactic.

Much the same judgment can be made regarding other grounds for objection. We would rarely grant someone else the right to lie, exaggerate, and so forth. Hence, Johnstone's concept of bilaterality can translate into a rather simple "golden rule" for argument: message strategies and procedures for argument that advocates would not allow their opponents or their audiences to use are unethical if used by the advocate.

Yoos' V-factor centers on an evaluation of the values embodied in public discussion. Like the E-factor, an investigation of both the arguments presented and the procedure for discussion is necessary. As we noted in Chapter 4, warrants frequently embody values. Consequently, analysts of public discussion may want to investigate the warrants of arguments not just to find the underlying values but to evaluate the ethical worth of those underlying values. Walter Fisher, a rhetorical theorist at the University of Southern California, has suggested that the values underlying arguments can be assessed according to a procedure that asks the following questions[7]:

1. What are the implicit and explicit values embedded in a message?

2. Are the values appropriate to the nature of the decision that the message bears upon?

3. What would be the effects of adhering to the values in regard to one's concept of oneself, to one's behavior, to one's relationship with others and society, and to the processes of rhetorical transaction?

4. Are the values confirmed or validated in one's personal experience, in the lives or statements of others whom one admires and respects, and/or in a conception of the best audience that one can conceive?

5. Even if an immediate need for belief or action has been demonstrated, would an outside observer/critic assess the values offered or assumed in the message as the ideal basis for human conduct?

An example of how Fisher's scheme works will illustrate the type of analysis he suggested. Consider, for example, a familiar argument from the abortion controversy. Pro-Life groups have consistently argued that abortion should be illegal because it constitutes the taking of a human life. These advocates present a variety of data concerning when life begins and why the fetus is properly classified as a human life to support their claim that abortion is wrong. The underlying value for this argument is an unconditional value in human life. Although the value is probably appropriate to the nature of the controversy, Fisher's last three questions make a judgment of the ethics of this message complex. The effects of adhering to the value expose a variety of uncomfortable contradictions. If human life is the supreme value, then how can we condone capital punishment, war, and other legally and communally sanctioned forms of taking life? What if it is a question of preserving the mother's life or the unborn's life? How does the value apply in such a mutually exclusive situation? As this example suggests, ethical evaluation of values may become confusing and may differ from analyst to analyst. Yet, such a scheme does point the way toward how an ethical evaluation can be made.

Another theorist, Karl Wallace, has suggested that the dominant values of a society are the ones relevant for an ethical evaluation of values.[8] Thus, in democratic societies, democratic values should underlay arguments and procedures. Wallace identified four values basic to our democratic system: respect for the dignity and worth of the individual, fairness, freedom and responsible exercise of freedom, and belief in each person's ability to participate in democracy. His suggestion is that the values that ground any particular argument and the procedure for advocacy itself should reflect these four values. Consequently, he set four guidelines for ethical communication:

1. Habit of Search
2. Habit of Justice
3. Preference for Public over Private Motivations
4. Habit of Respect

Habit of search requires that advocates reflect a thorough knowledge of the subject and sensitivity to both sides of the issue in a public controversy. Habit of justice requires that advocates present fact and opinion fairly. Preference for public over private motivations requires reliance on community interests over selfish interests as the motivation for claims. Habit of respect for dissent requires encouraging disagreement rather than closing off discussion as a means for reaching consensus or compromise. We can use Wallace's perspective both as a yardstick by which to measure the values implicit in arguments as presented and as a standard by which to evaluate the procedure used in arguing.

In general, then, both the reasons presented and the procedure for presenting reasons can be evaluated according to four ethical standards. An analyst may compare the substance of the arguments and the procedure to the situation to see if mutual agreement is being sought. The data and reasoning of arguments may be examined to see if rational choice is promoted. The situation and the strategies of particular messages can be investigated to see if equal opportunity is being given to all participants and to determine if the Golden Rule of argument is being adhered to. Finally, the values reflected by individual arguments and the process of advocacy alike may be uncovered in order to determine if those values are ideal, given the circumstances, or conform to democratic values generally.

Ethos as a Product of Ethical Advocacy

Thus far our discussion has centered on what constitutes ethical arguments and how an analyst may uncover unethical arguments. Just as important is an explanation of why ethical reasons are effective in public persuasion. Obviously, the foregoing discussion provides some explanation of why ethical considerations are important. If an advocate violates the social contract established by choosing unethical rhetoric as a means to resolve disputes, that seems like a bad thing in and of itself. Such violations of the social contract usually result in a feeling of betrayal by the audience, a judgment that the advocate in question is not to be trusted. It is this implication that explains why ethical arguments are important to public advocacy. If the reasons presented are ethical, then advocates are likely to be judged trustworthy, and, as a result, their persuasive power is enhanced. This idea was discussed by Aristotle. He termed the persuasive power derived from an advocate's personal trustworthiness, *ethos*.[9]

It is not unusual for contemporary communication scholars to equate Aristotle's concept of ethos with the more contemporary concept of credibility. However, there is a difference between the two and understanding the difference provides the key to understanding how ethos results from ethical argument. Credibility is the term generally used to describe the believability and trustworthiness of a particular speaker. If a speaker is credible, she is believable. Public opinion polls have frequently attempted to survey public attitudes regarding which public figures are perceived as credible and which are not. For many years, the most credible, believable person in the United States, according to these polls, was Walter Cronkite, long-time anchorman for the CBS Evening News. The idea that someone, like Cronkite, can be trusted to tell us the truth arises from a variety of factors. Simple familiarity accounts for some measure of credibility. We tend to believe our friends and acquaintances more than we believe strangers or enemies. Similarly, some people gain credibility because of their status or position in the world. We assume that if a person is given the job of anchorman for a national network then they must know what they're talking about (the movie "Broadcast News" notwithstanding). Newman and Newman's indices of credibility, discussed in Chapter 4, illustrate a number of factors that sensibly contribute to an audience's perception of a particular source's believability. Among those factors were situational factors, characteristics of the message, characteristics of the writer, and characteristics of the sources quoted by the author. Various studies of credibility have demonstrated the importance of this dimension to the persuasiveness of any message. For example, one famous experiment presented the very same messages to different audiences.[10] In one case the message was attributed to a credible source. In the other case, the same message was attributed to a source with low credibility. The results indicated that when the message was attributed to a source with high credibility, audiences believed the message; when the message was attributed to a source with low credibility the message was dismissed as irrelevant, wrong, or inaccurate.

Although credibility is important to the persuasiveness of any particular source, it is not the same concept as ethos. Aristotle explained that ethos was not the result of factors prior to, or outside of, the rhetorical transaction but was the personal power created during the speaker-audience interaction. Aristotle identified three dimensions of ethos that could be created during a rhetorical transaction: (1) good sense, (2) good character, and (3) good will.[11]

Good sense is displayed by an advocate who uses sound evidence and reasoning to support his arguments, thereby providing the audience with sensible grounds for rational choice. In addition to meeting the standards for good argument reviewed in the previous chapter, several of the indices of credibility listed by Newman and Newman bear on an audience's perception that the advocate is arguing with good sense. First, the higher the internal consistency of a source, the higher the credibility of testimony. Second, the more careful the advocate is in generalizing, the more likely it is that the argument is trustworthy. Third, the greater the objectivity in an advocate's message, the greater the likelihood that a credible case sensitive to opposing points of view is being presented. Fourth, the more accurate citations of other sources of testimony are, the more believable they will be, as the audience perceives the careful, sensible presentation. Fifth, the more discerning an advocate is in selecting sources to quote, the more credible the testimony. Again, the advocate's selection of sources provides insight into whether or not he or she is a person of good sense. If advocates fail to provide sound evidence or use sensible reasoning, they will probably lose credibility and fail to establish ethos. For example, during the 1976 Presidential campaign, incumbent President Gerald Ford made a number of misstatements and confused his facts. The most famous incident was when he referred to Poland as a non-Communist country. Numerous political commentators have suggested that his loss in the election to Jimmy Carter was, in part, a result of public perceptions that Ford was not a man of good sense.

Good character is demonstrated by the use of arguments that rely on values that the audience recognizes as virtuous. Aristotle identified seven virtues common in Greek culture during this time: justice, courage, temperance, generosity, magnanimity, magnificence, and prudence. The list of standard American values discussed in Chapter 4 provides a similar index to contemporary standards regarding virtue. By presenting arguments that conform to one or more of those values, advocates illustrate that they are arguing from community values rather than private self interest. As with good sense, if an advocate relies on values that are not indicative of good moral character, she may lose credibility. For example, following the indictment of Ivan Boesky for "insider trading" on Wall Street, many commentators pointed to a speech he had delivered during commencement ceremonies at Harvard. In the speech, Boesky had argued that greed was good and was what made America great. The value of money, to the exclusion of more traditional American values concerning God, hard work, and generosity, was identified as a sign that Boesky was not to be trusted.

Good will requires the advocate to somehow suggest that she has the audience's best interests in mind. In part, by presenting sensible arguments that rely on accepted values, the advocate can accomplish this task. However, good will also is demonstrated by following procedures for argument that allow the audience an opportunity to respond and generally allow for equal opportunity in public discussion. In his famous "Checkers Speech," Richard Nixon not only appealed to traditional values, but also explicitly asked for audience participation in the controversy by urging his listeners to respond to his message. Nixon had been accused of accumulating and using money from a political fund that made him susceptible to the same charges of corruption as he had been levelling toward his opponents in the Democratic party. Following a lengthy explanation of the nature of the fund and his financial history, Nixon appealed to the audience to decide whether or not he should remain on the Republican ticket as the vice presidential candidate. By asking the audience to write or wire someone with their judgment regarding his fitness for public office, Nixon demonstrated his goodwill, his willingness to do whatever the audience thought was in their best interest.

As the discussion of Aristotle's dimensions of ethos suggests, ethos is a product of ethical argument, argument that seeks mutual agreement by appealing to the audience's rational autonomy and their accepted values, while at the same time using a procedure that guarantees fairness and equal opportunity for all parties in public discussion. Unlike credibility, which may be established prior to the speaker-audience interaction by virtue of an advocate's expertise or station in life, ethos is the product of that interaction. If ethos is constructed by way of ethical argument, then the advocate has added another source of persuasion to his or her strategic arsenal, the persuasive power that derives from the fact that the audience perceives him or her as trustworthy.

Summary

Ethical considerations are important in public discussion for two primary reasons. First, unethical advocacy violates the social contract that is established when people choose argument as their preferred means for resolving disputes. Second, ethical advocacy not only preserves the social contract but produces ethos, the personal persuasive power of advocates. The social contract forged in public controversy is characterized by three factors inherent in the rhetorical transaction: recognition that the audience is beyond the control of the advocate, respect for human choice that requires an open mind and good faith on the part of all participants to the discussion, and shared commitment to the outcome of advocacy. To evaluate the ethics of advocacy requires attention to both the procedure or circumstances of public discussion and the actual messages as presented. Both procedure and substance should reflect a commitment to mutual agreement, rational choice, equality of opportunity, and shared values.

Notes

[1] Henry W. Johnstone, Jr., "Some Reflections on Argumentation," in *Philosophy, Rhetoric, and Argumentation,* eds. Maurice Natanson and Henry W. Johnstone, Jr. (University Park: Pennsylvania State University Press, 1965), pp. 1-10.

[2] Kenneth Burke, "Dramatism," in *Communication: Concepts and Perspectives,* ed. Lee Thayer (Washington: Spartan, 1967), p. 336.

[3] Details of the Atomic Energy Commission's public relations campaign and the Congressional investigation that followed nearly thirty years later are found in Stephen Hilgartner, Richard C. Bell, and Rory O'Connor, *Nukespeak* (San Francisco: Sierra Club Books, 1982).

[4] Richard L. Johannesen, *Ethics in Human Communication,* 2nd ed. (Prospect Heights: Waveland, 1983), especially pp. 11-28.

[5] George Yoos, "A Revision of the Concept of Ethical Appeal," *Philosophy and Rhetoric* 12 (1979): 41-58.

[6] Henry W. Johnstone, Jr., "Bilaterality in Argument and Communication," in *Advances in Argumentation Theory and Research,* eds. J. Robert Cox and Charles Arthur Willard (Carbondale: Southern Illinois University Press, 1982), pp. 95-102.

[7] Walter R. Fisher, "Toward a Logic of Good Reasons," *Quarterly Journal of Speech* 64 (1978): 376-84.

[8] Karl R. Wallace, "An Ethical Basis of Communication," *Speech Teacher* 4 (1955): 1-9.

[9] Aristotle, *Rhetoric,* trans. Rhys Roberts (Cambridge: Modern Library, 1954), 1355b-1356a.

[10] C.I. Hovland and W. Weiss, "The Influence of Source Credibility on Communication Effectiveness," *Public Opinion Quarterly* 15 (1951): 635-50.

[11] Aristotle, 1378a.

Suggested Readings

Fisher, Walter R., 1978. "Toward a Logic of Good Reasons." *Quarterly Journal of Speech* 64:376-84.

Johannesen, Richard L., 1983. *Ethics in Human Communication,* 2nd Ed. Prospect Heights: Waveland.

Johnstone, Henry W., Jr., 1982. "Bilaterality in Argument and Communication." In *Advances in Argumentation Theory and Research,* pp. 95-102. Eds. J. Robert Cox and Charles Arthur Willard. Carbondale: Southern Illinois University Press.

Johnstone, Henry W., Jr., 1965. "Some Reflections on Argumentation." In *Philosophy, Rhetoric, and Argumentation,* pp. 1-10. Eds. Maurice Natanson and Henry W. Johnstone, Jr. University Park: Pennsylvania State University Press.

Johnstone, Henry W., Jr., 1981. "Towards an Ethics of Rhetoric." *Communication* 6:305-14.

Nilsen, Thomas R., 1974. *Ethics of Speech Communication,* 2nd Ed. Indianapolis: Bobbs-Merrill.

Wallace, Karl R., 1955. "An Ethical Basis of Communication." *Speech Teacher* 4:1-9.

Wallace, Karl R., 1963. "The Substance of Rhetoric: Good Reasons." *Quarterly Journal of Speech* 49:239-49.

Yoos, George, 1979. "A Revision of the Concept of Ethical Appeal." *Philosophy and Rhetoric* 12:41-58.

Chapter 8

Ideology, Propaganda and Implicit Discussion of Public Issues

Thus far, our discussion has centered primarily on explicit discussion of public issues. Because a rhetorical perspective toward public discussion recognizes that both advocates and audiences act strategically, the most obvious form of public discussion occurs when advocates and audiences intentionally produce and attend to arguments in order to resolve controversy. Even within this context, however, sometimes a part of the argument is implicit. The power of enthymemes, discussed in Chapter 3, derives from their use of implicit premises or conclusions. Similarly, the values on which many arguments are based operate implicitly during a communication event. Not only do individual messages frequently incorporate implicit premises or conclusions, but sometimes the totality of a message may function implicitly in the context of the larger public discussion of an issue. In other words, sometimes advocates mask their persuasive intentions by presenting messages that, although not obviously persuasive, still have the effect of coordinating social action. At other times, producers of messages who have no intention to be persuasive may have their messages interpreted by audiences in ways that influence social action. In both cases, we are dealing with implicit rhetoric, rhetoric that is not obviously persuasive but nonetheless is a management of symbols that results in a coordination of social action.

Reviewing some examples of implicit rhetoric will help to clarify the phenomena with which this chapter is concerned. During the discussion of factual claims in Chapter 3, an example of background reports presented by the news media was reviewed. Background reports are a good example of implicit rhetoric because these reports appear to be only informative, describing the reality in which controversy arises. Yet, the background report influences our view of what the facts are and, thereby, has a persuasive impact as well. Similarly, news articles in either newspapers or magazines frequently appear as, and attempt to be, unbiased accounts of what is happening. They too present only one version of the facts, or what is happening. Studies of eyewitness testimony suggest that the likelihood of identical reports of an accident by two different witnesses is very small.[1] Thus, it was not surprising to learn, in Chapter 2, that news reports of the Jeanette Rankin Brigade presented very different visions of what happened. Commercial advertisements are obviously persuasive, but are usually perceived as aimed toward private buying habits rather than social action and the resolution of public controversy. Yet, one of the suggested side effects of such advertising is an influence on how viewers see reality and what they perceive to be the prevailing values in society.[2] Similarly, although most of us read novels and watch movies and television shows for entertainment purposes, these too present us with visions of reality and suggestions about appropriate values and actions. As these brief examples suggest, any message may function persuasively despite the conscious intention of its source or audience that it is performing an informative or entertaining purpose.

The purpose of this chapter is to investigate why and how messages can function implicitly as means for coordinating social action. We will begin by exploring the characteristics of symbols and meaning that allow rhetoric to function implicitly. Then we will turn to two important aspects of public discourse that result from the implicit capacity of symbol use: ideology and propaganda.

The Persuasive Nature of Symbolic Activity

Symbols, whether verbal or nonverbal, are usually thought of as representative. In other words, when we make sentences or produce gestures, we usually think that what we are doing is representing our ideas, feelings or attitudes. In addition, we generally believe that these ideas, feelings, or attitudes are related somehow to external reality as we experience it. For example, if I write a sentence ("My dog is lying on the floor beside the desk") I think that I'm describing one aspect of what is happening right now (incidentally, "the dog just moved"). In this example, the words, as they are put together in the sentence, represent what is happening. These words are clearly an imperfect representation. As you read the sentence, you don't know what either the dog or the desk look like. Moreover, you also know that I'm writing the sentence at the same time that I'm telling you about the dog. Thus you can be assured that I've only chosen one thing to tell you about in the larger context of all that is happening. At best, my words are an imperfect, partial representation of what is happening both in reality as I experience it and in my head and body as I experience that reality. Symbols, therefore, have a complex relationship with both things and thoughts.

I.A. Richards, a philosopher and teacher of English, described this complex relationship with a diagram he called the "semantic triangle."[3]

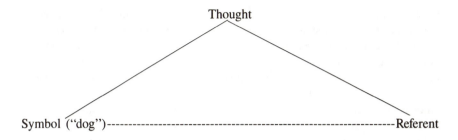

According to Richards, when we use language, or symbols, there is usually a referent, something outside of ourselves that provokes a thought, something inside of ourselves. We use the symbol to represent the thought, which in turn is related to the referent. However, the symbol does not have a direct relationship with the referent because our thought has already mediated or transformed the referent by focusing on particular details of the referent and omitting others.

Most of us have experience with the fuzzy relationship between symbol and referent that Richards described. Several years ago, for example, a friend invited me to spend a weekend at her family's "cabin" in Michigan. I grew up in the Appalachian mountains; "cabin" referred to a wooden building with no indoor plumbing and probably no electricity. When we arrived that weekend to a charming house with not only electricity and plumbing but also a dishwasher, I was surprised. My confusion, of course, resulted from my failure to remember that symbols do not have a direct relationship with the things to which they refer, but are always the product of an intervening thought. Similar examples abound.

We are all taught as children that "sticks and stones will break your bones, but words will never hurt you." However, when someone calls us a "jerk," a "dummy," or refers to us by some other derogatory symbol, we still feel the pain. Therefore, recognition of the imprecise connection between symbols and referents does not explain fully the nature of symbols. Just as important is an explanation of the relationship between symbols and meaning, or the thoughts of those who produce and receive the symbols. With the example of the "cabin" and the case of calling names, the meaning that is carried by the symbol is the key for investigating the resulting confusion and pain. Consequently, it is helpful to remember how it is that we attribute meaning to symbols.

By the time children reach the age of six, they are altogether accustomed to attributing meaning to new and unfamiliar symbols. By adulthood, we are so practiced in figuring out the meaning of new words that it is sometimes difficult to explain just how we do it. We sometimes, mistakenly I think, explain to others that the way to determine the meaning of a word is to look it up in the dictionary. While we may follow this advice on occasion, more usually we determine the meaning of a word, or other symbol, by using the context. Richard's calls this the "contextual theorem of meaning" and contrasts it with a "proper meaning superstition," that holds that words have *a* proper meaning that does not change with context.[4] The contextual theorum of meaning is probably most apparent in those rare instances in which we encounter a symbol for which we have no referent. For example, while reading a science fiction novel, we might come upon a fictitious language. Although some such novels do have glossaries, more usually the reader is expected to figure out the meaning by using the context. Some part of the enjoyment of reading such novels is no doubt derived from our natural delight in discovering the meaning of these "new" words.

Just how we use the context to attribute meaning to symbols is not as simple as it might first appear. A brief example, borrowed from S.I. Hayakawa, a student of language and former U.S. Senator, illustrates the point.[5] Consider the word, "gyxpyx." Following are several sentences in which the word is used:

> Bill's gyxpyx is twenty years old, but it still works.
> Yesterday, I bought a new, electric gyxpyx.
> My father's secretary was fast as blazes on the gyxpyx.
> One of the keys on the gyxpyx is stuck.
> The gyxpyx is certainly better than an abacus, but I really prefer the
>   new solar-powered calculators that do everything.

As you have surmised by now, a gyxpyx is an adding machine. But more important than determining the meaning of this word, is understanding how you arrived at that meaning. Early on, the grammatical context signals the type of referent that the symbol represents. By the time the first sentence is read, you probably know that the gyxpyx is a thing, as opposed to a process or a concept or a feeling. In other words, the placement of the word in the sentence reveals that it is a noun, rather than a verb, adjective or adverb. As the sentences progress, most people start constructing mental images of things with keys that secretaries use and that run on electricity. These mental images are refined by the last sentence when the gyxpyx is contrasted with an abacus and a solar-powered calculator. Thus, some of the context is supplied by the surrounding words, and some of the context is supplied by our mental images that are provoked by these surrounding words. As we imagine electric office equipment, our images are concrete and mirror actual offices in which we have spent time. When we finally arrive at an image of an adding machine, chances are that each of us has a slightly different mental picture. Your adding machine may be gray with tan keys and a black handle. Mine may be half the size of yours and navy blue with pale yellow keys and no handle at all. Similarly, as I recall the office setting I may experience a warm feeling associated with my childhood as I spent time at my parent's office. You, on the other hand, may recall how bored you were as you waited for your parent to finish working on the machine before going home. The differing pictures of the thing that the symbol represents are illustrative of how we arrive at the denotative meaning for the symbol. The differing experiences we recall as we arrive at that *denotative* meaning are illustrative of how we arrive at the *connotative* meaning for the symbol. Thus, using the context to determine the meaning of symbols does not just involve concern for grammatical context, but also concern for the differing human experiences that contribute to contextual meaning.

When communicators share common experience, the likelihood of confusion and misunderstanding is sharply reduced. However, much of the time experience varies from individual to individual and, as a consequence, what a symbol means to one person is unlikely to be identical with what the same symbol means to another. For the purpose of analyzing public discussion, the importance of human experience for how meaning is attributed to symbols explains how rhetoric can operate implicitly. Because symbols are imperfect representations of real world referents, messages composed of symbols necessarily reflect only a partial view of reality. Because meaning is attached to those symbols by reference to context and that context may differ among different individuals, messages necessarily evoke a subjective view of reality. Therefore, any message may be examined to uncover the view of reality that it presents. In place of the more ordinary understanding of symbols as representing reality, we can substitute an understanding of symbols as presenting a view of reality.

The notion that symbols present a view of reality has been discussed by numerous scholars. Two points of view are of particular interest. One was presented by Richard Weaver, a long-time professor of English at the University of Chicago, and the other by Kenneth Burke. Weaver argued that all language was "sermonic."[6] In other words, every linguistic construction suggests a particular way of viewing the world because language reflects values. The connotative dimension of meaning supplies a collection of associations to symbols that range from relatively positive to relatively negative. Values, as discussed in Chapter 4, are those things that we understand as good, as ideals to which we aspire. A composition, or speech, or any set of verbal symbols, consequently, may manifest what is good, what is bad, and what is in between these two extremes. Weaver's point is illustrated by a simple exercise. Using any topic, try to construct a sentence that says something neutral about the topic, a sentence that is free of any bias. It is difficult, if not impossible, to do. Assume we are discussing women. We might say, "women are the fairer sex." The positive connotation of "fairer" is obvious. We might say, "women are equal to men." Again, positive connotations abound. "Equality" is usually considered to be a good quality, at least in contemporary American culture. If "men" is understood as the standard for personhood that embodies strength, autonomy, and integrity, then this term also manifests a positive value for the sentence. The same type of analysis could be used for nearly any sentence about women that we might construct. Some sentences, of course, would embody a negative connotation and imply a badness rather than a goodness. Finding a neutral sentence, given the condition that the sentence must actually say something about women, is next to impossible. If, as Weaver argued, all language is sermonic, then any message that uses symbols can be analyzed to determine the point of view that it suggests. Any message can be analyzed to uncover the values manifest by it. Thus, messages that are explicitly designed to be informative or entertaining, but not persuasive, may function implicitly as persuasion.

Kenneth Burke discussed the nature of symbol use in much the same way as Weaver. Burke argued that "you persuade a man only insofar as you can talk his language by speech, gesture, tonality, order, image, attitude, idea, *identifying* your ways with his."[7] Identification, or shared understanding that results in a mutual feeling of oneness, is a matter of shared ways of viewing the world. One shares a view of the world with others only through the use of symbols. Any message, therefore, may promote identification, by presenting a view of the world that can be shared by receivers, or may promote division, by presenting a view of the world that is not shared by receivers.

Among the many suggestions that Burke provided for analyzing messages to investigate identification, one method is particularly valuable for application to implicit rhetoric. Arguing that human action, including human symbolic action may be interpreted dramatically, Burke proposed a dramatistic interpretation of messages.[8] Burke's dramatic interpretation of human action is similar to Shakespeare's suggestion that "all the world is a stage." Many of us tend to interpret our life as a whole and our daily actions in ways that resemble a drama. An example is provided by the familiar fantasies that most of us construct as we move through a particular day. As the day goes along, we may treat particular parts like episodes in a drama. Such treatment is clearest during those moments when we reflect on what has been happening and plan what we will say to our friends, roommates, or family when we return home at the end of the day. We may think of ourselves as the main character, usually the hero or heroine, who has struggled in many battles during the course of the day.

Consider, for example, the student who didn't hear the alarm and awoke with only twenty minutes to get ready and make her first class. She scrambled and arrived at class only five minutes late. The class was uneventful, but as she listened to the lecture, she suddenly remembered that she had forgotten to make her final fee payment to the Bursar the day before, the last day to pay without a late charge. With only fifty minutes between the class she was in and her next one, she realized she would need to hustle, to blaze across campus and speak with the Bursar before her next class. To top off the problem, it had started raining. Following a mad dash across campus, she arrived at the Bursar's Office. Her initial conversation with the clerk was less than successful as she was told there was no alternative but to pay the $25.00 late fee. **But**, she had taken a course in advocacy the semester before and quickly assembled a case for why the rule should be bent in her case. The clerk was unimpressed. She asked to speak to the clerk's supervisor. While she waited, she refined her arguments. With only fifteen minutes before she had to leave to make her next class, the Bursar emerged from the inside office. "What seems to be the problem," he asked. She responded with the polished explanation she had been rehearsing mentally for the last five minutes. Confronted with such a reasonable explanation, the Bursar relented: "Just write a check for the amount you owe, and we'll forego the late fee." Success. As she raced to her next class, she rehearsed the story of the Bursar's Office that she would tell her friend at lunch. As this example illustrates, even mundane activities of daily life can constitute the material for narratives about our lives. More dramatic events provide even richer ground for such narratives.

If we often construct symbolic messages that take a dramatic view, then the categories of a drama can be used to uncover the view of reality presented by those messages. One method for analyzing symbols from a dramatic perspective that Burke suggested was the use of the *dramatic pentad.*[9] The pentad includes five elements common to drama: *act, agent, agency, scene,* and *purpose.* In the example above, our student was an agent, the main character who acted by pleading her case at the Bursar's Office. The clerk and the Bursaw were, of course, other characters, or agents, in this drama. The student's purpose was to avoid the late fee. She accomplished her purpose through the agency, or means, of persuasion. The action took place in a scene dominated by urgency and inclement weather. Burke explained that by determining which elements of the drama were emphasized in relation to other elements, the analyst could provide a clear picture of the view or perspective of a message. In the foregoing message, the agent (student) is clearly important, but her shrewd use of agency (persuasive technique) is what allows her to overcome the various obstacles provided by the scene. The moral of the story seems to be that assertiveness and persuasive facility can overcome problems that seem otherwise insurmountable. Although the story does not seem to be obviously persuasive, the fact that it is so easy to derive a moral for the story suggests that there exists an implicit claim. By using the pentad to analyze the story, we may arrive at that implicit claim.

Numerous critics have used Burke's pentadic analysis to examine both explicit and implicit rhetoric. One of the more notable critiques concerned Edward Kennedy's explanation of the Chappaquidick incident.[10] In 1969, Kennedy, a Senator for the state of Massachusetts, attended a party on Chappaquidick Island off Martha's Vineyard. When he left the party, he was accompanied by his secretary, Mary Jo Kopeckne. During the drive back to the mainland, an accident occurred. Kennedy survived, but Kopeckne drowned in the waters of a deep pond. Following this incident, Kennedy found it necessary to appear on national television to explain what had happened. Ling analyzed his televised address using Burke's pentad. What Ling found was that the first half of the speech, the explanation of the tragedy, was dominated by scenic elements. For example, Kennedy explained that "the car drove off the bridge." Cars, of course, do not drive. However, by phrasing his explanation as he did, the view presented by Kennedy downplayed his role as an agent. In contrast, the second half of the speech, in which Kennedy appealed for continuing support of his political career, emphasized agent. Kennedy recounted his effective work as a Senator and the political competency of his family as a whole. Ling's analysis, thus, provided insight into some of the implicit claims at work in Kennedy's address.

As the explanation of Burke's pentad suggests, symbols can be analyzed for their implicit presentation of a perspective as well as for their explicit presentation of a viewpoint. The very nature of symbols, as described by scholars such as Richards and Weaver, suggests that all symbolic messages will present a perspective. Consequently, any symbolic construction may function rhetorically to present a point of view. If the view of the world presented by a message bears on an audience's understanding or orientation toward a public controversy, then it may need examination as a relevant part of public discussion. News reports, textbooks, historical accounts, scientific explanations, entertainment, and so forth may all furnish an audience with a particular perspective from which to view and understand the world. As a consequence, any of these messages may be examined for their bearing on public controversy.

Ideology

The importance of a world view to public argument has been suggested throughout this book. An audience's view of the facts plays an important role in proscribing what data an advocate may productively use in constructing arguments. Similarly, an audience's values are a crucial factor in determining whether they will accept a particular argument as warranted. The preceding discussion of implicit rhetoric suggests that any symbolic message may present a world view. Systematic examination of messages to determine the world view manifest in them is assisted by an understanding of three related concepts: *culture, myth,* and *ideology.*

To say that audiences may share a particular view of the world is to suggest that in addition to maintaining an individualistic sense of the world, there exists the possibility of a mass consciousness. The very idea of public opinion, discussed in Chapter 1, suggests that within a society, despite individual differences, there exist common views concerning what is important or valuable. Relying on the work of cultural anthropologists and rhetoricians alike, William Balthrop, a professor of argument at the University of North Carolina, has defined culture as "the pattern of meanings into which individuals are born and socialized" and which provide a "reservoir of interpretation from which individuals make sense of their environments."[11] In other words, the essence of a culture is its shared world view from which individuals are able to understand and explain why things happen as they do. Furthermore, any individual culture, or shared world view, is comprised of "beliefs, values, and social myths that coalesce around and are infused by a dominating hierarchical ideal." In other words, individuals within a particular culture share a common set of understandings about what is and what ought to be that are frequently symbolized in a social myth that suggests which value, or ideal, is most important for a culture. A couple of examples may illustrate the concepts of culture and myth that Balthrop identified.

American culture is dominated by a set of beliefs and values that emphasize a myth of the individual. Myth does not refer here to a fantasy or "make-believe," but rather to a dramatic vision that serves to organize everyday experience and give meaning to life. We have already discussed the list of standard American values in Chapter 4 and may recall that Americans place a high value on the individual and individualism. Success is valued and thought to be the result of honest, hard work in a land where all have an equal opportunity. Although we recognize that tragedies do occur and unfairness sometimes happens, most of the time we believe that if a person is not successful, it is their own fault. One of the dominant myths of our culture is that an individual can be successful regardless of their humble beginnings through hard work and initiative. This myth and its attendant beliefs and values are so common that it is difficult to imagine a different world view in which the individual's success is not related to hard work and measured by the fruits of that labor. However, the myth of the American dream stands in contrast to similar myths from other cultures.

A culture's beliefs, values, and myths are often easier to recognize if we are visitors in another culture. As visitors or tourists in a foreign land, our attention is often directed to the symbols that seem to mark the new territory as unique. For example, if you visit several of the countries in western Europe, you soon discover that among the most notable tourist attractions are cathedrals, castles, and museums. In West Germany, for example, castles and many museums display enormous wealth and power amassed by royalty, an aristocratic class. The power and influence of the church, particularly the Catholic Church, is similarly displayed in the many magnificent cathedrals. Compare these tourist attractions with those in the United States. A visit to Chicago is hardly complete without a ride to the top of the Sears Tower. Other buildings that demand attention, like the John Hancock Building or the Standard Oil Building, similarly draw attention to business and industry. In place of castles, the visitor in American may tour mansions belonging to the rich and famous. Instead of hearing the history of royalty during a cruise along the Rhine, the foreign traveler aboard a cruise of Lake Geneva in Wisconsin will hear about a variety of self-made men. The Wrigley mansion, built by the baron of Wrigley chewing gum, is followed by the Brach estate, a product of the candy company. In Paris, the Louvre may be the most visited museum, but in Chicago the Museum of Science and Industry takes that honor. The visitor in Rome may visit the Roman ruins, but the visitor to Hollywood sees the homes of the stars, individual celebrities. The visitor to Disneyland may enjoy the rides and exhibits, but most of them bear the names of their corporate sponsor. Firestone and Goodyear bring us the joys of such entertainment.

Although success, in terms of material wealth, and the fruits of hard work by ambitious individuals connected to science and industry comprise a major part of American culture, there are other myths at work as well. For our purpose, more important than the particular myths themselves are the symbolic messages that embody those cultural ideals. Symbolic statements of those cultural ideals provide the background for public argument. The unique beliefs, values, and myths of a culture provide the common sense for a community that allows its members to interpret and decide about the validity of particular claims advanced during public discussions. In contemporary American society, for example, if a policy is shown to violate the rights of the individual it may be dismissed because of its inconsistency with a dominant aspect of our culture. Similarly, if a particular problem is shown to result in large economic losses, the necessity for correcting the problem is clear. In short, when advocates are able to link their cause to something generally accepted as good or bad, they will usually convince their audience that the cause is likewise good or bad. It just makes common sense.

Whenever discussion invokes common sense, it is likely that such discussion is based on *ideological* grounds. The term, *ideology* has been used by various scholars to refer to diverse concepts. Therefore, a brief discussion of what the term means to an analyst of public discussion is in order. For many scholars, *ideology refers to the set of background beliefs and values that define a culture.* Thus, ideology is considered as equivalent to culture, as was defined in the foregoing paragraphs.

For other scholars, particularly those following the teachings of Karl Marx, ideology is defined as a "false consciousness." Instead of being just a world view that is shared by members of a culture, ideology is described as a partial world view, partial because the world view represents and advances the privileges and powers of only a part of the culture and, thereby, is repressive to other members of the culture. For example, by presenting a world view that hard work will lead to success, members of a culture who reap profits from those who labor may accumulate wealth while the actual laborers have limited room for advancement and rarely realize the profits of their labors. Such a perspective is typical of the statements by labor during many negotiations with management. Auto workers, for example, may argue that managers are getting salary increases at the same time that workers are asked to take pay cuts in order to improve the efficiency of the firm so that it may compete more effectively with foreign automakers. Management, of course, argues that the necessity for maintaining a competitive edge is real and that the world view they present is accurate, not false.

Common to both descriptions of ideology is the notion that *ideology is a coherent world view.* Regardless of whether or not we accept the idea that such a world view is false, the Marxist notion that such a world view serves to provide an interpretation of events that justifies the exercise of power and guides choices of action is an important one. In the context of public discussion, the implication is that ideology constitutes a world view that determines how arguments will be received and interpreted. The common sense of the world view provides the basis for determining what is good, bad, right, wrong, and so forth. Balthrop pointed out that ideology is often invoked to defend a cultural myth that comes under attack.

He described, for example, the Cavalier and Plantation Myths common to southern culture following the Civil War and argued that during the 1950s and '60s when the Civil Rights movements attacked these myths many southerners invoked an ideology of white supremacy, an ideology commonly used during the earlier abolitionist movement, to justify continued segregation and reinforce the myths of southern culture. An ideological statement is often the last statement of justification in a controversy. In other words, if an advocate is repeatedly asked to defend her position, the ideological statement may be the final answer, beyond which she can say no more. Thus, during the time of heightened racial tension in the south, those resistant to granting Blacks the rights accorded to white citizens often ended their defense by suggesting that, "you just can't mix the races; if you lived in the South, you'd understand."

A third characteristic of ideology, most commonly discussed among Marxist thinkers, is that *ideology is resistant to inspection*. In other words, the coherent world view is rarely open to debate or argument. This is partly a result of the function that ideology plays in the larger argumentative context. If, finally, the argument rests on common sense, then how does one argue about common sense. For example, when the law requiring drivers and their passengers to wear seatbelts was debated in many state legislatures, advocates were expected to provide reasons why such a law was needed. The most typical reason was that a seatbelt law would save lives because the chances of death from an accident were greater if a person was not wearing a seatbelt than if they were buckled up. There was controversy about whether or not seatbelts would really save lives. Opponents argued that in certain types of crashes seatbelts were useless and suggested that in some cases the time required to get out of the seatbelt would endanger the life of the motorist if the vehicle caught fire. However, the basic value of saving lives, the common sense that saving lives was a good thing, was not a matter of controversy. The sanctity of human life, therefore, acted in an ideological manner; the idea was resistant to inspection. This makes so much common sense that it may be difficult to imagine why anyone would want to argue about whether or not saving lives was a good thing. Yet, if such a value were absolute, wouldn't it make sense just to eliminate automobiles as a mode of transportation? After all, if no one drove, there would be no automobile accidents and none of the resulting injuries or deaths. As this example illustrates, an ideological belief and an argument based on ideology may make sense, but we rarely inquire into its sensibleness. Instead, we take it for granted.

Ideology, then, is the symbolic expression of a coherent world view that is accepted as common sense in a culture. Common sense provides the ground for interpreting, rejecting, and accepting arguments generally and provides a discursive defense for the beliefs, values, and myths accepted by members of the cultural community. Common sense also resists inspection because it is taken for granted. Those outside the culture and those who find fault with the dominant culture may judge the ideology to be a false consciousness that represses some groups of individuals, but those immersed in the culture will likely accept the ideology as an accurate representation of the way the world works.

While it is possible to examine any symbolic message for the implicit claims it makes regarding how the world works, some messages are more likely sources for identifying the ideology common to a culture. Classic works, whether they are revered political documents like the U.S. Constitution, long-remembered public orations like the Gettysburg Address, or enduring literary works like Steinbeck's *Grapes of Wrath*, often provide coherent statements of cultural ideals. Frequently the explicit purpose of these messages is something other than advocacy regarding a public controversy. However, their enduring and revered quality indicates their implicit function as statements of a culture's ideology.

Explicit advocacy also frequently incorporates ideological statements. Because of the consonance of ideology with the culture, investigation of the ideological component of public discourse is warranted. Michael McGee, a professor of communication, provided a method for conducting such investigation.[12] He suggested that the analyst look for *ideographs*, the one-term sums of a perspective or world view. McGee described ideographs as similar to Chinese symbols, in that these singular words or phrases signify a complex gestalt of an orientation by representing a collection of beliefs, values, and myths that taken together provided a coherent view of the world. Both Richard Weaver and Kenneth Burke, whose views of language were discussed earlier in this chapter, described a similar concept. Weaver described "God terms," those words that symbolize the ideals of a culture.[13] Burke wrote about "ultimate terms," that expressed the universality of a perspective.[14] According to McGee, "such terms as 'property,' 'religion,' 'right of privacy,' 'freedom of speech,' 'rule of law,' and 'liberty'" function as ideographs insofar as they refer to a complex set of beliefs, values, and myths in American culture.[15]

Several characteristics of ideographs deserve mention. First, ideographs provide "the symbolic bridge through which specific ideological statements are related to, and infused by, the cultural ideal's aura."[16] In other words, these terms express and reinforce the ideals of a culture. Such terms unite and divide people into communities. Those who understand and attach significance to ideographs recognize each other as belonging to the same culture, while those who do not respond to these ideographs are recognizable as standing apart from the culture. For example, "equality" as an ideograph provides a vocabulary that, if understood, identifies members of American culture. Soviet citizens, who might not understand the concept or respond to it with the same understanding as Americans, would stand outside the American culture.

Second, ideographs are abstract terms that reify, or make concrete and visible, concepts and ideas that in themselves are not concrete or visible. Imagine, for example, how you would define the ideograph, "freedom." You cannot point to something in the real world that is "freedom." "Freedom" is not a thing or a process but a concept. You might give examples of freedom, but any particular example would be an incomplete representation of the concept. Yet "freedom" is something that most, if not all, Americans purport to understand and value. "Freedom" may provide the grounds for committing actions that risk death as people fight to defend "freedom." The term, thus, represents a complex of beliefs and values. We treat the term as if it had a concrete referent when, in fact its referent is a set of abstract concepts and potentially concrete and emotion-laden actions.

Third, ideographs command a sort of allegiance that renders them impervious to logical investigation. Just as it is difficult to argue about whether or not $2+2=4$ because the rules of arithmetic demand that we take the equation for granted, so it is difficult to argue about the value of "freedom" because the rules of our culture demand that we take the concept for granted. McGee recounted an example from the time of the Vietnam War. He noted that a vocabulary of ideographs extolling patriotism made a majority of Americans view as sensible the willingness of tens of thousands of young men "to go halfway around the world to kill for God, country, apple pie, and no other particularly good reason."[17] At the same time, those who objected to U.S. involvement in Vietnam and chose to flee to Canada were labeled as unpatriotic and cowardly because the ideographs were not a subject of inspection. Thus, when terms are used as ideographs, those terms take on a level of social commitment that allow them to dominate the consciousness of citizens.

The analyst of public discourse, then, may uncover the ideologies at work within public argument by identifying those ultimate terms that represent a complex of cultural beliefs, values, and myths. Those terms that function as ideographs will provide a symbolic means for members of a culture to identify with one another and furnish the symbolic reason for condemning those who appear to reject the culture. In addition, these ideographs will seldom be called into question as the subject for argumentation and debate.

On some occasions, and in some forums, ideology does act as the topic for argument. Individuals may sometimes discuss what it means "to be patriotic" or what constitutes "freedom" or "justice." However, such discussions are generally confined to the academy, while discussion in the public sphere comes no closer than arguing about whether a particular action is or is not patriotic or what constitutes "justice" in a particular case. In the ancient world, Plato suggested that philosophical argument, a systematic method of question-and-answer he called "dialectic," was the means for determining the validity of those beliefs that are generally taken for granted.[18] In *The Republic*, for example, Plato used arguments by his main character, Socrates, to question the assumption that women should not be allowed to engage in combat for the Greek City States. Socrates, following an elaborate set of questions and answers, finally gained the assent of his partners in conversation that the typical belief about women being unfit for combat was incorrect. The possibility for such argument in the public sphere is more limited. However, such possibility will be explored at greater length in the following chapter. At present, what is important is to recognize and identify the ideological bases for public argument.

Propaganda

In some ways, a discussion of propaganda within a chapter that began with a discussion of implicit advocacy and proceeded with an explanation of ideology may seem out of place. Historically, propaganda has constituted the most explicit form of persuasion. However, as will soon be clear, propaganda in contemporary society often appears as subtle, authorless, implicit advocacy. Before detailing the characteristics of contemporary propaganda, it is helpful to review the standard treatment of this subject.

Traditionally, propaganda has been identified as a quite explicit form of advocacy, often produced within a particular social institution in order to manipulate the ideas and actions of the masses. In their review of the history of propaganda, Jowett and O'Donnell point out that "propaganda, in the most neutral sense, means to disseminate or promote particular ideas. The word is derived from the Latin— 'congregation de propaganda fide'—meaning congregation for propagating the faith of the Roman Catholic Church."[19] As they explain, in 1622, Pope Gregory XV established the Congregation for the Propagation of the Faith, whose mission was to revive and strengthen the Church in Europe and carry out missionary work in the New World. Based on the educational and missionary work of the Jesuits and assisted by Pope Urban VII's founding of a seminary to train propagandists, workers in the Catholic Church set about to bring others to a voluntary acceptance of Church doctrine.

Important to the Catholic Church's initial use of propaganda was the idea that their mission was securing adherence to doctrine. Doctrine, as a body of principles that constitute a particular world view in addition to providing guidelines for behavior, shares many of the characteristics of ideology. Thus, the earliest propaganda was aimed toward spreading an ideology. Later uses of propaganda have similarly aimed toward securing adherence to a particular view of the world that will influence the actual behavior of those who keep the faith. Consequently, a defining characteristic of propaganda that persists to the present is its relationship to ideology, or doctrine.

Through the centuries, propaganda has been institutionalized in many locations other than the Catholic Church. Perhaps most famous was Adolph Hitler's establishment of the Ministry of Propaganda during the Third Reich. Hitler had described a collection of rules for successful propaganda in his book, *Mein Kampf.* He explained that appeals to the emotions should be used rather than discussion of abstract ideas, that a few ideas should be constantly repeated, that objectivity should be avoided in favor of presenting only one side of the argument, and that one special enemy should be chosen as the object of consistent vilification. Goebbels, as Hitler's Minister of Propaganda, followed these rules as he orchestrated a barrage of messages in the form of radio broadcasts, printed fliers, posters, films, and spectacles that featured Hitler presenting stirring orations under gigantic banners that displayed the Nazi swastika to massive audiences. The messages centered on the vilification of Germany's alleged enemies, primarily the Jewish race, and exaltation of Aryan superiority. Hitler's rules of propaganda may be characterized as formula for unethical advocacy as described in the previous chapter. Not surprisingly, a second typical characteristic associated with propaganda that persists to the present is the use of unethical, deceptive means of advocacy.

The study of propaganda, then, has typically been located somewhere on the continuum between relatively neutral descriptions of propaganda as persuasion that aims toward influencing the world view of an audience and pejorative descriptions of propaganda as the use of unethical means for securing adherence to a world view. Common to both perspectives is the idea that propaganda is produced intentionally and operates explicitly. The intentional and explicit production of messages described as propagandistic is worthy of further exploration.

Historical studies of propaganda have frequently focused on the use of propaganda during wartime.[20] Less famous, but probably equal in importance to Nazi propaganda, is the use of propaganda by many other governments, including the United States government. Although scholars have described the documents and other symbolic activities surrounding the American and French Revolutions as techniques of propaganda, clearer cases are furnished by the open and explicit efforts of various governments during World War I and World War II. Until very recently, energetic study of propaganda was dominated by these two time periods.

During World War I, the Committee on Public Information (CPI), headed by George Creel, a journalist, was established to "sell the war to America." According to Creel's later exposé of the operation of this committee, *How We Advertised America: The First Telling of the Amazing Story of the Committee on Public Information*, CPI attempted to use all available means of communication to mobilize public opinion behind the war effort.[21] Speakers' bureaus were established in many localities making available volunteer speakers, known as "The Four Minute Men," who would lecture about the war. Pamphlets that detailed atrocities by the German "huns" were distributed. Posters promoting America and freedom and attacking the enemy were printed and distributed. In addition, Creel and his compatriots worked with filmmakers in Hollywood, encouraging them to make movies with patriotic content and offering military expertise and props to enhance the likelihood that studios would produce propagandistic films. Finally, CPI was allowed to disseminate information concerning the war to the press, both in the United States and abroad. Bordering on censorship, the CPI's activities in relation to the press approximated a policy of managed news.

Following World War I, revelations about the activities of CPI, such as the lack of evidence for many of the stories regarding German atrocities, combined with the sadness that accompanied the many American casualties during the war and the peace settlement that was unsatisfying to many provoked a high degree of interest in propaganda and skepticism of such organized attempts at persuasion. The interest and skepticism was heightened by news of Lenin's new propaganda campaign following the Russian Revolution and Hitler's rise to power in Germany. Among the most notable attempts to deal with what was perceived as the growing problem of propaganda was the formation at Columbia University of the Institute for Propaganda Analysis in 1936-37. In addition to helping Americans cope with political and war propaganda, the Institute also identified the growth of commercial advertising as a new form of propaganda. In the second issue of the Institute's bulletin, their collection of social scientists produced a list of seven propaganda devices that later appeared in their 1939 publication, *The Fine Art of Propaganda* as "the ABCs of Propaganda Analysis."[22] The seven devices they identified were:

1. *Name Calling:* gives an idea a bad label, and therefore rejects and condemns it without examining the evidence.
2. *Glittering Generality:* associates something with a "virtue word" and creating acceptance and approval without examination of the evidence.
3. *Transfer:* carries the respect and authority of something respected to something else to make the latter accepted. Also works with something that is disrespected to make the latter rejected.
4. *Testimonial:* consists in having some respected or hated person say that a given idea or program or product or person is good or bad.
5. *Plain Folks:* the method by which a speaker attempts to convince the audience that he and his ideas are good because they are "of the people," the "plain folks."
6. *Card Stacking:* involves the selection and use of facts or falsehoods, illustrations or distractions, and logical or illogical statements in order to give the best or the worst possible case for an idea, program, person, or product.
7. *Band Wagon:* has as its theme "everybody — at least all of us — is doing it," and thereby tries to convince the members of a group that their peers are accepting the program, and that we should all jump on the band wagon rather than be left out.

Many of these devices, of course, resemble the logical fallacies that operate as natural lines of objection to arguments as discussed in Chapter 6. However, they provide a concrete illustration of the recognition by the Institute that too often propaganda used distorted, unreasonable means of advocacy.

Just as important and certainly more tragic than the growth of techniques for analyzing propaganda was a second result of the use of propaganda during and after World War I. Assaulted by propagandistic messages that were later revealed as misleading, the American public grew skeptical of messages that vilified an enemy and recounted the atrocities that he had supposedly perpetrated on helpless victims. At least one scholar has suggested that part of the reason that so little was done so late in coming to the aid of European Jews who were the target of

Hitler's Nazi genocide was the skepticism of the masses to believe the stories.[23] Interestingly, Americans had little difficulty subscribing to efforts by government during World War II to portray the Japanese as "yellow hordes" who were capable of the most despicable crimes, but were reluctant for some time to share similar images of the German soldiers. Today, such stereotypical and negative images of Japanese or German citizens seems absurd. Yet many Americans probably have little difficulty imagining Arabs as fanatical terrorists, testimony to the power of symbolic messages to shape our perceptions of the world.

Despite skepticism on the part of audiences, American involvement in World War II following the Japanese attack on Pearl Harbor had the effect of curtailing investigation of propaganda at the same time that various government agencies began to mobilize efforts to conduct such campaigns to insure domestic support for the war effort. The Institute for Propaganda Analysis announced that it would suspend its activities for the duration of the war crisis. At the conclusion of World War II, research regarding the process, techniques, and effects of persuasion and advertising continued, but studies of propaganda, specifically, waned.

In contrast to standard treatments of propaganda that emphasize its intentional and explicit uses, contemporary theorists, particularly in Europe, have suggested that propaganda in contemporary society frequently operates implicitly. Jacques Ellul, a French social theorist, has suggested that while previous studies concentrated on "agitative" propaganda, explicitly propagandistic messages designed to lead people to resentment, rebellion, and even war, a second type of propaganda, "integrative" propaganda has received less attention. Generally operating at a more implicit level, "integrative" propaganda functions so as to make people more docile, less questioning, and more likely to adjust themselves to desired patterns.[24]

According to Ellul, integrative propaganda works by depending on a "prepropaganda" stage, during which people are conditioned by, and socialized into, a particular world view, or ideology. He identifies education as the primary means by which such conditioning is accomplished. It is through education, formal or informal, that citizens became acquainted with cultural ideals, myths, and the body of "facts" that explain and assist in interpreting the world. The propagandists then extend, use, and modify the ideological tenets already subscribed to by a populace to squelch expression of individual, diverse points of view, thereby keeping the masses quiet and essentially controlled. Thus, from Ellul's perspective, propaganda serves the interests of established parties, states, and commercial entities by literally commanding the participation of the masses in actions that the masses think make common sense while insulating the masses from any real reflection on the validity, consistency, or worth of that supposed common sense. Ellul's argument will be discussed in greater detail in the last chapter of this book, but for now, it is sufficient to note that he points directly toward the implicit functions of propaganda in contemporary society. In other words, propaganda often operates subtly, outside or beyond our conscious awareness, because of its relationship to ideology, to what seems to be common sense.

As the foregoing review suggests, definitions of propaganda are often slippery, changing according to the practices and functions that accompany a particular time period. However, some general characterizations of propaganda can be made. Fundamentally, *propaganda is the presentation of an ideological message, a one-dimensional world view.* Whether such presentation is designed explicitly to propagate a particular doctrine or operates implicitly to reinforce a dominant ideology, propaganda insulates itself from critique. Frequently, explicit uses of propaganda to bolster a war effort or establish a new political system have relied on unethical techniques of advocacy in order to conceal the weaknesses and inconsistencies of the message, thereby minimizing the possibility of opposing points of view. Implicit uses of propaganda in the form of education or entertainment similarly resist analysis, but not so much because unethical means of advocacy are used as because the audience operates under the illusion that these messages are not persuasive, but informative or entertaining reviews of the facts, of common sense. This characterization of propaganda holds several implications for analyzing public discourse.

First, analysts should not limit their object of analysis to instances of explicit advocacy. Any message for public consumption, from textbooks to movies, may function implicitly to state or restate an ideology. Therefore, secondly, any public message may be examined to uncover the world view that it reflects. Such examination should concentrate on uncovering the ideographs that signal the presence of cultural values and myths. Third, the world view manifested by those messages should be subjected to scrutiny. What are the opposing points of view that the message omits or eludes as it conceals from the audience its persuasive power?

Summary

The very nature of symbols—their relationship to meaning and context and their ability to present reality as surely as they represent reality—suggests that any message may function persuasively, even if that was not the intention of the source. Because any message may influence an audience's view of the world, analysis of implicit rhetoric is important to the analysis of public controversy. Burke's pentad provides one way to uncover the world view manifested by messages that do not openly claim to be persuasive. In uncovering the world view of such messages, an analyst should pay particular attention to the cultural values and myths that are promoted by the ideology that grounds the message. Ideology is the coherent world view that is accepted as common sense within a culture. Ideographs are the one-term sums of that common sense. Ideographs are inherent to cultures and reify abstract concepts while providing powerful guides for interpreting experience.

Ideographs and the ideologies they represent are resistant to analysis and critique. Propaganda, the presentation of messages that foster one-dimensional world views, tends to promote or use ideology. Although much propaganda has been explicit and has often depended on unethical means of advocacy, contemporary propaganda tends to operate implicitly, reinforcing and using ideologies that promote existing social structures.

Notes

[1] Elizabeth F. Loftus, *Eyewitness Testimony* (New Haven: Harvard University Press, 1980).

[2] Vance Packard, *The Hidden Persuaders* (New York: Pocket Books, 1957). See also, Gary C. Woodward and Robert E. Denton, Jr., *Persuasion and Social Influence in American Life* (Prospect Heights: Waveland, 1988), pp. 204-11.

[3] C.K. Ogden and I.A. Richards, *The Meaning of Meaning,* 8th ed. (New York: Harcourt, Brace, 1946), especially Chapter 2.

[4] I.A. Richards, *The Philosophy of Rhetoric* (London: Oxford University Press, 1936), pp. 31-43.

[5] S.I. Hayakawa, *Language, Thought, and Action,* 3rd ed. (New York: Harcourt Brace Jovanovich, 1972), p. 58.

[6] Richard Weaver, *Language is Sermonic,* eds. Richard L. Johannesen, Rennard Strickland, and Ralph T. Eubanks (Baton Rouge: Louisiana State University Press, 1970), especially pp. 201-225.

[7] Kenneth Burke, *A Rhetoric of Motives* (Berkeley: University of California Press, 1969), p. 55.

[8] Kenneth Burke, *A Grammar of Motives* (Berkeley: University of California Press, 1969), especially pp. xv-xxiii.

[9] Burke, *Grammar* especially pp. 3-20.

[10] David Ling, "A Pentadic Analysis of Senator Edward Kennedy's Address to the People of massachusetts, July 25, 1969," *Central States Speech Journal* 21 (1970): 81-86.

[11] V. William Balthrop, "Culture, Myth, and Ideology as Public Argument: An Interpretation of the Ascent and Demise of 'Southern Culture,'" *Communication Monographs* 51 (1984): 340.

[12] Michael Calvin McGee, "The 'Ideograph': A Link Between Rhetoric and Ideology," *Quarterly Journal of Speech* 66 (1980): 1-16.

[13] Weaver, *Language,* pp. 88-99.

[14] Burke, *Rhetoric,* pp. 188-190.

[15] McGee, 6-7.

[16] Balthrop, 344.

[17] McGee, 6.

[18] Plato, *The Republic,* trans. Desmond Lee, 2nd ed. (New York: Penguin, 1987).

[19] Garth S. Jowett and Victoria O'Donnell, *Propaganda and Persuasion* (Beverly Hills: Sage, 1986), p. 15.

[20] See, for example, Jowett and O'Donnell, pp. 38-62 and 118-152.

[21] George Creel, *How We Advertised America: The First Telling of the Amazing Story of the Committee on Public Information* (New York: Harper and Row, 1920).

[22] Reported in Jowett and O'Donnell, p. 136.

[23] Jowett and O'Donnell, p. 137.

[24] Jacques Ellul, *Propaganda: The Formation of Men's Attitudes,* trans. Konrad Kellen and Jean Lerner (New York: Vintage, 1973), pp. 70-84.

Suggested Readings

Balthrop, V. William, 1984. "Culture, Myth, and Ideology as Public Argument: An Interpretation of the Ascent and Demise of 'Southern Culture.'" *Communication Monographs,* 51:339-352.

Burke, Kenneth, 1969. *A Rhetoric of Motives.* Berkeley: University of California Press.

Doob, L.W., 1948. *Public Opinion and Propaganda.* New York: Holt.

Ellul, Jacques, 1973. *Propaganda: The Formation of Men's Attitudes.* Trans. Konrad Kellen and Jean Lerner. New York: Vintage.

Jowett, Garth S. and Victoria O'Donnell, 1986. *Propaganda and Persuasion.* Beverly Hills: Sage.

Lasswell, H.D., D. Lerner, and H. Speier, Eds., 1980. *Propaganda and Communication in World History,* Vols. 1-3. Honolulu: University of Hawaii Press.

McGee, Michael Calvin, 1980. "The 'Ideograph': A Link Between Rhetoric and Ideology." *Quarterly Journal of Speech,* 66:1-16.

Plato, 1987. *The Republic.* Trans. Desmond Lee. 2nd Ed. New York: Penguin.

Richards, E.A., 1936. *The Philosophy of Rhetoric.* London: Oxford University Press.

Sproule, J. Michael, 1983. "The Institute for Propaganda Analysis: Public Education in Argumentation, 1937-1942." *Argument in Transition.* Eds. David Zarefsky, Malcolm O. Sillars, and Jack Rhodes. Annandale, Virginia: SCA.

Weaver, Richard, 1970. *Language is Sermonic.* Eds. Richard L. Johannesen, Rennard Strickland, and Ralph T. Eubanks. Baton Rouge: Louisiana State University Press.

Chapter 9

Free Speech and Discussion of Public Issues

What, if anything, saves a society from oppression through propaganda techniques, from the perpetuation of misguided ideologies? The answer lies in a concept familiar to the Age of Enlightenment. Thinkers such as John Locke, Jean Jacques Rousseau, and Thomas Jefferson believed that democracy could best be insured by maintenance of a free marketplace of ideas. A similar conception, of course, has grounded the entire discussion thus far in this book. Without the possibility of free discussion, there is no possibility for the resolution of controversy through the means of communication.

Partly as a result of becoming a nation state during the Eighteenth Century, the United States has long held a unique faith in the possibilities of free and open discussion. Despite the fact that the U.S. Constitution itself was written in secret session, the Founding Fathers manifested the belief that freedom of inquiry was not only an inherent human right but basic to the advancement of knowledge and the discovery of truth. The American political philosophy of popular sovereignty and democratic rule, even if it is representative democracy, required involvement by the many as opposed to the few. Such involvement necessarily entails the potential for discussion and resolution of controversy by the many as opposed to the few.

The durability of that enlightened idea of free and open discussion is illustrated by a variety of contemporary developments. The American fascination with, and endorsement of, the new policy of Glasnost, initiated in the Soviet Union by Mikhail Gorbachev, testifies to our continuing appreciation for open and free debate. Similarly, governmental restrictions on the freedom of press throughout the world, from South Africa to Nicaragua, unite conservatives and liberals alike in this country in protest against the oppressors. In short, our continuing commitment to an ideal of free expression explains why we often take for granted our right to say what we like and to critique what others say.

The justification for such commitment has already been suggested. By maintaining an atmosphere of free and open discussion we assume that the discovery of truth will be easier, that eventual decisions about public matters will be better, that the political system will be forced to respond to the will of the people, that government by the many will flourish. More specifically, free and open discussion seems to insure that ideologies will be exposed, that propaganda may be resisted, and that by resolving controversial matters *in* public the public's interests will be served.

This chapter will explore the nature of free and open discussion in our society. The exploration begins with a careful analysis of the guarantee of our right to free expression. Following a discussion of the First Amendment and the grounds for its limitations is a brief review of various ways in which the government generally encourages public discussion of public issues. Because a free flow of information is a prerequisite for free discussion, the next section of the chapter concerns the available means for securing information within our society. The chapter ends on a note of circumspection. By reviewing the limitations as well as the opportunities for public discussion, the dangers of silence can be compared to the possibilities of an ideal speech situation, the possibilities for empowerment.

The First Amendment and the
Freedom to Engage in Controversy

The First Amendment to the United States Constitution guarantees the right of people, individually or collectively, to engage in discussion of controversial issues. The Amendment reads: "Congress shall make no law . . . abridging the freedom of speech, or of the press; or the right of the people peaceably to assemble and to petition the Government for a redress of grievances."[1] One of the most detailed explanations and comprehensive treatments of the meaning and application of this amendment for the purposes of public discussion is provided by Franklyn Haiman, a professor at Northwestern University.[2] The discussion here will rely on Haiman's work.

To understand the meaning of the First Amendment, it is helpful to analyze the words of the amendment systematically. As Haiman has pointed out, "Congress," the agent in the amendment, typically refers to all government. Consequently, the amendment is presumed to insure that not only will Congress not abridge these rights, but neither will any other branch of government at any level—federal, state, or local. By specifying both "freedom of speech" and a free "press," the amendment issues a sort of double guarantee. "Speech" is generally recognized as referring to oral statements made by individuals, while "press" is typically assumed to refer to written statements made by institutions—newspapers, magazines, and other publishers. The existence of contemporary communication technologies have blurred these distinctions some. With the assistance of personal computers, for example, individuals may now play the role of "desktop publishers." Similarly, broadcast journalists operate in a mode closer to classic oral communication than written communication. However, the inclusion of both speech and press provides a double guarantee that seems to cover even contemporary communication practices. The "right of assembly" appears to recognize that collectives, or communities of communicators, are just as important as individuals, and as a result adds the guarantee of a protected forum, where people may talk or write together, as a group.

Like the rest of the Constitution and Bill of Rights, the guarantees of the First Amendment have been subject to continuing interpretation during the course of U.S. history. Although the spirit of the amendment assumes unrestricted discussion by individuals, alone or in assemblies, and by the press, the language of the amendment specifies that no law will be made that abridges such discussion. As a consequence, interpretation of the amendment occurs when laws, or public ordinances, are made that appear to some as potentially restrictive, or abridging, of free speech, press, or assembly. In other words, the meaning of the amendment is reexamined whenever a governmental body adopts a law that seems to violate the amendment and a concerned citizen questions the validity of that law by petitioning to the judiciary for an evaluation of whether or not the amendment has been violated. This has happened on numerous occasions. Although recounting all the cases of First Amendment questions is a project larger than this chapter, an understanding of the types of restrictions that have been questioned and the types of issues that influence judicial interpretation of the amendment is in order.

Whenever a question of interpretation arises, what must be determined is whether or not the particular instance of speech, press, or assembly falls under the protection of the First Amendment. If so, and if the law in question does restrict speech, press, or assembly in that instance, then the law is struck down as unconstitutional. As a result of the court's explanation, another instance of what may be defined as free speech and another instance of what may be defined as a restriction of that freedom is added to the list from previous cases. Because interpretation proceeds on this case by case basis, there is no general policy or law that identifies what restrictions are constitutional or what specific types of communication are protected.

There are various types of restrictions that governmental authorities have attempted to place on free speech, press, and assembly. The most obvious type of restriction, simply outlawing public speech by individuals or groups or journalists, is apparently at odds with the amendment and consequently not a typical restriction. Instead, government officials have been more inclined to enact legislation designed to control, or manage, the discussion that occurs. By requiring communicators to fulfill some prior condition in order to engage in discussion, officials have frequently tried to manage the discussion and sometimes violated the amendment. Three typical sorts of laws are ones that require fees, advance notice, or liability insurance for a person or persons to engage in communication. For example, some communities have required that persons wishing to speak in public places pay a fee to use the public facilities. During the 1960s, when many public streets and parks became the scene for mass demonstrations and rallies for a variety of social causes, a number of communities passed ordinances that required advance notice. In other words, prospective participants were asked to file notice of their assemblies with local officials. Similarly, some governmental units have required members of the press to provide advance notice of what stories they plan to publish and, especially in times of war, have even required the press to seek prior approval from government officials for their reports. Especially when communities were concerned that public discussion or assembly might result in damage to public property or private property within their jurisdiction, requirements for liability insurance have been enacted. In most of these instances, a question regarding violation of the First Amendment has been raised.

Restrictive legislation is typically justified by governmental authorities along one or more of four possible lines. Restrictions on free discussion cluster around questions of (1) who communicates (2) about what (3) by what means (4) to what effect. These four elements are characteristic as well of the judiciary's explanations of how a case is resolved and how the amendment should be interpreted. By reviewing each element, the dynamics of the interpretation of the amendment become clearer.

Questions about *who may communicate* are most common when the person or group that attempts to exercise their right to free discussion is a religious group or a discriminatory group. Because the First Amendment also includes the clause regarding separation of church and state, some restrictions have been enacted and upheld in relation to religious groups. For example, managers of some public buildings, like public schools or public libraries, have argued that religious groups may not use these facilities for assemblies and discussions. Similarly, some localities have attempted to prohibit public demonstrations and rallies by groups who are discriminatory and will not allow other citizens to attend their assemblies. For example, in 1977 the village of Skokie, Illinois attempted to prohibit a rally by the American Nazi Party partly on the grounds that the Party would not allow Jews or Blacks to attend. In both cases, the judicial issue concerns whether or not the exercise of First Amendment rights conflicts with other protections, such as separation of church and state or freedom from discrimination.

Other restrictions are often justified because of *what the communicators talk or write about*. Controversies regarding obscenity and pornography are typical of this type. For example, communities may prohibit "obscene material" from being sold in local stores, or the federal government may restrict the use of the postal system for distribution of obscenity. Similarly, radio or television stations may be subject to losing their operating licenses if broadcasters use "obscene language" or air "obscene programs." In addition to communication about obscenity, communication about matters of "national security" is often the target of restrictions, particularly during a state of declared war. In 1971, for example, the Nixon administration tried to halt publication of news stories about U.S. involvement in Vietnam because the stories included material that was classified as "top secret-sensitive" and later known as the "Pentagon Papers." A similar case occurred when, in 1979, the government attempted to halt publication of an issue of *The Progressive* magazine. *The Progressive* published an article concerning the making of a hydrogen bomb that included material the government had deemed vital to "national security." In the cases of obscenity and national security, the court was faced with determining whether or not exercise of free discussion in these cases conflicted with other case law in which concerns about local standards for acceptable messages or concerns about national security had been paramount.

A third element, the *means by which the message is communicated*, is also frequently used as the justification for restrictions and thereby becomes a subject for judicial interpretation and resolution. Because communication may take many forms, include both verbal and nonverbal actions, and use a variety of tactics, the means of communication sometimes become the object of restrictions. A prime example of such an emphasis concerns the act of heckling. Hecklers, by interrupting and otherwise taunting a public speaker, seem to interfere with the exercise of free speech. But when legislation designed to prohibit or inhibit heckling is enacted, a primary concern is whether or not the right to free speech of the heckler has been abridged. Similar questions have been raised concerning the display of signs and the use of nonviolent resistance techniques. For example, students at my university argued that their right to free speech and assembly had been violated when they were arrested for blocking a state highway (and main drag through town). Their argument was that they were exercising their First Amendment rights as they sat, sometimes quietly and sometimes chanting opposition to proposed tuition increases, on the road.

The *potential effect of engaging in public discussion* is also a source of objection that leads to restrictions and requires consideration by the judiciary. The concern for effects becomes most apparent in those cases where the effect of the exercise of free speech seems antithetical, or opposite, of the intent of the amendment. For example, part of the arguments offered by the village of Skokie, when village officials attempted to inhibit the assembly of Nazis in their community, centered on the intended effect of the Nazi message. Community leaders pointed out that the message of the Nazis was aimed toward denying Constitutional rights to nonwhite peoples, particularly Jews. The argument was particularly salient in Skokie, a village where many citizens belonged to the Jewish religion and a number of survivors of the Holocaust resided. They argued that one of the intended effects of the Nazi's message was to remove the freedom of speech and assembly for a number of citizens in the village, to deny first amendment rights. In addition, and probably more important later in the dispute, officials argued that other effects, not necessarily related to Constitutional rights, might ensue from the Nazi march. They argued that the demonstration posed a "clear and present danger" to the citizens of Skokie because the clash of values that would probably result from the interaction between residents and marchers would likely be followed by violence. Their "clear and present danger" argument mirrored the standard explanation for when restrictions on free speech have been allowed, namely when the lack of restrictions would violate other, often more basic, rights. The classic example is contained in the explanation that people have freedom of speech, but not the freedom to yell "Fire" in a crowded theatre.

The instances cited as examples in the last few paragraphs all raised questions concerning the validity of government actions or ordinances that attempted to restrict freedom of speech, press, and assembly. In many cases, once the issue is raised, government restrictions are withdrawn. However, in other cases, the question has proceeded to courtrooms where judges have ruled. Most cases that have reached the Supreme Court have resulted in confirmation of a broad interpretation of the First Amendment. In other words, in general, restrictions are not tolerated. However, from time to time, restrictions are upheld.

Official and Legislative Encouragement of Public Discussion

In addition to guaranteeing that restrictions of public discussion will not be allowed except under extraordinary circumstances, a number of legislative actions and court cases relevant to the First Amendment have actually encouraged public discussion. These legislative acts and court decisions serve an enabling function as they help provide means by which citizens are enabled to engage in public discussion. Such acts and decisions may be classified into two categories: those that help provide a place, or *forum*, in which public issues may be discussed and those that enable discussion by assuring citizens *access* to the information needed to engage in discussions of the public interest.

The establishment of places in which to engage in public discussions has a long history. Haiman pointed out that all public places and buildings are generally assumed to serve a function as a "public forum." Thus, whenever a public park, street, auditorium, library, school, or other building is erected, citizens may assume that their right to free speech may be exercised in that place. Haiman explained that the language used by former Justice Owen Roberts in a 1939 Supreme Court Decision expressed the principle that "was reiterated by later majorities and has come to be accepted as the prevailing precedent in this field."[3] Roberts expressed the principle as follows:

> Wherever the title of streets and parks may rest, they have immemorially been held in trust for the use of the public and, time out of mind, have been used for purposes of assembly, communicating thoughts between citizens and discussing public questions. . . . The privilege of a citizen of the U.S. to use

the streets and parks for the communication of views on national questions may be regulated in the interest of all; it is not absolute, but relative, and must be exercised in subordination to the general comfort and convenience, and in consonance with peace and good order; but it must not, in the guise of regulation, be abridged or denied.

Not only are public forums for oral communication established, but the U.S. government has also established means to encourage written and mediated communication. Among the arguments for establishment of the U.S. postal system was the idea that such a system would encourage citizen participation in discussion of public issues. Haiman explained that: "A postal system was recognized by our Founding Fathers as vitally important to the functioning of a free society and became a part of the initial framework of government which they established. Lower rates, in the form of second- and third-class mailing privileges, have even been built into the system to ease the financial burden on those who distribute newspapers, magazines, books, and solicitations for the support of nonprofit causes."[4]

While various forms of written communication have been assumed to be available to all citizens, the advent of technological innovations such as radio and television posed a different sort of problem for a government that wanted to encourage public discussion. Although the public forum of the airwaves was assumed to belong to anyone and everyone, the capital expenditures required to set up a broadcasting station and the capabilities of the airwaves to handle only a limited number of broadcasting stations within a given geographic area threatened to inhibit the likelihood that the new communication technologies would be used in the public interest. Therefore policies were implemented to ensure that those media would program in the public interest and allow for public access. The 1924 Radio Broadcasting Act and rules that followed were designed to do exactly that. Contemporary media scholars have pointed out that, "Regulations promulgated subsequent to the act such as the equal time provision, the requirement for broadcaster ascertainment of community needs, ceilings on the frequency of advertisements, and minimal requirements for news and public affair programming, are responses to this public interest, an interest which can be summarized in one word—fairness."[5]

The Federal Communications Commission (FCC) was established by the Communications Act of 1934 to distribute licenses to broadcasters and to supervise broadcasting operations in a way that would insure that they operated in the public interest. When television broadcasting began in the 1930s and 1940s, the FCC assumed responsibility for that activity as well. In 1941, when the FCC authorized the start of television broadcasting, most of the rules that had been earlier applied to radio broadcasting were similarly applied to television.

Among the various regulations and rules of the FCC, probably the most important for public controversy was the recently repealed Fairness Doctrine. The Fairness

Doctrine provided a legal answer or compromise to the question of how to reconcile the First Amendment's guarantee to broadcasters and the government dictate that broadcasters serve the public interest. The doctrine explained that broadcasters had an "affirmative duty" to seek out controversial issues and provide programming that dealt with those issues. Not only did broadcasters need to air controversial issues of public importance, but they also had to provide reasonable opportunity for contrasting or opposing points of view. Because the public's right to hear was described as more important than the broadcaster's right to make money by offering programs that were profitable, but not necessarily in the public interest, broadcasters were required to make time available for opposing views even if no commercial sponsor could be found for such programming. For years, editorial comments and requests for opposing points of view, public service announcements, and general news and public affairs programming were the obvious responses to the demands of the Fairness Doctrine. If stations did not abide by this doctrine, as well as other regulations designed to protect the public interest, they could lose their licenses when the FCC performed regular evaluations and renewal of licensing procedures.

The Fairness Doctrine was repealed in 1988 amid some controversy. However, as advocates of its repeal argued, other changes in mediated communication had obviated the need for official government legislation that ensured a mediated public forum. The likelihood of commercial broadcasters abandoning programming that deals with public issues seems small as many such programs attract large audiences. Daytime programs like "The Phil Donahue Show" and "The Oprah Winfrey Show" are quite profitable, and the nightly news programs that have been expanded from fifteen minutes to thirty minutes during the development of television attract many viewers. Special public issue programs like CBS' "Sixty Minutes," ABC's "Nightline," and NBC's special documentary reports will probably continue as staples of commercial television. In addition, several profitable and publicly-minded innovations have occurred. C-Span, the cable network that broadcasts live political events and other public happenings unedited, and the Cable News Network (CNN) that provides all news programming both have a large and devoted audience. C-Span, in particular, regularly incorporates a call-in feature with its programming that encourages viewers to ask questions or air their views. However, even if public issue programming is not now endangered, it is reasonable to consider whether or not there exist any safeguards should public issue programming and public access become less profitable and less attractive in the future.

The Public Broadcasting Act of 1967 was designed to insure the continuing existence of a mediated public forum. The act established the Corporation for Public Broadcasting, which was mandated to develop educational and public issue programs and a system of distribution that would encourage local public access. Supported by a minimal amount of public funds, the Public Broadcasting System (PBS) has relied on private contributions from individuals and corporations alike. PBS provides a wealth of programming in the public interest, including the popular

"MacNeil/Lehrer News Hour" that has furnished several examples noted earlier in this book. In addition, PBS stations and local public access stations afford ordinary citizens an opportunity to produce their own shows and air their own opinions. Such opportunities are not limitless, however, as such productions require funding that is often beyond the means of local stations to provide. However, independent filmmakers with a particularly "good idea" and the assistance of charitable foundations or their own resources do find a forum with such stations. Many of the documentaries concerning public issues that find their way onto the "Frontline" series of PBS are the products of such efforts.

From places to speak, to places through which to distribute printed messages, to places to broadcast ideas, then, there is official encouragement of public discussion. However, in order to participate in such public discussion, at least a modicum of information is necessary. If information about public problems is kept secret or if policies are made behind closed doors, the right to free expression loses its meaning. Therefore, investigation of the availability and accessibility to the information needed to engage in discussion is in order. Again, there is a fair amount of official encouragement of public discussion.

Like the availability of forums for discussion, the availability of the means by which discussion could occur was a concern of the Founding Fathers. In part, they viewed the existence of a free press as an insurance policy for the free flow of information. In anticipation of the inclusion of a right to free press in the Constitution, Thomas Jefferson wrote that "the people are the only censors of their governors," and therefore it was necessary that the people be provided "full information of their affairs through the channel of public papers."[6]

But a free press was not the only way that access to information was encouraged. The establishment of both a public education system and a public library system served a similar function. Haiman noted that "the architects of democracy recognized the need for public schools and public libraries which provide the training and resources needed for competent participation in the marketplace of ideas."[7] The first public library of any size was opened in Boston in 1854.[8] Before that time, however, a number of subscription libraries were formed. These libraries allowed members, or subscribers, to use printed material in much the same way as the later public libraries but at some cost. Benjamin Franklin commented on the importance of such libraries to intelligent public discussion in his *Autobiography*: "[Subscription] libraries have improved the general conversation of Americans, made the common tradesmen and farmers as intelligent as most gentlemen from other countries, and perhaps have contributed . . . to the stand so generally made throughout the colonies in defense of their privileges."[9] After public libraries began to replace the subscription libraries, Melvil Dewey, one of the founders of the American Library Association, voiced a comment similar to Franklin's. He wrote: "The school teaches [people] to read; the library must supply them with [information] which will serve to educate."[10] Both the availability of education through the public school system and the availability of information through the public library system thus enable citizens to engage in public discussion and influence public decision making.

In contemporary society, the mushrooming of informative materials available through diverse agencies, both public and private, is staggering. Part of the reason that contemporary society has been dubbed the "information age" is captured by the words of a recent report on the nature of information in society.

> The production and dissemination of information has replaced manufacturing as the principle activity of the U.S. economy. Information-oriented businesses, ranging from publishing and recordkeeping to typing, are said to be growing at an annual rate of around 10 percent, or double the rate of growth for the economy as a whole.[11]

Interestingly, the government is probably the major source for much of this information. The Library of Congress is, of course, the largest and most comprehensive public library in the country. If some bit of information cannot be located elsewhere, it is probably obtainable through the Library of Congress. Among the holdings of the Library of Congress are the volumes of information produced by government agencies and bureaus. One report suggests that even private "companies in the business of supplying information rely to a large extent on the U.S. government and its vast data-producing resources."[12] However, not all information possessed by government has been readily available to the public.

Two recent acts of Congress have facilitated greater openness and accessibility to previously unaccessible information. The first, the Freedom of Information Act, was passed into law in 1966. The second, called the "Government in the Sunshine Act," was signed into law in 1976.

The Freedom of Information Act was in part a reaction to the continuing struggle between some government officials who wished to keep government secrets and the press who wished to expose government secrets. Early in American history, despite the faith of Jefferson and others regarding a free press, government officials found a need to protect national security particularly as it related to foreign policy by withholding some information from the press and the people. In 1798, the Congress passed the Sedition Act that made publication or speech that defamed government a punishable crime. Later, during the Civil War, the federal government and the Union army censored news in an effort to foil the efforts of Confederate spies. During both world wars, government agencies were responsible for overseeing the flow of public information about the war effort and issued regulations concerning what should and should not be published. In 1941, President Roosevelt created the Office of Censorship, an office that performed censorship duties generally and was particularly important in maintaining the secrecy that surrounded development of the atomic and hydrogen bombs. Although government censorship officially ended with the end of World War II, many of the justifications for maintaining the secrecy of some government information were reflected in the Administrative Procedure Act of 1946 that, among other details, indicated how government information could be released to the public.

During the 1950s and early 1960s, many government officials as well as groups like the American Civil Liberties Union and the American Bar Association expressed concern about the vague language of the Administrative Procedures Act that "permitted agencies at their discretion to exempt from [disclosure] material required for good cause to be held confidential."[13] In 1966, the Freedom of Information Act "required agencies to publish procedures and rules in the Federal Register, to make publicly available all final opinions, statements of policy and staff manuals, and to maintain an index of these."[14] In addition, the new act replaced the vague wording for possible exceptions to the 1946 act with nine more specific requirements. Material that was exempted from disclosure was described by the following nine requirements:

1. "Specifically required by executive order to be kept secret in the interest of the national defense or foreign policy.

2. Related "solely" to agencies' internal personnel rules and practices.

3. Specifically exempted from disclosure by statute.

4. Privileged or confidential trade secrets or financial information.

5. Inter- or intra-agency memoranda or letters which would be unavailable by law to a person in litigation with the agency.

6. Personnel and medical files "the disclosure of which would constitute a clearly unwarranted invasion of personal privacy."

7. Investigatory files compiled for law enforcement purposes except to the extent available to private parties.

8. Contained in or related to examination or condition reports of agencies regulating financial institutions.

9. Geological and geophysical information and data, including maps concerning wells.[15]

As the list of exemptions suggests,the new Freedom of Information Act was designed to open almost all government information, except where such disclosure would violate other rights or conflict with existing law regarding confidentiality or the time honored policy of protecting national security. Thus the act represented an advance in openness, but some retention of the idea that some secrets were necessary.

During the early 1970s, proponents of openness and disclosure observed that even the new Freedom of Information Act was not facilitating enough disclosure. There appeared to be bureaucratic delay and sometimes prohibitive expenses when citizens attempted to obtain information under the act, and there seemed to be no way to review an agency's decision to "classify" a particular item of information. As a consequence, Congress passed amendments to the Freedom of Information Act in 1974. Those amendments streamlined the process for requesting information as well as minimizing the financial burden of such requests. In addition, and perhaps most importantly, the amendments altered the wording of the foreign policy and national security exclusion so as to allow judicial review of whether or not the label, "classified," had been properly applied. Since 1975, when the amendments took effect, the number of requests for information has grown substantially from members of the press, members of citizens' action groups, and private individuals. As a consequence, people are more able to raise questions regarding public policies and uncover social problems that would otherwise remain hidden.

A second Congressional act that has facilitated the flow of information is the "Government in the Sunshine Act." While the Freedom of Information Act facilitated access to information generated by government agencies, the Government in the Sunshine Act facilitated access to those government agencies themselves by requiring that "all agencies headed by two or more persons . . . conduct their business regularly in public session."[16] As a result, interested persons may actually attend meetings and obtain information firsthand, rather than waiting for the information to be processed by an agency and then filing for its disclosure through the Freedom of Information Act. Like the FOIA, this "open meetings law," has not always worked to perfection. The public interest group Common Cause, for example, released a study in 1978 that indicated "many government agencies were following neither the letter nor the spirit of the law."[17] Even so, with the legislation in place, court cases remain a means for redress and challenge for those persons wishing to obtain the information available from agency meetings.

In summary, then, the U.S. government has in many ways facilitated public discussion of controversial issues. Public places, whether buildings or parks or airwaves, are protected as places where citizens may find access and a forum for discussion. Accessibility is not totally unlimited and may be restricted from time to time as necessary for the well being of the citizenry, but the assumption is that these places belong to the people rather than to government. Similarly, many public institutions, like the system of public education and public libraries, enable citizens to obtain the information necessary to participate effectively in public discussion. Access to both public forums and public information has been facilitated by a variety of legislative acts, from regulations that insure broadcasters operate in the public interest to laws that require public agencies to disclose their information. Although access to information is not totally unlimited, the assumption is that public information also belongs to the public rather than solely to the government. With these laws and the First Amendment as a basis, the court system provides a continuing means by which to expand the citizenry's ability to engage in public controversy and to hold public officials accountable for maintaining an atmosphere of full and open discussion.

A Final Plea for Public Discussion

This book began with an argument that diverse and isolated people become members of a community by communicating. This chapter began with a description of the typical justification for free and open discussion of controversial issues, a political philosophy of popular sovereignty and a faith in the quality of decisions that emerge from discussion and debate. These claims are both familiar to, and consistent with, the political tradition of the United States. As was suggested in the discussion of ideology contained in Chapter 8, however, it is often helpful to reexamine the set of background beliefs, like those just mentioned, from which a culture operates. Consequently, this last section will provide a justification for engaging in public discussion that emanates from thinkers outside of American culture. The problems and ideals set forth by these thinkers expand and enrich the justification for, and ideal of, free and open discussion.

First, the problem: Why is public discussion so important? An interesting answer to this question has been suggested by the work of Elisabeth Noelle-Neumann. Noelle-Neumann is a Professor of Communication Research in Germany who has studied the connections among philosophy, history, journalism, and American studies for over forty years. From that study, she has developed a theory of public opinion known as *the spiral of silence*.[18]

In its simplest form, the theory of the spiral of silence hypothesizes that when people believe that their opinions represent a minority perspective, they are less likely to express those opinions publicly. As a consequence of their silence, others who hold similar opinions are more likely to perceive their own opinions as out of step with the majority and thus the silence spirals. The theory has been tested extensively by Noelle-Neumann and her colleagues in Germany, but has only recently become an object of study in the United States.

By investigating Noelle-Neumann's understanding of several concepts, her theory of the spiral of silence becomes clearer. Noelle-Neumann defines public opinion somewhat differently than is usual and was the case in the first chapter of this book. Her historical research indicated that prior to the eighteenth century, public opinion was "taken to be pressure to conform."[19] She notes that writers from the Classical world to Rousseau thought of public opinion in a similar way, as "unwritten laws." The pressure to conform, or public opinion, caused rulers to seek the consent of the governed and caused individuals to seek acceptance by the community in which they lived. Hence, public opinion served an integrative function in that expression of public opinion, or expression of opinions in public, was done primarily in order to reinforce the cohesion of the community, to indicate that the individual belonged because he or she shared the perspective common to others in the community.

Noelle-Neumann has pointed out that many contemporary psychological theories and studies support the importance of conformity as a motivating factor. In these quarters, as well as in Noelle-Neumann's work, conformity is explained "as the assumption of most people that what the majority thinks must constitute the best judgments."[20] Studies of conformity (even in the case of the famous Asch experiment where many subjects identified a longer line as the shortest line as a result of the pressure to conform exerted by a number of confederates who all identified the longer line as shorter) have shown that some people are less likely to give into the pressure to conform and in some situations the pressure to conform is weakened. However, Noelle-Neumann points out that in cases where there is no right or wrong answer, in areas of contingent matters such as public controversies that require value judgments, pressure to conform is greatest. She wrote:

> What is at issue is not "correct" or "incorrect" but good or bad. It is the fact that public opinion is morally loaded that makes it so powerful in pressing for conformity. Thus it would not be enough for normal people to find just one or two others of a like mind in order to lose their fear of isolation and their fear of appearing contemptible to others.[21]

This idea, that matters of public controversy because they entail a heightened pressure to conform as a result of their moral implications, provides the basis for her suggestion that what is perceived as the "majority" opinion is important.

Noelle-Neumann explains that individuals use a "quasi-statistical ability" to keep track of what seems to be the majority opinion at any given time. In other words, people keep track of the climate of opinion on particular matters. She also points out that one of the primary ways people keep track of the climate of opinion, because such a climate involves more than the opinions of a few friends or relatives, is through the messages of the mass media. Not just by results of polls or surveys that are aired, but by general news coverage, people get a sense for which problems are important and which are not, which policies are popular and which are not, and so on. Even when issues are covered in ways that show two or more sides to the controversy, her position is that the result will be a greater willingness on the part of individuals to express an opinion about those issues because the majority seems to perceive the issue as important. So, if coverage of an issue identifies a majority and minority point of view, members of the citizenry who identify with the minority perspective may still express their opinions because they see the media coverage of that minority perspective as evidence that they will not become totally isolated by expressing their opinion. However, if the media does not cover the issue at all or provides no coverage of the minority viewpoint, these same individuals will likely remain silent. Furthermore, "[w]hen the media preponderantly take one point of view, which is opposed to the majority view, this changes the process of the spiral of silence and the 'silent majority' emerges."[22]

In tests of the theory in Germany, people were found to be much more willing to express and to talk about their opinions if those opinions were in line with the perceived climate of opinion. Even more interesting, in studies of election results in Germany, Noelle-Neumann found that the actual results of elections, as determined by vote counts, more closely resembled people's assessments of the climate of opinion than people's voter preferences. So impressive were the results of her studies, that in subsequent elections, "the Christian Democrats, who were in a minority position as regards both the population and the media, made it the cores of their strategy to explain the mechanism of the spiral of silence to their followers and to encourage them to fight the spiral of silence."[23]

The implication of Noelle-Neumann's theory for the public discussion of controversial issues seems clear. Silence begets silence. Under the pressure to conform, alternative points of view may not be expressed even with official encouragement of, and Constitutional guarantees against the abridgement of, free and open discussion. As a consequence, citizens themselves must take responsibility for breaking the silence and raising issues even when the climate of opinion appears to be hostile if the benefits of free discussion are to be realized.

Another contemporary European perspective that bears on the benefits of free and open discussion appeared in the work of a French scholar, Michel Foucault. Foucault was interested in the relationship among discourse, knowledge, and power. His description of discursive practice across time and cultures emphasized the various ways in which some people are silenced, or even if allowed to speak are not accorded legitimacy and thereby ignored. In an essay entitled "The Discourse on Language," Foucault summarized the various ways in which societies manage discourse so as to control who speaks about what in what circumstances.[24] Foucault's description centered not so much on formal, governmental restraints on free discussion but, instead, on the informal, unwritten laws that sometimes control discussion.

Unlike many thinkers who conceptualize discourse as a vehicle for transmitting ideas or information, Foucault recognized that the production of discourse always entails the production of ideas and human relationships. When a speaker or writer verbalizes something, that object becomes an idea for consideration, or a thought about which others may make judgments. If an idea is not said, how can people think about it or evaluate it? Because of this inventive function of discourse, according to Foucault discourse becomes the means by which people form human relationships—cooperative, competitive, or otherwise. In terms familiar to this book, when an advocate offers reasons, she is constructing objects for the audience's consideration and, in doing so, initiating a relationship with that audience.

According to Foucault, the ability to construct such objects and human relationships makes discourse a valuable commodity. The right, or potential for producing discourse, becomes a center for power struggles. This idea is consonant with a variety of everyday experiences in the marketplace of public controversy. For example, when opposing advocates fight for the floor in meetings, or when interest groups vie for media coverage of their activities and ideas, it is clear that the right to speak and be heard is a valued commodity.

From Foucault's perspective then, a certain measure of power accompanies the right to speak and be heard. Those with the means for getting their message out are empowered; those who do not may be impotent. This idea is probably clearest in the case of political campaigns. Candidates who find a forum, draw an audience, and obtain media coverage assume a position in which they may wield power. The case of Jesse Jackson's successful move into the ranks of power within the Democratic party during the course of the 1988 campaign is illustrative. On the other hand, candidates who cannot find a place or an audience, like Gary Hart after his reentry into the campaign, are quickly dismissed from the ranks of the powerful.

Similar to Noelle-Neumann's theory of the spiral of silence, Foucault believed that by examining who was silent, what topics were not raised, what forums were not accorded legitimacy in the public sphere, a social critic could determine who was not empowered in a society. In illustration, he pointed out how informal norms at various levels of society work to silence certain speakers, certain topics, and certain forums. For example, madmen, prisoners, and the like are not accorded legitimacy when they speak and are thereby effectively silenced. Similarly, the various institutional forums described in Chapter 2 are treated as legitimate public forums, while the meeting rooms of women's clubs or the streets of the barrios are not. Similarly, while the reports of academicians and members of "think tanks" may be plumbed for the wisdom they offer, the writings of obscure fringe groups or the comments of a welfare mother may be dismissed.

Foucault's position was that only by paying attention to *the people, topics, and places of silence* could people free themselves from otherwise unnoticed ideologies that restrained their options and worked almost like propaganda to restrict their thinking along narrow lines. Foucault's argument points toward a potential path for freer and more open discussion of public issues. By searching for the silences, citizens concerned with the public interest may find problems, issues, or policies that have been ignored simply because they have not been suggested by the powerful. A contemporary scholar of communication at Northwestern, Thomas Goodnight, has pointed out that the impetus for two contemporary public controversies was just this sort of process, by which advocates gave voice to an otherwise silenced concern. Goodnight described the fundamental importance of two books, *Silent Spring* and *Fate of the Earth*, to the environmental and nuclear freeze movements respectively.[25] In the case of *Silent Spring*, the author, Rachel Carson, gave voice to the environment which could not speak on its own behalf. Similarly, Jonathon Schell, author of *Fate of the Earth*, gave voice to the generations of human beings yet unborn who had the most to lose from a nuclear catastrophe.

The implication of Foucault's idea, then, is also clear. Like the implication of Noelle-Neumann's work, Foucault's work suggests the need to break the silence, to engage in public discussion. But Foucault goes beyond suggesting that advocates should express their opinions even when those opinions are at odds with the climate of opinion. In addition, advocates should seek out the ideas, the views, of those who would otherwise remain silent because of the operative norms concerning who may speak when and about what. In addition to the responsibility to speak, there is a responsibility to speak for those who cannot, for those without power.

The challenges for expanded discussion suggested by Noelle-Neumann and Foucault are supplemented by the suggestions of yet a third contemporary scholar from Europe. Jurgen Habermas, a contemporary German social critic and philosopher, has spent considerable time investigating how communication about public issues results in the formation of public will or public opinion. His concern has been with how modern societies develop a world view or background consensus regarding community affairs. Habermas' studies are in part a reaction to the frightening era of fascism in Germany during Hitler's reign when the government controlled public discussion through massive propaganda campaigns. However, his work also reflects an interest in how people can avoid the repressive effects of contemporary Communism and the extensive governmental hold on information common in some contemporary Democracies. As a result, Habermas describes the public sphere in terms of an ideal vision that he labels *the ideal speech situation*.[26]

The ideal speech situation is a rhetorical situation in which maximum opportunity for public discussion of public issues is realized. Habermas identifies two primary requirements for the ideal speech situation. First, he says that all people must have equal opportunity and access to participate in public discussion. This requirement entails the need for an open society in which all have the ability and the means, both formal and informal, to speak or write and to be heard or read.

Secondly, Habermas suggests that ideally discourse must always be open to criticism. Furthermore, such criticism should be oriented in four important areas. First, the comprehensibility of a message should be open to question. Like the objections to procedure reviewed in Chapter 6, discourse that is confusing or otherwise incomprehensible should not be tolerated. Advocates should be expected and ultimately required to be understandable. Second, the truth of discourse should be open to question. In other words, discourse should be examined for its relationship to reality as we know, understand and experience it. Third, the truthfulness of discourse should be open to challenge. The intentions of advocates should be examined to insure that their claims and reasons for those claims reflect genuine public interests. Finally, the appropriateness of discourse should be open to examination. Common sense, background beliefs, frame of reference, and the like should not just be accepted, but should be open to debate just as other issues are open to debate. Only in this way, can the trap of ideological argument be avoided.

Terming Habermas' suggestions the "ideal speech situation" is apt as his ideas reflect an ideal, a perfect form of free and open discussion. Many of his critics have attacked his position on the grounds that such ideals do not exist. However, Habermas' ideal speech situation suggests a third challenge for students and participants of public argument alike. The implication is that advocates have a responsibility to attempt to create more ideal procedures wherein all people may participate with equal opportunity and access and all aspects of the discussion remain open to objection and debate.

Summary

The political ideal of popular sovereignty on which the United States was founded and the faith in discussion as a preferred means for resolving controversy that pervades our society provide the justification for free and open public discussion of controversial matters. Constitutionally, the right to free expression is protected by the First Amendment. In addition, a variety of laws and court decisions have worked to enable freer and more open discussion. Still there exist challenges for advocates to realize the full potential of free discussion by volunteering their opinions, even when unpopular, by seeking out the voices that are silenced and empowering those silences through discourse, and by establishing procedures that move closer to the ideal of free and open discussion for all.

Notes

[1] U.S. Constitution, Amendments, Article I.

[2] Franklyn S. Haiman, *Speech and Law in a Free Society* (Chicago: University of Chicago Press, 1981).

[3] Haiman, p. 298. The following excerpt of Roberts' opinion is cited by Haiman.

[4] Haiman, p. 310.

[5] Gaven Duffy, "The Normative Ground of Spectrum Policy Debates," in *Progress in Communication Sciences: Volume VII*, eds. Brends Dervin and Melvin J. Voigt (Norwood: Ablex, 1986), p. 74.

[6] Quoted by Elder Witt, "Supreme Court and the Press," in *The Public's Right to Know*, ed. Hoyt Gimlin (Washington: Congressional Quarterly, 1980), p. 29.

[7] Haiman, p. 312.

[8] William V. Thomas, "America's Information Boom," in *Public's Right to Know*, p. 149.

[9] Benjamin Franklin, *The Autobiography* (Cambridge: Modern Library, 1950), p. 88.

[10] Quoted in Thomas, "Information Boom," p. 149.

[11] Thomas, "Information Boom," p. 143.

[12] Thomas, "Information Boom," p. 144.

[13] Thomas, "Freedom of Information Act: A Reappraisal," in *Public's Right to Know*, p. 131.

[14] Thomas, "Freedom," p. 131.

[15] Thomas, "Freedom," pp. 131-2.

[16] Thomas, "Freedom," p. 137.

[17] Cited in Thomas, "Freedom," p. 137.

[18] Elisabeth Noelle-Neumann, *The Spiral of Silence* (Chicago: University of Chicago Press, 1984). See also, Noelle-Neumann, "The Spiral of Silence: A Response," in *Political Communication Yearbook 1984*, eds. Keith R. Sanders, Lynda Lee Kaid, and Dan Nimmo (Carbondale: Southern Illinois University Press, 1985), pp. 66-94.

[19] Noelle-Neumann, "Spiral: A Response," p. 69.

[20] Noelle-Neumann, "Spiral: A Response," p. 71.

[21] Noelle-Neumann, "Spiral: A Response," p. 72.

[22] Noelle-Neumann, "Spiral: A Response," p. 82.

[23] Noelle-Neumann, "Spiral: A Response," p. 88.

[24] Michel Foucault, "Discourse on Language," trans. Rupert Swyer, appendix to *Archaeology of Knowledge*, trans. A.M. Sheridan Smith (London: Tavistock, 1972).

[25] G. Thomas Goodnight, "Public Discourse," *Critical Studies in Mass Communication* 4 (1987): 428-32.

[26]Jurgen Habermas, *Communication and the Evolution of Society*, trans. Thomas McCarthy (Boston: Beacon, 1979); see also, "Towards a Theory of Communicative Competence," in *Recent Sociology #2*, ed. Hans Peter Dreitzel (London: Collier Macmillan, 1970), pp. 114-48.

Suggested Readings

Gimlin, Hoyt, Ed., 1980. *The Public's Right to Know.* Washington: Congressional Quarterly.

Haiman, Franklyn S., 1981. *Speech and Law in a Free Society.* Chicago: University of Chicago Press.

Noelle-Neumann, Elisabeth, 1984. *The Spiral of Silence.* Chicago: University of Chicago Press.

Chapter 10

Conclusion and Application
Controversy over Nuclear War

In this book, we have reviewed the nature of public discussion about controversial public issues. Chapters 1 and 2 provided general context for the subject by explaining the importance of public opinion, the relationship between public opinion and public discussion, and the general features of a rhetorical perspective toward the investigation of public opinion formation. Chapter 3 detailed a method for uncovering and describing the anatomy of a public dispute according to the communication about the issue. In Chapters 4 through 7, a variety of methods for analyzing particular messages and arguments presented by advocates in support of their positions on an issue were provided. In each case, a standard for evaluating the reasons offered by an advocate was explained. The standards for evaluating messages and the arguments presented in those messages were: (1) Good reasons should fit the audience. (2) Good reasons should strategically structure the audience's response. (3) Good reasons should withstand objections. (4) Good reasons should be ethical. In Chapter 8, our attention shifted from the more straightforward, explicit presentation of reasons on behalf of a position in controversy to more implicit discussion of public issues. Thus, the nature of ideology and propaganda was reviewed and additional methods for analyzing messages in order to reveal the argumentative and persuasive potential of ideological and propagandistic public communication were described. In Chapter 9, the importance of free speech and open public discussion was explained in reference to the type of problems described in Chapter 8. The suggestion of Chapter 9 was that only through free and open discussion could the power and potential dangers of ideological thinking and propagandistic communication be countered. In this final chapter, the major points of this text as just described will be reviewed by applying them to a public issue of major importance.

Richard McKeon, one of the authors cited in Chapter 1 as concerned with the relationship between communication and the formation of communities, wrote that "the problems of an age arise in what is said — in the communications of the age."[1]

Perhaps the most threatening problem of the contemporary period is the threat of nuclear holocaust, the virtual extinction of the planet. Our age has been dubbed the "atomic age." Therefore, the controversy surrounding the threat of nuclear war suggests itself as a public issue by which to illustrate the principles of this text. This chapter begins with a general description of the nuclear controversy that draws on the ideas contained in Chapters 1, 2, 8 and 9. Various notable rhetorical events—some involving explicit rhetoric and others involving implicit rhetoric—are described. The description uses concepts like "rhetorical situation" and "free speech" to chronicle the controversy. After the general description, a single message from the mosaic of discussion about nuclear war is analyzed in closer detail using ideas presented in Chapters 3 through 7. The "data-warrant-claim" scheme describes the message, and the four standards for "good reasons" evaluate it. The discussion then returns to a more general level of abstraction, incorporating the ideas from Chapters 8 and 9 to comment on the nuclear controversy generally and to focus on the importance of continued discussion of this issue.

A Rhetorical Perspective Toward the Issue of Nuclear War

The United States is the only sovereign nation to have engaged in nuclear warfare. Since 1945, the issue of nuclear warfare has captured the spotlight of public attention on several occasions. At other times, controversy and concern receded to the background of the public's collective conscience. From our current vantage point, classifying nuclear warfare as a "public issue" is not a matter of controversy. The destructive power of nuclear weapons makes the issue of their use paramount regarding the survival of millions if not the survival of the planet itself. Questions concerning both the legitimacy of the existence of these weapons as well as the appropriate conditions for their use transcend private interests. Moreover, various formal institutions (both governmental and grassroots) have been established to facilitate decision making about this issue, thereby creating various "publics" in the wake of discussion about the issue. In short, nuclear warfare appears to be an issue with probably the largest public—that is, the largest number of interested and concerned parties—in existence. Let us turn to a description of the multiplicity of messages about this issue and the history of its emergence as a public issue.

With few exceptions, most historical studies have concentrated on one of four periods of development of nuclear weapons policies: 1) events leading to the massive effort to develop atomic bombs during World War II, 2) events including and immediately following the United States' detonation of bombs in 1945 over Hiroshima and Nagasaki, 3) the Cold War era, and 4) events surrounding the Nuclear Test Ban Treaty of 1963. Future historians will no doubt add to this list the contemporary period during which the United States and the Soviet Union agreed to begin to reduce the world's nuclear weapons arsenals. During the few years prior to this historic agreement, public discussion of the issue reached a peak.

Reports of the first period, development of the bomb, indicate that public discussion of the issue was severely restricted. Prior to 1939, discussion of atomic warfare was limited to science fiction novels. After the publication of *The Interpretation of Radium and the Structure of the Atom* by Frederick Soddy in 1909, H.G. Wells forecast the use of the atom for production of atomic bombs in his 1914 novel, *The World Set Free*.[2] *The World Set Free* predicted that the discovery of atomic bombs and their use in war would make war so devastating that the world would be forced to establish an international government to control atomic energy and outlaw war. Between 1909 and 1940, scholars and scientists discussed atoms and fission in the context of the factual issue of what was scientifically possible, but little discourse regarding atomic warfare, other than science fiction novels, existed.[3] Of the 61 entries in the *Reader's Guide* under the headings of "atomic power" and "atoms," only three discussed the possible effects of atom-smashing; none speculated about nuclear warfare.

In 1939, Albert Einstein wrote the now famous letter to President Roosevelt, warning him of the danger of Nazi research into atomic bomb production. Leo Szilard was a close associate of Einstein's at the University of Berlin and had read *The World Set Free* in 1932. He convinced Einstein to send the letter to Roosevelt. Thus, a limited number of scientists and governmental officials formed an interested public regarding the issue in response to the fear that the Nazis might produce an atomic bomb. The result was not only an elaborate program by the United States Government to produce an atomic bomb first, but also a system of government classification and secrecy that severely restricted the flow of public discussion about atomic warfare.[4]

The *Reader's Guide* indicates that from 1940 to 1945 only 31 articles were entered under "atoms" or "atomic power," compared to the 61 entries for the period 1939-40. Government censorship had reduced the number by half. Perhaps the major exceptions to this lack of public discourse were several articles written by William L. Laurence, the only journalist to witness the first atomic explosion in New Mexico. Even these articles, which appeared in the *New York Times* and *The Saturday Evening Post*, were written in 1939 and 1940 and discussed atomic energy generally, rather than atomic warfare specifically.

The second period, immediately after Hiroshima and Nagasaki, is characterized by a surge of discourse on the subject and an expansion of the audience for that discourse. On August 6, 1945, President Truman broke the nearly five year silence with his press release indicating that the bomb had been dropped on Hiroshima. The issue thus became salient for ordinary citizens. The issue was no longer limited to the *possibility* that the Nazis would develop an atomic bomb during the war and to the elite group of scientists and government officials who had responded to a perceived crisis. Now the issue penetrated the structure of society. The bomb had been produced, detonated, and the technology for its existence could not be erased. Even so, continued government censorship[5] and public rapture over the end of the war stifled a more complete public discussion of the issue. However, several discursive events of this period bear noting.

Between August of 1945 and April of 1947, the *Reader's Guide* listed 371 articles on the subject. The categories had expanded from "atom" and "atomic power" to "atomic bombs," "atomic bomb tests," "atomic power control," "atomic power terminology," "atomic research," and "atomic warfare." Discussion of the issue had grown from the feasibility of making atomic bombs to include a range of factual, value, and policy questions. Despite this increased discussion, government secrecy and censorship still prevailed. At least one historian has suggested that "the administration's initial monopoly on the facts about Hiroshima and Nagasaki and its subsequent censorship practices—whatever the administration's actual intentions— produced certain effects resembling those resulting from a policy of managed news."[6]

Yavenditti's study of American reactions to use of the atomic bomb indicates that John Hersey's *Hiroshima* was the single most important item of "unmanaged" discourse during the two years following Hiroshima and Nagasaki.[7] In addition to Hersey's book, two other notable discursive events took place. The Senate commenced hearings on atomic energy in November 1945, and the scientific community founded the *Bulletin of the Atomic Scientists*. In keeping with its role as "the Paul Revere of the post-war period," the *Bulletin* invented the doomsday clock in 1947. The clock symbolized the danger of the outbreak of nuclear war.[8] While scientists entered into evaluative and policy discourse on the subject, the religious community also began to question the morality of war, particularly atomic war, thereby initiating another arena of discourse and additional questions of value. At the same time, many academics and businessmen hailed the coming of a new age, generating a variety of descriptive discourse designed to explain and to promote the policy of continued atomic development.

"For the most part, the press either sympathized with American decisionmakers or at least printed little that would foster misgivings among Americans."[9] The average American rarely discussed atomic energy and, according to a Social Science Research Council survey in 1947, only about one-quarter of the Americans responding said they were particularly worried about the atomic bomb. A survey of articles during this period indicates that the major topics of interest centered around what the bomb was, how it had been developed, how its secret might be kept, and what promise its development held for domestic progress—mostly factual questions. The only major exceptions to this characterization were Hersey's book and essays by scholars such as Albert Einstein and Bertrand Russell published by the *Bulletin of the Atomic Scientists*. In these writings, questions regarding the value of atomic warfare were raised that pointed directly to questions of policy.

The third frequently studied period of nuclear warfare discourse, the Cold War Era, marks a shift from the discourse of the second period. In the middle fifties, the United States Government conducted numerous weapons tests and devised a public relations campaign known as "Atoms for Peace" to coincide with continued development of atomic energy and nuclear weapons.[10] At the same time, a number of foreign policy experts devised strategies of diplomacy which necessitated allegiance to doctrines ranging from deterrence to a flexible response posture for NATO. A number of books discussing East-West relations and the link between nuclear weapons and foreign policy were published; however few received much attention from ordinary citizens. As with the first period, discussion seemed to reside mostly in elite circles. In contrast to the earlier period, the elites were more often foreign policy analysts and political scientists instead of physical scientists.

Efforts by Adlai Stevenson between 1954 and 1956 to make fallout and a test-ban important issues in his presidential campaign failed. Despite widespread fear regarding the Soviet Union's successful production of a hydrogen bomb, "more Americans responded 'don't know' to public opinion surveys about testing, fallout, and disarmament than those responding favorably or unfavorably."[11] A *New York Times* election survey indicated that discussion of the subject by Eisenhower and Stevenson had left the public "numb, bewildered, or indifferent."[12] A few special interest groups for disarmament and a complex of government officials and foreign policy elites provided the main arenas for the serious discourse that occurred at this time.

Two messages from this period were exemplary of an attitude of reflection and concern about nuclear weapons. One of these was a full page advertisement that appeared in the *New York Times*, November 15, 1957. The advertisement was entitled, "We are facing a danger unlike any danger that has ever existed," and was signed by a number of prominent individuals including Norman Cousins, Erich Fromm, and Eleanor Roosevelt. Readers were encouraged to sponsor a newly-formed group in New York called the National Committee for Sane Nuclear Policy (SANE). The response was declared "overwhelming" by the organization.[13] Thus, another elite group evolved as an interested public and a forum for potential advocacy. The second discursive event was the continuation of essays in the *Bulletin* regarding the need to prevent nuclear warfare. Notable among these was the Einstein-Russell Manifesto printed in the September 1955 issue which called on the international community of scientists to seek means for preventing another world war. This marked the beginning of the Pugwash Conferences designed to foster a world community of scientists.

For American citizens, however, imaginative discourse on the subject may have been far more influential than the agenda issues promoted by elite groups. Perhaps the message most widely attended to during this period was Nevile Shute's novel, *On the Beach*, one of only four books on this subject ever to make the annual best-seller's list. The book was made into a movie that was released in 1959 and subsequently has been listed by *Variety* as one of the most widely distributed films in history. This fictional account probably furnished the most explicit descriptions and definitions of nuclear war to ordinary citizens and prompted them to consider value and policy implications of the issue.

In many respects, the discussions of the fourth period resembled those of the Cold War Period. The main difference was that average people appeared to attend to the controversy surrounding testing. Government control of information persisted and discussion of foreign policy generally remained directed toward special audiences. However, the popular media discussed testing and fallout at length and preceded official concern about testing by one to five years.[14] As with the previous period, imaginative literature again assumed importance in terms of public attention.[15]

Fail-Safe, a best-selling novel by Eugene Burdick and Harvey Wheeler in 1962, was transformed into a top money-making film in 1964. With its release, a new topic of discussion, accidental nuclear war, received wide public attention. The first satirical work concerning nuclear war, "Dr. Strangelove" was released the same year. This film remains the most-seen film on the subject to date. A variety of political discourse by governmental officials and foreign policy experts appeared around the time of the Cuban missile crisis. The Kennedy Administration launched an ambitious program for civil defense that was accompanied by a plethora of discourse concerning bomb shelters. As was true of the earlier periods, most discourse was practiced by an elite group of experts—government officials, foreign policy experts, and scientific experts. The American citizenry remained relatively passive and attended to imaginative discourse on the subject much more frequently than they attended to serious, non-fiction discourse. As one study of the rhetoric from Hiroshima to the Nuclear Test Ban Treaty put it:

> . . . it should be of particular interest to note the relative absence of involvement by the people of the United States in a matter which so vitally concerns their very existence. Indeed, due to the nature of the problems involved, it was considered impossible to give the people an active and meaningful role in the decision-making on this issue. Thus, in a formal sense, the people simply were not consulted in the series of decisions made to further the development of nuclear weapons.[16]

During the early 1980s, a radical shift in discursive practice occurred. Suddenly, the American public not only attended to but generated, discourse on the subject of nuclear warfare. During this period, the nuclear issue made the cover story of the two most widely circulated news periodicals in the country, *Newsweek* and *Time*. A Gallup Poll in March of 1982 indicated that 72% of Americans knew about and favored a United States-Soviet pact not to build any more nuclear weapons.[17] Following an unprecedented House debate on the arms race, seven different joint resolutions on the subject were introduced in the Senate and House. *Time* magazine reported on March 29, 1982:

> The resolutions on Capitol Hill are the small tip of a very large iceberg. In part, the Senators who favor the motions are responding to an unprecedented flood of teach-ins, referenda, legislative proposals, letter-writing campaigns, petitions, and books addressing the peril of nuclear war.[18]

A group of 35 world religious leaders—including the Dalai Lama, the Secretary General of the World Muslim Congress and the President of the National Council of Churches—called on all nations to "freeze and reverse the arms-race as a first and crucial step toward disarmament."[19] The editor of the *Bulletin of the Atomic Scientists* summed up the proliferation of public discourse during this period:

> For 37 years the *Bulletin* addressed and was listened to by a small audience. Quite suddenly, the arms race has become everybody's concern, the clergy, physicians, students, business people, ordinary women and men, and God help us, even some Senators and Congressmen, are realizing that the arms race is expensive, dangerous, and can have only one outcome if it is not stopped.[20]

A review of news articles during this period indicated that the discourse on this subject peaked in 1982 through a series of events. In February, Jonathan Schell's book, *The Fate of the Earth* was serialized in *The New Yorker*. In the first week of March, 161 town meetings in Vermont passed resolutions calling for a mutual and verifiable freeze on testing, production, and deployment of nuclear weapons. The following week, Congress held an open debate on the arms race and Senators Kennedy and Hatfield introduced a similar resolution in the Senate and House. Secretary of State Alexander Haig immediately dismissed the resolution as naive and preposterous. During the same week, Premier Brezhnev announced the willingness of the Soviet Union to participate in a bilateral freeze in Europe. Brezhnev's proposal met with little response from the Reagan Administration except an announcement at an April 1 press conference that United States military forces were inferior to Soviet forces. Exactly one week later, *Foreign Affairs* published an essay by four former foreign policy experts (MacNamara, Bundy, Kennan, and Smith) who had helped to fashion NATO's first strike policy-option. These four experts now advocated abandonment of that option. Throughout April, a variety of religious leaders, including the National Council of Churches and the United States Bishops of the Catholic Church, called for worldwide nuclear disarmament. During the last week of April, a newly formed organization conducted lectures, seminars and a variety of educational activities across the nation in an educational campaign known as Ground Zero Week. A variety of anti-nuclear organizations, including Physicians for Social Responsibility, the Union of Concerned Scientists, Citizens for Survival, and others, conducted educational meetings and circulated nuclear freeze petitions throughout the months of April and May. On Memorial Day, President Reagan presented his first speech dealing exclusively with nuclear weapons policy to the graduating class of Eureka College, his alma mater. June 7 marked the beginning of a special United Nations session on disarmament. At the end of the first week of this session, over 700,000 people from across the country and the world participated in the largest rally against nuclear weapons ever held in the United States.

Despite the initiation of Reagan's START talks on June 29, anti-nuclear activities continued throughout the summer and fall. November 11, 1982, was declared a Nuclear Convocation Day in most cities and on most college campuses in the United States. By that date, over forty books on the subject of nuclear warfare had been rushed to press. Over 200 national, state, and local anti-nuclear organizations had been established and had accumulated or produced a wide range of films, pamphlets, addresses, and articles concerning the nuclear warfare issue.

In the several years that followed, discussion of factual, value, and policy questions concerning nuclear warfare continued at a high level. Serious discourse on the subject by academics pursuing "peace studies" and news reports regarding governmental policies were in abundance. The new Strategic Defense Initiative (SDI) spawned much commentary. Imaginative literature was still of importance, most notably in the form of "The Day After," the first made-for-television movie that attempted to present the horror of nuclear war during prime time. With the signing of the INF Treaty that signalled the first mutual dismantling of nuclear weapons by the superpowers and continued arms talks, the discussion seemed to move toward more focused determination of policy issues that would reduce the threat of nuclear annihilation.

Viewed from a historical perspective, then, the topic of nuclear warfare has been a persistent issue of public controversy during the twentieth century. The topic has spawned a multiplicity of messages that entailed factual, value, and policy disputes. The issue was sometimes salient for only a small group of people who formed a public to discuss the controversy. Often due to governmental restrictions on discussion, the messages about the issue were not available for wider public view. However, at other times, interested parties formed publics and produced messages intended to reach a larger public and to encourage ordinary citizens to become interested and able participants in the controversy. Sometimes the discussion occurred within formal institutions for advocacy, such as in Congressional Hearings, at international negotiations, or at academic and professional conferences. At other times, the discussion occurred quite informally in the popular press. The messages surrounding the issue were sometimes prompted by perceived crises, such as the danger of an enemy obtaining nuclear capabilities or the possibility of accidental nuclear holocaust. At other times, discussion emerged because of the concerted efforts of an elite group, such as the atomic scientists or the Bishops of the American Catholic Church. Of course, once the United States had developed and used the bomb, the issue evolved into a structural one that was likely to emerge, recede, and emerge again as it became a fixture of our foreign policy. Just as the exigencies and advocates for the issue change over time, so the messages themselves differ. From actual face-to-face negotiations and public addresses to feature films and newspaper advertisements, the multiplicity of messages about this issue that confront an ordinary citizen are diverse.

Analyzing a Single Message:
The Case of "The War Game"

Among the multiplicity of messages regarding nuclear warfare is an award-winning documentary film entitled "The War Game."[21] Commissioned for production by the British Broadcasting Corporation (BBC), this film was awarded an Oscar as "Best Feature Documentary" in 1966. Despite its apparent artistic merit, however, "The War Game" has never appeared on any public or commercial television network anywhere in the world.[22] It has the dubious distinction of being the only documentary ever censored from showing by the BBC. Yet, the film did find an audience. It is available at many college, university, and large public film libraries and was shown frequently at public meetings sponsored by "anti-nuclear" advocates during the early 1980s. Obviously these advocates disagreed with the conclusion of the BBC, that the film was "fatalistic, bitter, hopeless, and cruel," and suspected that the film would be effective in increasing the salience of the problem of nuclear warfare to a wider public audience.

Before analyzing the film according to the four standards for good reasons discussed in this book, a description of the film is in order. The ideas suggested in Chapter 3 that detailed the anatomy of disputes can be used to describe the film. "The War Game" presents a variety of data. The documentary mixes live interviews with carefully staged vignettes and quotations from military, scientific, and religious authorities. In addition to the staged vignettes, footage of the actual destruction at Hiroshima and Nagasaki is included. Thus, the data appears in three familiar forms: examples, testimony, and statistics.

The footage from Hiroshima and Nagasaki provides examples of the destructive power of nuclear weapons. Similarly, the staged vignettes follow a story-line of a hypothetical attack on Great Britain, thereby providing a dramatized and extended example of the effects of nuclear war. The live interviews with ordinary citizens provide testimony regarding topics that range from whether or not they know the effects of radioactive fallout to what they think about the first strike policy of NATO (if western Europe were invaded by conventional forces of the Warsaw Pact, then NATO would respond with nuclear weapons). Live interviews with military, scientific, and religious authorities provide additional testimony regarding the value of nuclear weapons, the probable effects of their use, and appropriate policy regarding their use. These authorities often provide statistical data concerning factual issues such as the number of weapons and their potential destructive effects as well. In addition, an off-screen narrator provides similar statistical data at several junctures in the film.

Although both the testimony included in the film and the narration include explicit statements that act as claims, most of the major claims of the film are implicit. Thus, the documentary works enthymematically, providing the viewer with much data that points toward several primary claims. In the order of their appearance, each of the following is introduced as a claim by the narrator and elaborated by one or more of the types of data described above:

1. The present policy of deterrence makes weapons installations targets for the enemy.
2. Civil Defense policies (such as evacuation and civil defense) are problematic and perhaps wholly unworkable.
3. NATO's "First Strike Option" makes escalation to nuclear war likely.
4. Immediate physical effects of a nuclear attack are horrible.
5. Retaliation against civilians which will broaden these horrible effects is inevitable.
6. Civil Defense measures are hopelessly inadequate to deal with these horrible effects.
7. Long-term physical and psychological effects on individuals are just as bad, if not worse, than the immediate effects.
8. The only prevention for these horrible effects is for the world to turn to peace.
9. The problem is urgent because of present policies.
10. In the aftermath of nuclear war, the human spirit would be destroyed.
11. Silence in the press and the public diminishes hope that this problem will be avoided.

These are the explicit claims, and as the reader will notice there is a preponderance of factual (descriptive and designative) claims. Claims 1-3 describe the effects of current policies. Similarly, claims 5 and 6 describe the effects of pursuing those current policies in the event of a nuclear attack. Then in claims 9 and 11 the effects of current policies are redescribed in light of the prior descriptions. Claims 4, 7, and 10 move beyond mere description to include designation. The immediate and long-term effects of nuclear war are defined as "horrible" as a consequence of how they are depicted. Given the nature of the data, which will be reviewed shortly, perhaps "horrible" is an inadequate term for the designation provided here. For the effects of nuclear war are depicted as being so terrible that these claims almost take on the characteristics of an evaluation. The human destruction is so complete that the viewer must reach the conclusion that nuclear holocaust is absolutely inhumane. Only claim 8 deviates from this pattern of factual claims. Here, the film suggests a course of action—policies that work for peace.

Because of the preponderance of factual claims, it is tempting to characterize the main claim of the film as a designative claim about the nature of nuclear war— Nuclear war is horrible (using the most intense meaning of the term, "horror"). This temptation is reinforced by the narrator of the film who, throughout the middle of the film, interrupts the action to repeat a single line—"This is nuclear war." However, such analysis neglects the several factual claims that point toward the potential causes of nuclear war—nuclear policy in general, the first strike option of NATO, and silence among the citizenry in particular—and the single policy claim that we must work toward world peace. Therefore, probably a more accurate statement of the main claim is one that recognizes the policy claim: We must work for peace by breaking the silence about the issue and changing our foreign policy. Viewed in this way, the collection of factual claims act as subclaims in support of the main claim. In other words, the reason that we must work for peace is because present policies encourage the likelihood of nuclear attack and retaliation that would result in horrible effects to human beings. This description of the main claim and its relationship to supporting claims assumes that the film is working enthymematically rather than only explicitly.

We may then investigate the arguments within the film in light of the issues that are relevant to a policy dispute as outlined in Chapter 3. There, Hultzen explained that a policy issue turns on four questions: ill, blame, reformability, and cost. Analyzed from this perspective, we find that the documentary devotes most of its time to presentation of data concerning the ill — the likelihood and effects of nuclear war. Secondary attention is given to blame — current policies of deterrence, first strike, and silence appear to perpetuate the problem. Very little time is given to the issue of reformability other than the narrator's suggestion that we should work for peace. Reference to what was said about blame does suggest some avenues that might be pursued to remedy the problem (e.g., we could start talking about it and renounce our first strike option), but there is no explicit discussion of this issue, no testimony, no examples of how the reform might proceed. And, finally, there is no discussion of cost (the disadvantages that might ensue from breaking the silence or renouncing first strike or no longer depending on the policy of deterrence). The concentration of the message on the issues of ill and blame suggest that it is most appropriate for the stage of the issue when the problem is becoming salient, rather than when particular policies become the focus of debate and discussion or the objects of implementation. This description of what type of rhetorical situation the message fits is consistent with when the film was actually produced. In 1966, as the earlier review of public discussion suggested, ordinary citizens were just beginning to take the problem seriously and were obtaining their images of the effects of nuclear war from feature films such as "Fail-Safe" and "Dr. Strangelove."

Individual arguments within the film may be assessed as to their merit as good reasons by applying the standards from Chapter 4 that concern whether or not the reasons fit the audience. To determine if the reasons fit the audience, however, we must first know who the audience is. It is here that the first complication in the analysis emerges. Do we conceptualize the audience as British citizens in 1966, even though few of them saw the film at that time, or do we identify the audience as United States citizens in the early 1980s, many of whom actually viewed the film as public concern with nuclear policy was growing? There are other options for defining the audience as well. This is an important question because of the nature of the analysis suggested in Chapter 4. For example, to determine if the argument fits the audience, we must be able to determine whether or not the data presented by the advocate is consistent with what the audience generally perceives as the facts of the situation. The level of knowledge regarding radioactive fallout, effects of nuclear war, and so on had changed considerably between 1966 and 1988. Thus, what might have been inconsistent in 1966 could easily be quite consistent in 1982. In order to stabilize the analysis, then, the audience must be identified. For the purposes of this illustration, we will define the audience as Americans who viewed the film during the early to mid-1980s.

Because the film was typically shown at public meetings sponsored by groups who were advocating a nuclear freeze or some other comparable policy at that time, we can assume that the audience was predisposed to accept the claim that nuclear war was a horror that should be prevented. However, because alternative policy options were being suggested with much regularity at that time, the audience may have expected more explicit discussion of potential remedies for the threat depicted in the film. Keeping these predispositions in mind, we can examine particular arguments to determine if they fit the audience.

The film devotes much of its time to the subclaim that the effects of nuclear war are horrible. In support of this claim, the film provides a variety of dramatic vignettes showing scenes of people suffocating from the firestorm, burning to death, bleeding from radiation sickness, and screaming with terror. In addition, the claim is supported by footage that shows actual burn victims from Japan and the squalor and immense destruction that characterized the aftermath in Hiroshima and Nagasaki. To accept the claim on the basis of these dramatic and real examples, the audience would need to believe that the examples were typical. The mixing of the real with the dramatic as well as the authority conferred on these scenes by the nature of the film as "documentary," rather than fictional, makes the likelihood that audiences will accept the examples very high. So high is the believability that after showing the film to several classes of students, this writer is no longer surprised when an occasional student asks how the cameraman kept the film from melting when the film was shot. It is apparently easy for reality and drama to blur such that viewers clearly imagine that the dramatized attack is real and credit the hypothetical example with the same legitimacy as the real examples.

In addition to accepting the example as typical, the audience must also supply a definition concerning what constitutes "horrible" in order for the claim to carry its designative force—defining the effects as horrible. The many scenes that show children whose eyeballs were melted or who are suffering from the ravages of radiation sickness nearly guarantee that the audience will supply the appropriate definition of the horrible. Testimony by doctors who describe the gory effects of radiation on the intestinal system violate the standards of acceptability so completely that there is little doubt that the audience will supply the necessary definitional warrant to complete the argument.

One of the effects of nuclear war that is depicted in the film is the absolute breakdown of normal law and order. The film shows a food supply center after the explosion that is being ravaged by tattered, but otherwise ordinary, housewives.

The narrator explains that "this woman," who we see in a close-up clutching an armload of canned goods, has just shot and killed the three workers who were guarding the center. The scene and its accompanying sound track, composed of screams and sirens, cannot help but evoke a disconcerting feeling that encourages the viewer to define the situation as horrible.

In addition to describing the effects, the film also presents a number of claims concerning the causes of nuclear war. Among these is the explicit claim that silence diminishes the chances of preventing war and its implicit counterpart that the "wrong" people are discussing the issue. Throughout the film, live testimony from ordinary citizens and experts alike is intercut with dramatizations of the destruction. For example, while developing the claim that civil defense policies are unlikely to be very helpful in the event of nuclear war, the film cuts to a statement by an American scientist. The scientist proclaims that although we might not have ranch houses, electric freezers, and so forth, there would be survivors of a nuclear war. Immediately, the film moves to a dramatized vignette of a firestorm in which the viewer sees a woman slowly and agonizingly suffocate as the narrator describes in graphic detail the effects of the lack of oxygen. This enthymeme encourages the viewer to supply the claim that "the wrong people are talking and as a consequence deceiving us as to the 'real' effects of nuclear war." The proximity of the live testimony with the dramatized effects encourages a cause-effect sort of orientation that invites the viewer to conclude that if we don't begin to widen the discussion we will be misinformed to the point that the dramatization may become a reality.

Each individual bit of data can be analyzed to determine the warrants required to link it to the several claims in the film. Although too lengthy for inclusion here, such analysis reveals that the arguments rely on patterns of thinking that are dominated by causal reasoning and patterns of similarity. Viewers are consistently invited to see the government officials and experts who precede the scenes of destruction as the causal forces of the holocaust and are encouraged to identify with the hypothetical British and real Japanese victims as comparable to themselves. While frequently not meeting the tests of logic, these patterns are still compelling because of the persistent mixture of reality and drama in the film.

Probably the only exception to the characterization of the sensibleness of the claims discussed thus far is the claim regarding the likelihood of nuclear war. This claim is supported in the film by live testimony and dramatizations of battle in West Germany. In addition, the narrator explains a scenario that would lead to nuclear war by reference to United States policy (with an accompanying picture of former President Lyndon Johnson) and predictions that such a war will occur by 1980. The datedness of the scenario and the obvious fallacy of the prediction probably undercuts the believability of this claim because of its inconsistency with the audience's frame of reference.

Still, many of the claims are compelling. The persuasiveness of the arguments relies on their motivational appeal even more than on their sensibleness. Scene after scene evokes a variety of the needs discussed by Packard in Chapter 4. Probably the need for immortality is given the most emphasis by the film in that scene after scene reminds the viewing audience that mega-death is a very real consequence of nuclear attack. Both the close-up shots of individuals dying and the statistics that appear in the testimony by various people reinforce the possibility of mortality and thereby evoke the need for immortality. The long shots that show mounds of corpses waiting to be buried plus the wounded crying for help have a similar effect.

In addition to evoking the need for immortality, the film also reinforces needs for emotional security, reassurance of worth, love objects, power, and roots. Various dramatic vignettes display fathers, mothers, and children searching through the carnage in the hopes of locating members of their families. The insecurity revealed in the mock testimony of these victims comes to a head with the narrator's explanation of the neuroses that result from the sudden loss of loved ones. Later vignettes show devastated, neurotic individuals unable to bring a spoon to their mouths because their hands are shaking so badly. The clatter of the spoon against the bowl as the result of these nervous hands dominates the sound track, underscoring the insecurity.

The film plays on both the need for emotional security and the need for love objects early in the vignettes designed to show the inadequacy of initial civil defense procedures. Anticipating an attack, civil defense authorities are shown managing evacuation of women and children. The narrator explains that these women and children are leaving their husbands and brothers behind as the viewer confronts the distraught faces of the evacuees. In a particularly disconcerting scene late in the film, a civil defense worker points to a bucket of wedding rings and explains that these rings are being taken from the bodies to use the inscriptions as a last resort for identifying the dead. Scenes like these, as well as others, reinforce the need for roots as well. Their homes destroyed, many of their relatives and friends dead, the survivors are depicted as roaming through an unfamiliar and rootless world.

The various vignettes showing lawlessness and the total breakdown of civil order call into question the relative worth of individuals. Various professionals are depicted performing duties which lead the viewer to question how these people maintain their sense of worth in the aftermath of nuclear attack. For example, doctors are shown separating the wounded into categories that will determine whether they will be shot or left to die a slow and painful death rather than providing medical care. Similarly, surviving soldiers who refused to burn additional corpses are shown before a firing squad. Like the scene described earlier in which housewives stormed a food depot, these scenes illustrate the radical changes in people's lives that follow nuclear attack and suggest that the prior standards for reassurance of worth are no longer applicable.

As need after need is invoked without any compensatory satisfaction, the viewer is likely to feel an intense need for power. Faced with the possibility of such utter destruction, viewers are likely driven to seek a solution to the problem. Watching so many helpless people may instill a feeling of impotence in the viewer. Especially when coupled with the negative visions of those with power (military, scientific, and religious authorities whose testimony regarding the viability of current nuclear policy is consistently followed by scenes of devastation), these scenes underscore the need for power.

As mentioned earlier in this analysis, the film gives little time and no visual support for the idea that we should work for peace to avoid the nuclear holocaust. Thus even though many needs are evoked, these needs are never satisfied in the film. Consequently, the film is likely to put the audience into a psychological frame dominated by despair and hopelessness. This was, of course, the conclusion reached by the BBC when they described the film as fatalistic and cruel. But is this conclusion similarly valid for the audience of the early 1980s? Perhaps not, as a number of concrete proposals for preventing nuclear war were being discussed at that time. Even so, the dissatisfaction inherent in the arousal of so many unmet needs may reduce the effectiveness of the film as an individual message. Dr. Robert J. Lifton, a contemporary psychologist who has studied the effects of living with the threat of nuclear war, has commented that concentration on the terrible effects of nuclear war can lead to "psychic numbing," a condition wherein people are somewhat immobilized and unable to feel compassion because of the depth of their fears.[23] Thus, while the audience will feel these needs, the reasons may fall short of fitting the audience completely as the needs go unsatisfied.

In addition to determining the sensibleness and motivational impact of the film, some attention needs to be given to the credibility of the data presented there. As mentioned earlier, the mixture of the real with drama tends to lend credibility to the drama. Similarly, the strategic explanations of the narrator, many of which were detailed earlier, help to make the dramatic vignettes believable. For example, in the scene concerning the use of wedding rings for identification of the dead, the narrator explains that such a procedure was actually used by the Germans after the bombing of Dresden during World War II and would probably be used again in the event of nuclear war.

Of special note in regard to the credibility of testimony is the consistent undermining of "official" testimony in this film. The juxtaposition of horrible deaths with the statements of clergymen and scientists regarding the viability of nuclear weapons undercuts the credibility of those experts. A case in point occurs just prior to the food depot scene. Just before we see the food riot and the housewife-turned-murderer, the film displays the words from a civil defense manual that describes a "typical meal following nuclear attack." The incongruity between the menu of pot roast and applesauce and the squalor of the food lines and the food riot encourage the viewer to discount the testimony of those who are currently in charge.

Warranting the various cause-effect relationships and the various needs evoked in this film are several of the standard American values detailed in Chapter 4. Probably the value of the individual is most dominant. Over and over again, individuals are depicted close-up, real, and suffering. The cause of their demise is somehow less individualistic as the film never really explains who devised the first strike option, why it is still in force, or how the destruction began. While the cause is clearly "governmental" policy, government officials are never really shown, certainly never depicted as among the suffering save for local firemen and police. Thus, policies — governmental actions that are larger and vaguer than concrete individuals — are blamed for the carnage to the real victims — individuals who lose their individuality in the event of nuclear war.

Values such as the value of the individual help to explain why so many of the scenes are so compelling. The dramatic vignettes frequently violate the viewer's sense of value, displaying in graphic detail the contours of a world in which the values of optimism, achievement and success, etc. are absent. For example, toward the end of the film, the camera directs our attention to a refugee center where surviving children are eking out an existence. An off-camera narrator asks these children what they want to be when they grow up. The consistent answer from child after child is simply: "nothing; I don't want to be nothing." And thus, the viewer is confronted with a hopeless, valueless society.

So, does the message fit the audience? Its arguments concerning the causes and effects of nuclear war are likely to be perceived as sensible. It evokes needs and values common to an American audience, even in the early 1980s. But the overwhelming effect is more likely to be hopelessness than inspiration for seeking a solution to the problem. The negativity of the film, however, may be modulated by the mosaic of messages to which the audience of the early 1980s was exposed in addition to this film. Because many of those other messages emphasized possible solutions, the audience might be able to avoid the psychic numbing of the film's depiction of unmet needs and absent values.

We can turn now to an analysis of the structure of the message to determine its strategic effect on the audience. The film follows a qualitative progression in which the viewer is introduced to a potential problem that increases in urgency and severity as the film proceeds. From beginning to end, the film leads the viewer through psychological states of concern, anxiety, hopefulness (that civil defense will take care of the situation), increasing horror (at the effects of nuclear war and the inadequacy of civil defense), and hopelessness (as the film ends with the despair of children).

The large structure of the film is filled out by a narrative sequence that dominates the intermediate structure of the film. Following a roughly chronological pattern, the film shows the preparation for, execution of, and aftermath of nuclear attack. This narrative pattern is interrupted occasionally by intercuts of testimony by experts and ordinary citizens, but these interruptions play more of a role in the small structure of the film than as a way of moving through the psychological states of the qualitative progression. The chronological sequence, even with interruptions, is conventional enough for an audience to follow unimpeded by much reflection or confusion. Repetitive form is used in the middle of the narrative as the various effects of the nuclear attack are detailed. The narrator repeatedly comments, "this is nuclear war," as the images shift from firestorms to hospitals to general devastation.

Probably most interesting in this film are some of the minor forms. Because many of the vignettes are dramatizations of what *could* happen, several techniques are used to convince the audience that these effects actually *would* happen. Usually, shocking scenes are accompanied by narrator explanations that encourage the audience to view a similarity. The scene of the wedding rings is an example. Other associative structures consist of quick cuts from newsreel footage to dramatized sequences. By preceding and following footage of Hiroshima and Nagasaki with dramatized scenes of destruction and squalor, the film encourages the viewer to accept these dramatizations as sufficiently similar to be believable. In addition, for American viewers in the early 1980s, it is probably easier to identify with the problem when confronted with mostly white, Anglo-Saxon, English-speaking victims as opposed to Japanese.

Another interesting associative structure that is used throughout the film concerns the visual techniques of the film itself. Filmed in black and white, shades of gray prevail in the images thereby reinforcing the bleakness of the disaster and the pessimism of the film. As noted by one analyst of nuclear war films, "[i]nstead of the expected dissolve or fade out, selected frames are frozen in a photograph, giving a memorial tone to the victims."[24] Again, the audience is invited to associate, but in these cases the association is between the victims portrayed on film and their prior experience with memorialized victims.

In addition to these associative structures, there also exist a number of disassociative and quasi-logical structures. The film repeatedly follows testimony regarding the viability of nuclear war with graphic and gory scenes of the destruction caused in nuclear war. The time sequence (statements about how deterrence is a reasonable policy followed by images of nuclear holocaust) suggest a causal relationship. The viewer is encouraged, therefore, to conclude that the cause of such destruction is talk that assumes the viability of current policies. Such juxtaposition not only encourages a causal connection but also suggests an irony. Thus viewers are encouraged to hear "official and expert" testimony as ironic and thereby deceptive. The message of these small structures is that experts lie and cannot therefore be trusted.

One of the most noticeable disassociative forms that encourages a reflection on the irony of nuclear war occurs at the end of the film. As the film moves from the pessimistic interviews with children regarding their future, the camera pans the desolate and bleak refugee center. In the background is the scratchy sound of a phonograph playing "Silent Night." As the words to the familiar song claim "all is calm, all is bright," the viewer is confronted with all destroyed and all bleak visuals. The narrator concludes with a plea to the viewers to break the silence that now prevails concerning nuclear war. This sequence, through its disassociative structure is likely to heighten the viewer's sense of anxiety as the irony is revealed while at the same time reinforcing quasi-logically the notion that silence is a contributing cause of the problem.

Structurally, then, the film begins by instilling anxiety, continues by consistently dashing any hopes of avoidance of the holocaust, and ends by heightening the audience's anxiety and making a plea for changes. This story of angst is carried through a narrative format that is interrupted only long enough to raise the skepticism and cynicism of the viewer regarding the good sense of those in positions of power regarding nuclear weapons policy. Quasi-logical structures that depend on disassociation underscore the deceptiveness of those in power throughout the film. Similarly, associative structures throughout the film encourage the viewer to accept as real what can only be dramatized. These conclusions about the structure of the film support our earlier conclusion that the film is more hopeless than hopeful, more blaming than constructive.

In addition to evaluating the message for its fit with the audience and its effect on the audience's perceptions, the film may be analyzed to determine if its arguments can withstand objection. If we begin by considering the potential objections to data, two lines of objection stand out as relevant. The film provides insufficient evidence for the claim that current policies increase the likelihood of nuclear war. Although the film presents a dramatic scenario concerning how a war might occur, no testimony or statistical calculation of probability is provided. Critical viewers may thus be unconvinced by the premise that leads to the horror depicted in the film. In addition, the film is probably guilty of suppressed evidence. The hindsight available to viewers in the 1980s clearly undermines the film's predictive claim that scenes such as these will probably occur before 1980 if a change in policy is not forthcoming. But even for the 1966 audience, there was considerable evidence that the policy of detente was working to prevent the types of military incursions that could escalate to nuclear war. These objections do not necessarily refute the need for a policy change, but certainly erode the claim of urgency in the film.

Probably more important than these objections to data are objections to some of the warrants in the film. Most obvious is an objection to questionable cause. As suggested earlier, the film attacks the credibility of experts by following their testimony with graphic scenes of destruction, thereby encouraging an attribution of blame to those experts who consider nuclear weapons a viable part of defense. This filmic argument displays the characteristics of a *post hoc* argument in which cause (or blame) is attributed simply because the talk of viability preceded the disastrous effect. If these effects could just as easily result from terrorist actions in a world in which East and West had dismantled their respective arsenals, then the causal connection can be viewed as only partial. Moreover, the implicit claim that experts cannot be trusted is probably weakened by this same objection. Just because a disaster follows the talk of experts on the film does not necessarily mean that all such talk is deceptive. Some talk regarding the viability of nuclear weapons may be necessary to maintain detente and thereby avoid war. Certainly, that is the claim likely to be made by those who support present policies. Thus, for viewers who hold similar faith in detente, the film may evoke an objection on the grounds of questionable cause.

Another potential objection to the film's arguments concerns the dramatized explanation of how a nuclear attack might occur. The film sets up a slippery slope that runs as follows. If tensions between East and West Germany were bad enough, the armies of the Warsaw Pact might invade West Germany. If NATO forces were unable to hold the line sufficiently, tactical nuclear weapons might be launched. If tactical nuclear weapons were launched, the Soviets might become fearful of losing any strategic advantage and therefore initiate a first strike of strategic weapons. If the Soviet Union launched their strategic force, the West would respond in kind. If all this happened, then the world as we know it would come to an end. There is a wealth of data, of course, available that if all these actions occurred, the planet would probably be destroyed. But as a sequence of events, there are many links in the causal chain, and consequently a critical viewer might object that somewhere along the line, someone might break the chain. For example, commanders on the battlefield might refuse to launch tactical nuclear weapons. Or even if launched, the Warsaw Pact might respond in kind rather than by unleashing their strategic force on civilian populations. The result might still be disastrous, but the magnitude of the disaster might be reduced. This objection, like many of the others, probably does not refute the entire message but does weaken some of the subclaims.

A similar objection might be raised to the mixture of the real with the dramatized. The analogy between the effects in Japan during World War II and the possible effects in Britain later may be questionable. The survivalists who believe in civil defense might argue that in 1945, nuclear bombs were unknown and the attack came as a complete surprise. Perhaps lives and property could be saved by a wary population who was prepared. But unlike some of the earlier objections, this one would probably not hold. In the film itself, the adequacy of civil defense procedures are questioned. In addition, sufficient evidence exists to suggest that the destructive power of a new generation of nuclear weapons makes defense against them impossible.

Finally, an objection might be raised to the procedure of argument in the film as it seems to construct straw men. The film proclaims that the first strike option and nuclear arsenals exist and proceeds to show the immense destruction that could result from such policies. There is likely to be little disagreement that nuclear war should be avoided. However, the film never explains why these policies exist. In other words, the proponents of current policy are never really given a voice in the film. Even the short interviews with experts tend to focus on their views concerning what life after nuclear attack would be like or whether or not a family should share their bomb shelter rather than plumbing their opinions of the value of a policy based on deterrence. Thus, the film avoids the thornier question of what exactly our nuclear policy should be in favor of emphasizing the enormity of effects should nuclear attack occur. The thoughtful viewer is therefore likely to experience some discomfort that the whole story is not being told, that the positions of those who favor continued maintenance of nuclear arsenals and the first strike option are not being represented accurately. In short, it may be difficult for critical viewers to believe that the various elite experts who fashioned nuclear policy are as naive and insensitive as the clips of testimony on the film suggest. While this objection may have been particularly problematic for viewers in 1966, its force may have eroded by the early 1980s. By that time, the architects of the first strike doctrine had repudiated the policy, and the arguments for continuing the arms race had lost their vigor. Still, the film is probably guilty of neglecting a thorough presentation of opposing arguments.

In summary, the main claim of the film that our policy towards nuclear weapons should be changed is eroded by objections to insufficient and suppressed evidence, questionable cause, and straw man. Subclaims regarding the horror of nuclear war and the need for more discussion of the problem withstand objection, but subclaims regarding the probability of nuclear attack and the probable cause of such attack are weakened.

Finally, we may analyze the film to determine if it presents an ethical message. Using the four factors of ethical argument supplied by Yoos, we can inquire into the film's confirmation of the autonomy, rationality, and values of the audience as well as its contribution to a public forum in which participants are given an equal opportunity for advocacy in seeking mutual agreement.

The film's emphasis on the claim that part of our change in policy should be expanded discussion of the issue (breaking the silence) suggests at least an implicit commitment to a search for mutual agreement and equal opportunity. However, this commitment is eroded slightly by the lack of time given in the film to opposing points of view regarding the benefit of nuclear arsenals and NATO's first strike option. Still, the strong plea for discussion presents an open rather than a closed appeal that seems to meet Yoos' requirements.

The question of whether or not the audience is recognized as autonomous and rational is less clear. The filmic form is more suited to the presentation of dramatic examples than intellectual, linear deductions, and therefore it is not surprising that the film plays more consistently with the passions than with the rationality of the audience. Still, the film does provide clips of testimony and the narrator does provide explanations that rely on facts and statistics, lending a rational quality to the arguments. The more important question is whether or not the audience is allowed to disagree with the film. Again, the film's suggestion of the need for discussion seems to emphasize this right and thereby promotes the audience's rational autonomy. Because the message takes the form of a film, equal exercise of this right is somewhat inhibited. Unlike a live, public discussion, viewers may not directly interact with the film. As mentioned earlier, representative spokespeople for the other side are relatively few in the film itself. The message may not be ideal in this regard but probably withstands the test of recognizing the audience's rational autonomy.

Concerning the V-factor, the question of whether the ends of the advocate share the values of the audience, the verdict seems particularly clear. The concern for humanity and its preservation is clear throughout the film. As with the other factors, the commitment to continued discussion reinforces the notion of community spirit in this message. Thus, the film generally seems to meet the requirements for ethical advocacy.

Much more analysis of this message could be done, but for the purposes of demonstrating the principles in Chapters 4 through 7, the foregoing will suffice. What we have found is a documentary film that works enthymematically to encourage the audience to accept several subclaims that lead to a main claim that we should break the silence concerning nuclear policy and consider changes in that policy. The arguments follow familiar patterns of thinking, evoke common needs, and rely on standard American values. The structure of the film reinforces the arguments. However, that same structure leads the audience to increasing heights of anxiety that, when combined with the plethora of unmet needs displayed in the film, may lead to psychic numbing of the audience. The film provides a less than accurate representation of opposing points of view as it fails sometimes to present sufficient evidence, suppresses some opposing evidence, produces some questionable causal links, and constructs some straw men. Although the filmic form does not allow for direct interaction by opposing advocates or unconvinced viewers, the film displays an ethical posture toward subject and audience. We may now consider the film in the context of the marketplace of ideas concerning nuclear warfare that was described earlier in this chapter.

Conclusion:
Moving Beyond Ideology and Propaganda with Free Speech

As the review of discussion of nuclear warfare at the beginning of this chapter suggested, "The War Game" is but one message within a mosaic of messages concerning this issue. While many of those messages are explicitly advocative, many more appeared as merely informative or entertaining discourse. News reports of how the atomic bomb was built, Truman's press release concerning its use at Hiroshima and Nagasaki, and feature films like "Fail-Safe" and "Dr. Strangelove" are examples of implicit rhetoric concerning nuclear war. Many of these messages help to shape our understanding of the nature of a world in which nuclear weapons exist. Some influence our common sense understanding of how the world should work and thereby operate ideologically. From time to time, public relations campaigns such as the "Atoms for Peace" campaign that was described in some detail in Chapter 7 take on the characteristics of propaganda. Throughout the history of this discussion, both formal government restrictions and informal societal norms have influenced the level of discussion.

Although complete analysis of the discussion would be too lengthy for this conclusion, a few examples may help to illustrate several of the concepts discussed in Chapters 8 and 9 of this book. In Chapter 8, the idea that a narrative could be examined to determine its influence on our world view was discussed. If we examined a narrative, such as the film "Fail-Safe," we would uncover a view of the world in which the superpowers (the United States and the Soviet Union) were the main agents in a scene dominated by the threat of nuclear holocaust. In this film, nuclear attack is accidental and the agents are depicted as reasonable, caring, but distrustful men who work to limit the degree of disaster. Is this world view reasonable? Does it take into account the other nations of the world with nuclear capabilities or the other citizens of the world who would suffer from nuclear detonations by the superpowers? Questions such as these would supplement our understanding of the world view revealed by the film.

"Fail-Safe," like many other visual messages concerning nuclear war suggests a common sense understanding that puts East and West in competition with one another and thus reveals a sort of Cold War ideology. Numerous ideographs, one-term sums of situations, dominate many of the messages about nuclear war. For example, the competitive relationship between East and West that feeds on mutual distrust as well as mutual assurance of destruction and leads to a continuing arms race is often summed up in the term "deterrence." Similarly, visual terms, such as the mushroom cloud, provide a summative symbol for nuclear holocaust. In contrast to the extended, graphic scenes of destruction and human suffering that were common in "The War Game," the mushroom cloud insulates us somewhat from the horror of nuclear war and thereby discourages investigation into the real effects. Even the term "peace" may function as an ideograph by encouraging us to accept the meaning of peace in a common sense way as merely the absence of war. Thus, "peace" resists inspection because its meaning is clear to all. Consequently, proponents of maintaining a nuclear arsenal may claim that while we have had the arsenal we have had "peace" just as easily as opponents may claim that if we destroyed the arsenal we would have "peace." In contrast, inspection of the ideograph of "peace" through discussion might reveal new and different relationships among people and nations that go beyond merely the absence of war.

The type of investigations just described are probably only realized in a situation where public discussion is encouraged and is free and open. However, as the earlier historical survey suggested, even in a society which guards against censorship and promotes discussion, the discussion of nuclear war has been episodic and less than complete. Not only did government censorship, classification of information, and propaganda campaigns restrict discussion, but distractions and disinterest on the part of citizens inhibited full discussion as well. A notable exception to this characterization has occurred only recently.

The dangers of a spiral of silence on the issue of nuclear war seems to have been at least implicitly recognized in "The War Game," which called for an end to the silence. However, ending the silence is not a simple matter. As Foucault suggested, even if the topic receives more attention as it has in the 1980s, some speakers and some contexts may still be silenced. You may have noticed that the speakers, the advocates, described during our most recent period tended to speak from institutions and roles characterized as expert. Senators and scientists speak and are listened to. Ordinary citizens speak but are usually listened to only if they represent an identifiable movement or provide dramatic and large rallys that attract the attention of the media. Perhaps there are people with valuable messages on this issue who lack the credentials and therefore the forum from which to find an audience. If this is so, then efforts to actualize Habermas' ideal speech situation and thereby to give voice to the silenced would be beneficial.

If discussion on this and countless other issues is to continue, then attention must be given to insuring open and equitable procedures for discussion. Moreover, participants in the marketplace of ideas must have the competence to analyze public discourse, their own and that of others. If this book assists in those endeavors, then its objective will be realized.

Notes

[1]Richard McKeon, "Communication, Truth and Society," *Ethics* 67 (1957): 91.

[2]H.G. Wells, *The World Set Free* (London: Macmillan, 1914), p. 203.

[3]A more complete description of messages concerning nuclear warfare is available in Martha Cooper, "The Implications of Foucault's Archaeological Theory of Discourse for Contemporary Rhetorical Theory and Criticism" unpub. diss. (Pennsylvania State University, 1984), Chapter 4 and Appendices A and B. The study analyzed sixty-nine articles from periodicals, six books, four documentary films, and seven miscellaneous statements, essays and documents. Much of the description of discourse in this chapter draws from that work.

[4]Stephen Hilgartner, Richard C. Bell, and Rory O'Connor, *Nukespeak* (San Francisco: Sierra Club, 1982), pp. 16-21; see also, Martin Sherwin, *A World Destroyed* (New York: Knopf, 1975), pp. 26-30.

[5]For example, Hersey reported in *Hiroshima* that: "Long before the American public had been told, most of the scientists and lots of the non-scientists in Japan knew that a uranium bomb had exploded at Hiroshima and a more powerful one, of plutonium at Nagasaki. They also knew that theoretically one ten times as powerful could be developed." See John Hersey, *Hiroshima* (New York: Bantam, 1948), p. 105. See also, Hilgartner, et al., pp. 57-71.

[6]Michael John Yavenditti, "American Reactions to the Use of Atomic Bombs on Japan 1945-1947," unpub. diss. (University of California-Berkeley, 1970), p. 287.

[7]Yavenditti, p. 303.

[8]Bernard T. Feld, "A Warning Not a Prophecy," *Bulletin of the Atomic Scientists* 38 (1982): 2.

[9]Yavenditti, p. 304.

[10]Hilgartner, et al., pp. 72-82.

[11]Eugene Joseph Rosi, "Public Opinion and Foreign Policy: Non-Governmental American Opinion Concerning the Cessation of Nuclear Weapons Tests 1954-1958," unpub. diss. (Columbia University, 1964), p. 132.

[12]Quoted by Rosi, p. 38.

[13]SANE, *Sane Organizer's Manual*, p. 1.

[14]Frederick Michael O'Hara, Jr., "Attitudes of American Magazines Toward Nuclear Testing, 1945-1965," unpub. diss. (University of Illinois, 1974), p. 22.

[15]Philip Duhan Segal, "Imaginative Literature and the Atomic Bomb: An Analysis of Representative Novels, Plays and films from 1945 to 1972," unpub. diss. (Yeshiva University, 1973), Ch. 1.

[16]Helen Ruth Harris Sands, "The Rhetoric of Survival in the Atomic Age: From Hiroshima to the Nuclear Test Ban Treaty," unpub. diss. (Southern Illinois University, 1969), p. 18.

[17]D.M. Richardson, "On the March—U.S. Version of Peace Crusade," *U.S. News and World Report* 92 (June 21, 1982): 24.

[18]"Thinking About the Unthinkable," *Time* 119 (March 29, 1982): 10.

[19]David M. Alpern, "Reagan Against the Freeze," *Newsweek* 99 (April 12, 1983): 19.

[20]Robert Gomer, "At Long Last," *Bulletin of the Atomic Scientists* 38 (1982): 3.

[21]"The War Game," Dir. Peter Watkins, BBC, 1966.

[22]Jack Shaheen, ed. *Nuclear War Films* (Carbondale: Southern Illinois University Press, 1978), p. 109. The quotation of the BBC reaction that follows may be found on p. 113.

[23]Eric Chivian, Susanna Chivian, Robert Jay Lifton, and John E. Mack, eds. *Last Aid: The Medical Dimensions of Nuclear War* (San Francisco: W.H. Freeman, 1982), pp. 287-92.

[24]Shaheen, pp. 110-112.

Suggested Readings

Hilgartner, Stephen, Richard C. Bell and Rory O'Connor. *Nukespeak*. San Francisco: Sierra Club, 1982.

Schell, Jonathon. *The Fate of the Earth*. New York: Knopf, 1982.

Shaheen, Jack G., ed. *Nuclear War Films*. Carbondale, Southern Illinois University P, 1978.

Index